HS

D0531161

WHEELS ROLLING
AT
EIGHT

by

Arthur Anderson

Grosvenor House
Publishing Limited

This book is published by
Grosvenor House Publishing Ltd
Link House
140 The Broadway, Tolworth, Surrey, KT6 7HT.
www.grosvenorhousepublishing.co.uk

A CIP record for this book
is available from the British Library

ISBN 978-1-78623-304-2

For
Andrea

Acknowledgements

Front cover design courtesy of Graham Lang

Photograph of Uswayford Farm, Northumberland,
by kind permission of Tom Pugh Photography

Photograph of Andrea in The Royal Hospital
for Sick Children, Edinburgh by kind permission of
"The Scotsman", Edinburgh

Photograph of the May Farm courtesy of Rhuna Barr

Photography layout and digitisation by Janusz Ostrowski

The author thanks the small army of BBC staff and
freelances who shared his journey and the farming families
of Scotland for their kindness and support over the years

Foreword

Wheels Rolling at Eight. There are many well-known phrases in the broadcasting business but that isn't one of them. It's special to me – and to the small team of cameraman, sound recordists, reporters and production assistants who spent 25 years following me to every corner of the UK and twenty-seven countries around the world.

Timing is critical in the broadcasting business. If you're a producer or director, clock-watching becomes an obsession. As you can't be a little bit pregnant, so you can't be a little late for a billed broadcast.

The title stems from a slight altercation on location early in my television career when I felt a member of my team had been a little too liberal in his interpretation of what I meant by an 8am scheduled start. I recall emphasising - as forcefully as I dared - that 8am did *not* mean checking in for breakfast or even having a final cup of coffee to kick-start the day. Nor did it mean a cue to start loading the camera car with the usual myriad collection of metal boxes. What 8am did mean, I gently insisted, was everyone breakfasted, hotel bills paid, cars loaded and – *wheels rolling!* It was a phrase that was to cling to me over the years.

I've heard it said that life is a bit like a toilet roll – the closer you come to the end, the faster it seems to go. For many years, a picture of our four young children playing in the snow has had pride of place on my bedside table. Today they have all grown to adulthood. How quickly the intervening years have passed. What have I missed of their growing up? What don't they know of their father? Perhaps this book will fill in some of the gaps and help explain why their father very often did not join them for supper.

The late Hollywood film star Cary Grant is alleged to have said that nobody is ever truthful about his own life – there are always ambiguities. George Orwell went further when he said that a man who gives a good account of himself is probably lying since any life viewed from the inside is simply a series of defeats. Hugh Cudlipp, the pioneering Fleet Street editor, put it succinctly when he said that most autobiographies share a common blemish – self-glory and self-justification. I'm sure they're all right. In the same way that childhood summers seemed always warmer and longer than today, other events in your life viewed from a distance can often take on a rosy glow. Nonetheless, what follows is an attempt to put on record an honest account of what has been a hectic but fortunate and fun-filled life.

Contents

Roots

November the 21st, 1944 was a Tuesday. It was a cold day with three inches of snow recorded in the Lanarkshire hills. The hit song of the time was the Mills Brothers' *You Always Hurt The One You Love* and 4000 tons of bombs were dropped by Allied planes on German oil stores. And one more thing – I came into the world at the Cresswell Maternity Hospital in Dumfries.

But I don't recall any of that. My earliest memory is climbing a hill. It was a thickly wooded hill deep in the south-west of Scotland and it's called the Doon of May. As hills go it isn't big but it played a large part in my early life. As a child, my father Jack and mother Frances would occasionally break off from their farming duties at the May Farm near Port William on the shores of Luce Bay and on a fine Sunday afternoon lead me over the Dam Field, across the boundary wall that separated our tenanted dairy farm from forestry land and up, ever upwards, until we reached the top of the Doon.

No matter how often we made the ascent, the excitement of the journey never grew less in the child breast. Maybe it was the stories my parents told me as we walked – tales of the School in the Wood with Mr Fox the teacher and Mr Squirrel the janitor who used his bushy tail to sweep the floors. They were stories that never palled no matter how often I heard them.

Maybe it was the prospect of a brief picnic of lemonade and a chocolate bar before beginning the descent and return to the farm in time for the afternoon milking. Or perhaps it was the view from the top of the Doon of May, surely one of the finest in Galloway. On a clear day the flat dark moorland stretched for miles eastward beyond the farm steading before being halted in its tracks by the sparkling waters of Wigtown Bay and the blue mass of Cairnsmore of Fleet in the Galloway hills beyond. Turn round to the west and there was Luce Bay and the distant coastlines of the Isle of Man and Northern Ireland in the far distance. Turn yet again and the chance to see the faraway smoke from a steam engine as it approached Kirkcowan railway station on the Stranraer-Dumfries line, all too soon to fall victim to the Beeching Axe, the name given to the wide-ranging cuts to Britain's national-ised rail system in the 1960s.

But in the summer of 1961 I climbed the Doon of May alone. As I looked out on the familiar scenes, I realised that my life was changing. I was 16 and had left Barnard Castle School in Co Durham with five "O" Levels to my name. There had been talk of my staying on for "A" Levels and then, maybe, to university but even though fees for a boarding school like Barnard Castle were low in those days, they were still a major commitment for a tenant farmer with 29 Ayrshire dairy cows. Going to boarding school in the first place had only proved possible thanks to a small legacy left to my parents in my maternal grandmother's will. At £65 13s 4d a term (£65.67p), an unbelievable small sum by today's stand-ards, that legacy just covered my five years at secondary school.

In any event, I was eager to stretch my wings. I wanted to be a journalist - despite some opposition from my English teacher at school. A fellow Scot, he had always been a supportive and enthusiastic teacher but when I confided my newspaper ambitions to him in my last months at school, he clearly felt I had made some kind of pact with the devil and barely spoke to me again. I suppose my wish to enter journalism stemmed from my enthusi-asm for the English language espoused by an earlier teacher at Barnard Castle. He was Arnold Snodgrass, a close friend of the poet W.H. Auden during their time together at Oxford University. I guess my commitment to words came from fierce penalties prom-ised by Arnold Snodgrass if we were found guilty of bad spelling, punctuation or grammar. "Boy," he would roar at the luckless offender of some such transgression, "I will thrash you with rusty barbed wire till the blood drips down your socks." Such threats tended to concentrate the mind wonderfully.

I was further enthused about a possible life in newspapers when in 1959 I read regular despatches on the progress of the 23-year-old Dalai Lama escaping from Chinese-controlled Tibet through the Himalayas into the safety of India. It was an exciting adventure story writ large and it sowed a seed within me. It never occurred to me that any journalistic beginnings I might aspire to were likely to be a little more mundane.

And so with the support of my parents, the decision had been made. I would leave school, sign up for Skerry's Commercial College in Edinburgh to learn typing and shorthand and wait to see what the next step might be.

One thing was for sure – despite the strong tradition of sons following in their father's farming footsteps, my parents believed that the future for their kind of farming was limited and that my best hopes of a career lay beyond slicing turnips for cattle and sheep on bitterly cold winter mornings. Despite my enthusiasm for working on the farm, I could see their point of view. It was a hard life.

Frances, my Galloway-born mother was from farming stock. Her father was Robert Skimming, a successful joiner and wood merchant in the village of Kirkinner near Wigtown– and by all accounts a formidable Scottish athlete in his youth - who had in his later years bought a dairy farm called Airyolland overlooking Port William village on the shores of Luce Bay. Her mother was Jeannie Simpson also from a farming family in the Garlieston area of Wigtownshire.

My father Jack, a Northumbrian lad, was from more distant farming stock. His great grandfather, George Anderson, had been a shepherd in the middle of the 19th Century at Uswayford Farm near the village of Alwinton in the foothills of the Cheviots. He was the father of eight children including five sons who were later to join him as shepherds at Uswayford in the valley of the River Coquet. Changed days. There's not a single sheep farm in Britain today that could support six shepherds.

Uswayford is no longer a sheep farm on the scale it was in my great great grandfather's time. Now surrounded by forestry plantations like so much of the uplands of the North of England and Southern Scotland, it remains one of the most remote farms in England but today offers a welcome sign of human habitation to passing long distance walkers trudging the weary miles of the Pennine Way. Stretching 260 miles from the Derbyshire Peak

District through the Yorkshire Dales and over Hadrian's Wall to the Cheviots, the Pennine Way is one of the great long distance walks in the UK and for walkers heading north, Uswayford offers a waymarker before journey's end at Kirk Yetholm just across the Border into Scotland.

But that link with the land on my father's side was broken when his father, Andrew Anderson, became an employee at Ratcheugh Whinstone Quarry near Longhoughton village in Northumberland until a variant of miner's lung disease claimed his life on April 20th, 1906. He was just 40 years old. As a result, Ellen, his schoolteacher widow, was left to bring up four sons – Norman, Edward, Arthur and John – with John, or Jack as he was always known, being my father. How she managed what must have seemed by today's standards a Herculean task is impossible to fathom. There was some fanciful suggestion that her family who were Forsters had links with a jockey who rode for the Duke of Bedford and went on to run a pub in London's Drury Lane. Sadly, I have never been able to discover any hard evidence to substantiate a family connection with either the aristocracy or the licensed trade – other than as a customer of the latter.

Times must have been hard for my widowed grandmother and the pressure to achieve independence in her four boys was strong. And so on May 15th, 1920, at the age of 16 my father Jack, the youngest son, began a four-year apprenticeship in the Merchant Navy with the Cairn Line. I have in my possession the linen apprenticeship document he signed which bears on its reverse side, in immaculate copperplate detail, the list of cash withdrawals from his wages over that four-year indenture period. The record notes that his first withdrawal from his wages was £1 13s 9d (£1.69p) on July 29th, 1920 and his final withdrawal was 13s 4d (67p) on May 18th, 1924. During his first year he received £4, in the second it was £8, in the third £16 until the final year of his apprenticeship when he earned the princely sum of £32 – a grand total of £60 for the four years of his training – and the cost of his uniform came out of his own pocket.

Having successfully completed his indenture with the Cairn Line, my father was to go on to earn his Master's ticket during the next 20 years sailing the oceans of the world before leaving the sea to pursue a second career as a farmer at the end of the Second World War shortly after marrying my mother. He was to exchange one tough life for another – no reflection on my mother.

Over those years he was to travel from one end of the world to the other on a succession of ships, mostly those owned by the Cairn Line based in Newcastle. His ships included the Cairndhu, Cairnross, Cairntorr, Cairnglen and Cairnesk. The one closest to his affections over the years, however, was the 4666-ton Cairnmona on which he served for 28 voyages mostly between the UK and Canada and the United States.

In truth, I guess he was glad to leave the sea at the end. He had begun the war by being torpedoed on October 30th, 1939, by the German submarine U-13 which five days earlier had left its Kriegsmarine base in Kiel in the north of Germany under the command of 30-year-old Kapitänleutnant Karl Daublebsky von Eichhain, a holder of the Iron Cross 1st Class, son of a Rear Admiral and scion of one of Austria's noble families.

Father's vessel, his beloved Cairnmona under the command of Master Frederick Wilkinson Fairley, was the last ship in HX-5, a small convoy en route for Leith and Newcastle from Montreal and Halifax, Nova Scotia, with a cargo of wheat, wool, copper, zinc and apples. The torpedo struck just before midnight three miles off Rattray Head north of Aberdeen and the Cairnmona took a direct hit in the engine room. Three firemen – George Barrett (39), Frank Thomas (29) and Richard Lynch (32), all from Leith – perished along with the black cat that had wandered aboard the vessel in Leith a few weeks earlier. When the torpedo struck, the officers and crew had barely enough time to throw on a coat and take to the lifeboats. Within 15 minutes of the explosion, the Cairnmona had sunk to the bottom of the North Sea. After 30 minutes the British drifter HMS River Lossie and its Skipper J.C Spence RNR and the Peterhead lifeboat Julia Park Barry picked up 41 survivors, including my father, First Mate Jack Anderson, and landed them safely at Peterhead. It proved to be one of the first rescues by the Peterhead lifeboat which had only recently been commissioned but over her years of service between June 1939 and January 1969 the Julia Park Barry was launched 162 times and saved 496 lives.

The first evidence the local population of the North-East of Scotland had of the sinking of the Cairnmona was the thousands of pippin apples carried onto the Aberdeenshire beaches by the incoming tide.

News of the sinking reached Germany and in one of his propaganda broadcasts from his studio in Hamburg during the last days of 1939 the Nazi collaborator and broadcaster Lord Haw Haw – later to be hanged for war crimes - jeered: "You had apples for Christmas but you'll have bombs for New Year."

On May 31st the following year, U-13 met her nemesis when HMS Weston, a Shoreham-Class sloop commanded by Lt. Cdr. Seymour Charles Tuke RN, put the U-Boat out of action for ever with depth charges eleven miles South-East of Lowestoft on the Suffolk coast. The British vessel rescued the U-13's 26-strong crew plus some Enigma rotors, an invaluable asset for Allied scientists at Bletchley Park in Buckinghamshire seeking to break the codes used by the Germans for the encryption and decryption of secret messages.

In the bitter war fought over the cold seas of the North Atlantic, lightning was to strike twice for the Cairnmona's Master, Frederick Wilkinson Fairley. Back at sea as Master of the Empire Sailor, returning from Canada he was torpedoed by U-518 on November 21st, 1942. Once again he and his crew were rescued, this time by HMCS Minas.

In yet another coincidence, when father's ship the Cairnmona sank below the grey waters of the North Sea it was a case of history repeating itself from the First World War for on June 15th, 1918, the original Cairnmona en route from Leith to Newcastle was torpedoed with the loss of four firemen.

As for Kapitänleutnant Karl Daublebsky von Eichhain, he was to finish the war as a prisoner of the allies but returned to his native Austria in 1945. He died in the small Austrian town of Pyrawang on the banks of the River Danube on October 8th, 2001. He was 92 years old.

After a short time helping run maritime training courses in South Shields in 1940, my father was to return to sea and become involved in the North Atlantic convoys carrying munitions and food to Murmansk in Northern Russia. A total of 78 convoys sailed to Murmansk taking supplies, including 7000 planes and 5000 tanks, to the Soviet forces. It was a perilous trade and thousands of Allied seamen lost their lives in the freezing conditions and by the time the war ended, the Battle of the Atlantic had claimed the lives of 24,000 men and women of Britain's merchant marine and fishing fleets. All of them who died with no known grave are remembered today at the Tower Hill Memorial in London.

The Public Records Office at Kew reveals that in June 1953, the British government salvaged much of the copper and zinc lost when the Cairnmona went down. At the time of her sinking in 1939, her cargo of 700 tons of zinc was worth £3525 and the 550 tons of copper worth £19,408. Official records show that 568 tons of zinc worth £41,358 at today's values and 399 tons of copper worth £104,000 were eventually reclaimed from the deep.

Many years after the war the British government bowed to pressure from veterans of the Arctic convoys and their supporters and agreed to strike a campaign medal for those who had risked or given their lives to brave the U boat packs and carry vital supplies to Murmansk. This was the Arctic Star, a six-pointed bronze medal for those who had served between September 3rd 1939 and May 8th 1945. Suspended by a ribbon with colours representing the services – red for the Merchant Navy and with a central white stripe, edged in black, representing the Arctic. Sadly, despite several letters to the Ministry of Defence and research at the National Records Office at Kew, I was unable to identify the name of any vessel that my father had sailed on in those troubled times. Without that information, there was no medal. I was disappointed – father was long dead but it would have been good to have the medal in the family to represent a tangible link with that significant period of British history. In truth though, had father known about this I suspect that in his own taciturn manner he wouldn't have cared one way or another. All that mattered was that he had come through that wartime ordeal with his life – and a future as a tenant farmer in Galloway lay ahead.

A combination of German U boats and a North Atlantic winter made it impossible for my mother and father to fix a precise wedding date. She didn't know where he was and when or even *if* he would ever return. But in his absence, the wedding invitations were duly sent out with the codicil that the ceremony would take place *at an early date*. Eventually, however, he did make it back in one piece and Frances and her Captain Jack were married in the village church at Mochrum near the May Farm on Thursday, December 31st, 1942. He was 39; she was 26.

By this time the tenancy of the May Farm had been taken out in my mother's name while father was part of the maritime war effort. Running a farm is tough work at the best of times but with a daily schedule of 29 cows to milk and a sheep flock to run, it was well nigh impossible to be done by my mother on her own. For that reason father applied to be released from his duties to join his new wife on the farm. The Ministry of Labour refused his request, arguing that as father was in possession of a Master's Certificate his services were required for the war effort.

His request for release went to appeal and was taken up by the Wigtownshire Agricultural Executive, part of a national network of agencies designed to keep the national farming industry working at maximum efficiency. This time his request for release was accepted and as the excitement of their Hogmanay wedding slipped away with the old year father and mother prepared for their new life together running the May Farm.

Despite forsaking the sea for the land at the end of the war, my father maintained his maritime friendships. One of his closest friends was Bill Livesay who had joined the Merchant Navy in the same year as my father in 1920. After the war, Bill and his wife Margaret would spend holidays at the May Farm, bringing with them from Middlesbrough their young son Michael and their daughter Ruth. In years to come, Michael too would follow a life at sea. But his choice would be the Royal Navy where he was to rise through the ranks to become Director of Naval Warfare during the Falklands conflict in 1982 before ending his career in 1993 as Admiral Sir Michael Livesay, the Second Sea Lord.

First Steps in Farming

Compared with the high-technology agribusiness units that dominate today's food production industry, it was a very different type of farming that filled my childhood days in the 1940s and 1950s.

The May Farm then extended to just over a thousand acres. This may seem like a large area of land but in reality most of it was low-lying wet and unproductive moor, useful for summering the sheep-stock but for little else.

Some of the history of the farm is contained in *Mochrum: The Land and Its People*, a scholarly work by John McFadzean who, together with his brother Stewart, was for many years one of our farming neighbours and friends at Airylick Farm.

Earliest records of the May Farm indicate that in 1578 it was part of the estate of Sir John Dunbar although by 1855 ownership had been passed to the Marquis of Bute, scions of whose family have continued to own Mochrum Estate ever since.

John McFadzean's diligent research reveals that one of the earliest tenants of the May was John Milligan, born in 1808 and who succeeded to the tenancy at the age of 24 on the death of his father who was killed by the kick from a horse.

John Milligan appears to have been a man of physical prowess. He apparently regularly drove sheep to Ayr market some 50 miles away, sleeping on the moor on the way. He then left Ayr immediately after transacting business and walked back without sleep.

He even told of one occasion of mowing hay at the May until two in the afternoon then setting out on foot for Lockerbie Lamb Fair, travelling all night. Breakfasting at Dumfries he reached Lockerbie in the forenoon and started his return journey in the same evening with a Mr Biggam of Barr. At Newton Stewart Mr Biggam was apparently overcome with fatigue and remained to rest but Mr Milligan finished back to the May alone having travelled a distance of about 120 miles. Even allowing for a little artistic licence Mr Milligan seems to have been a man of considerable stamina!

More than one hundred years later when my mother and father were tenants, the productive heart of the farm lay in the 200 acres or so of in-bye – better land lying close the farmhouse and farm buildings. This provided the grazing for the farm's main enterprise – a herd of brown and white Ayrshire cows housed in two byres known as the "wee byre" holding thirteen cows and the "big byre" for the remaining seventeen head. In fact, the larger of the two byres only ever housed sixteen cows; the seventeenth stall at the top of the byre was reserved for our Beef Shorthorn bull, in those days a popular crossing sire used on Ayrshire cows to produce beef from the dairy herds of South-West Scotland.

For more than 25 years, this small dairy herd was the centre of the farming business for my mother and father. Although they employed two full time workers for other farming tasks, milking was strictly a family-only affair. In part at least this was dictated by commercial demands imposed by Nestlé, the buyers of the milk that went for processing to the company's creamery at Dunragit near Stranraer. The May Farm was one of the most outlying sources of their supply and this meant that the lorry picked up our milk before any other farm, arriving each morning shortly after 6am.

To ensure the cows had been milked and their liquid contribution to the health of the nation was cooled and decanted into 10-gallon butts in time for the arrival of Geordie Graham, the driver of the milk lorry, meant that my parents had to rise each morning shortly after 3am.

In truth, there was little likelihood that they would ever sleep in and be late for the arrival of the milk lorry. A wake-up call invariably came from my maternal grandmother Jeannie Skimming. A large stern woman who dressed in black from head to toe, she slept in the room directly below my mother and father. Beside her bed she kept a thick walking stick and she would bang loudly on the ceiling to ensure my mother and father's wakefulness. Years later, I was to learn that on occasions when my mother and father retired for the night unusually early, any nocturnal bedroom noises that ensued - other than snoring - was met by another bout of furious banging on the ceiling. She couldn't have heard everything - I must have been conceived somehow.

But seven days drudgery each week for little tangible reward for my parents was far from my thoughts as a boy as I witnessed the twice-daily spectacle of the cows being milked. In winter especially I found the byres to be a warm and welcoming place to be – insulated from the cold and darkness outside by the body heat of the cows and the comfortable and familiar noise of the automatic milking machines pulsating gently in the dimly-lit buildings.

As I grew older, part of my daily winter task was to slice turnips for what my mother and father described as the "big bellies". This involved filling barrow-loads of turnips, often frozen to each other despite their insulating blanket of straw. The turnips were then decanted into a slicing machine that, long before the days of electrical power, was operated by hand like a giant mangle with the resulting bite-sized chunks taken to each cow in a wire basket. While the vigorous turning of the handle on the machine might have maintained upper body heat it did nothing to increase the flow of blood into my young hands.

To compensate, I used to look forward to feeding some of the more docile cows because I knew that, having fed them, I could pause before I left their stall and slip my hands between their udder and thigh which after a couple of minutes restored enough warmth to allow me to resume my feeding duties. If one or two of the cows looked around in some surprise when they felt two cold little hands on their warm udder who could blame them.

If milking proved a serious business for my father and mother there were occasional moments of humour that lightened the daily round and provided anecdotal material for years to come.

As a young girl my mother had grown up with her brother Peter and sisters Jean and Mary on the nearby dairy farm of Airyolland overlooking Luce Bay and had learned to milk cows almost as soon as she could walk. Consequently she was an expert at ensuring the flow of milk from each cow's teat by hand immediately prior to placing on the udder the automatic milking machine whose pulsating beat would reverberate round the byre. Not only was she expert at the task of squeezing the cows' teats to begin the milk flow but on many occasions, hidden from my view by the cow's flank, could accurately redirect a fine jet of warm creamy milk twenty or thirty feet down the byre to score a direct hit on an unsuspecting but soon to be startled little boy.

At times, it paid too to be aware of the cow's digestive system. This was especially true at spring when the cows were released from their winter quarters to enjoy the first flush of young grass. One afternoon a commercial traveller walked through the byre in an attempt to interest my mother and father in his latest agricultural product. If his smart suit, shirt and tie were singularly at odds with the working environment he found himself in, they proved even more so a few seconds later when he happened to pause behind one old cow at the precise moment she decided to combine a major bodily function with a vigorous cough and instantly enveloped him in a fine blizzard of bright green diarrhoea.

In today's high-tech and computerised farming world, dairy cows are identified by freeze-branding with transponders around their necks automatically ensuring they are given precise amounts of feed to match their milk yield when entering their chosen cubicle.

Things were a little more personal half a century ago at the May Farm where the Ayrshire cows entered their own stall. Be it Katie, Hilary, Monica, Muriel, Helen, Frances, Jean or Mary, each one was clearly identified with their names strikingly painted on the concrete wall in front of their feeding trough in bold red - emblazoned identities which were to last down the decades and a testimony to the artistic talent of a prisoner of war called Capperalli.

Capperalli was a young Italian solder who was incarcerated at the Holm Park prison camp at nearby Newton Stewart and was but one of 157,000 Italians and 402,000 German prisoners in the UK spread between 1500 camps from Cornwall to Orkney. Like many of his countrymen, Capperalli found the boredom of imprisonment was made more bearable by day release work on local farms. Painting cows' names on a small Galloway byre must have seemed like a heavenly release from the horrors of the global conflict that had destroyed so many millions of lives.

That Capperalli should choose my mother's name of Frances for one of the cows was understandable as were the names Jean and Mary, my mother's two elder sisters. Muriel and Helen were self-evident too – both fine young girls who were my father's nieces, the daughters of his eldest brother Norman. Settling on Monica, Katie and Hilary was more puzzling. Monica was to become my young sister but she didn't make her appearance in the world until years after Capperalli had worked his artistic magic with his paintbrush while Katie and Hilary were a generation later to become Monica's two daughters, my nieces, and who weren't even born in my father's lifetime – and more than likely not in Capperalli's lifetime either.

Whether prescient or just lucky with his choice of names of some girls not yet born, Capperalli was by all accounts a kind and personable young man who had an affinity for animals. Not only did he leave his legacy for generations to come by painting the names of the dairy cows on their stalls, he also made his mark by bonding with auntie Jean's dog Belle.

Despite her rural roots, auntie Jean, my mother's eldest sister, had forsaken her Galloway background when she married Bobby Bicketts, a local farmer's son from the village of Elrig. Together they had gone to London to forge a career in the Scotch drapery trade only for Bobby to fall victim to cancer in his 30s. Instead of returning to Scotland, however, my auntie Jean continued to carry on the small business that was concentrated in the East End of London.

As the years rolled on she and her dog Belle would make an annual pilgrimage to her childhood haunts in Galloway and stay with my mother and father at the May Farm. However, by now she was so inured to the buzz of London that it used to take her several days at the farm before she could get to sleep at night – too quiet, she used to reckon.

Even during the height of the London Blitz, Auntie Jean continued her small business but maintained her practice of an annual break on the farm. It was on one of these visits at the end of the war with Belle, a gentle yellow Labrador-type mutt with a few question marks over its lineage, that the dog and the young Italian struck up a bond.

In a short period they had become inseparable and when the time came for auntie Jean and her beloved Belle to return to

London and once more endure the privations of the war-torn city, Capperalli was inconsolable. As a final act of farewell, he took from around his neck a chain supporting a small Italian military medal and hung it around the neck of the dog.

History does not relate whether auntie Jean ever had to explain to the authorities how her dog came by a military medal from a member of the enemy forces but years later when I visited my aunt and an ageing Belle in London's Forest Gate the Italian medal still hung from the dog's neck.

Through the passing years I have often wondered what happened to Capperalli. Did he return safely to the land of his birth and enjoy a full life under a warm Italian sun. Despite my best endeavours I never found out. The Imperial War Museum in London does not hold any official documentation or listings of enemy Prisoners of War although it can offer plenty of advice on where to trace British and allied PoWs. The main source for information on enemy prisoners is held by the International Committee of the Red Cross in Geneva but even the efficiency of the Swiss failed to provide me with any information on what might have become of that artistic and kindly young Italian who left his mark on the cow stalls in the byres of the May Farm.

His personal war story remains incomplete and is likely to remain so. Despite my research at local, national and international level how Capperalli found his way to Scotland is not known. The best guess is that he was one of the 115,000 Italian soldiers taken prisoner in Operation Compass, the first major Allied military operation of the Western Desert Campaign when British and Commonwealth armies overwhelmed nine Italian divisions in western Egypt and eastern Libya from December 1940 to February 1941.

Despite her farming upbringing, auntie Jean increasingly seemed more at ease in the city than the countryside. On one of her holidays on the farm, she was called on to help during a difficult calving. Where my mother and father happened to be on this occasion is lost in the mists of time but the man in charge of proceedings was the farm shepherd, Bob Jardine.

The heifer was clearly in some distress although the calf appeared to be presenting properly with two small hooves protruding. As was normal in those days, binder twine was always readily available so clove hitches were tied above the calf's front hooves to allow a better grip by the human helpers.

Bob wound one piece of twine around his strong right hand while auntie Jean took the other. Each time the heifer heaved Bob took the strain – to no effect. Looking round he noticed auntie Jean had averted her eyes from the imminent birth in front of her and was pulling gently but intermittently and ineffectually while she stared steadfastly at her own feet, clearly unable to face the struggle for new life in front of her. Clearly urban life had erased some of her rural sensibilities.

This went on for some time with little progress being made until Bob lost his customary dignified restraint and shouted:

For God's sake wumman – dinnae pull till she pushes!

A healthy calf was delivered a short time later.

Away from helping with emergency deliveries in the dairy herd, Bob Jardine's main task was as shepherd, a role he accomplished with great skill and dedication over many years. Like many countrymen of his generation, he was taciturn but never sullen, friendly but never conversational. His day began early, particularly at lambing time, and before daylight had broken his arrival on duty could be determined by the gentle *putt-putt* of his auto-cycle as he rode into the courtyard of the farm buildings.

Bob had two distinguishing characteristics – his tuneless whistle and his tackety boots. His boots were of a type traditionally worn by farm labourers with upturned toes and serried rows of tackets which, when he walked along a hard surface, could convey the impression of an army of tap dancers advancing in perfect unison. And while he walked over the many miles of fields and moor, he whistled. Or rather, he believed he was whistling. He whistled as he breathed in and he whistled as he breathed out. Whether he thought he was giving vent to some popular tune remains unknown; in reality it conveyed the sense of a desperate breathlessness punctuated only occasionally by a brief snatch of what passed for a chill winter wind finding its way through a broken window pane.

At heart, he was a conscientious and able shepherd able to handle any given situation in all weathers. Not surprisingly, he was busiest during the main lambing season in April when his days began early and finished late. As a small boy I recall waking one beautiful spring morning and looking out of my bedroom window to the fields and the distant Galloway Hills. There in the bottom field walking towards the farm was Bob with a weakly lamb cradled gently in one arm and Nell his collie dog at his heels. I dressed in seconds and raced out of the house and down the road to meet him.

Good morning Bob, I ventured.

He looked down at me disdainfully but with a twinkle in his eye.

Aye, he said, When it *was* morning.

He took his pocket watch from his waistcoat and showed it to me. It was just after 7am. He'd been up for hours.

Years later when Bob Jardine had retired and I entered my teenage years I took an increasing involvement in the lambing and did my best to help mother and father in what was the busiest and most intensive time of their farming year. In those distant days part of our tenancy included what we called the "back hills" which lay about one and a half miles distant from the May and close by Drumwalt Castle, the home of our landlord Lord David Crichton Stuart. To get to and from these distant parts of the farm involved cycling and with one of our collie dogs panting in our wake we would follow the narrow tarmac road past the calm waters of Mochrum Loch with its catkins galore and the scent of spring in the air. In such rural beauty it was easy to forget the cruelty of nature because it was this same loch that took the lives of two youngsters – one of them the son of a previous tenant at the May Farm – who perished when they fell through the ice while playing on their way to Culshabbin School on December 9th, 1909. The first to fall through the ice was Alexander Chesney, aged 14, and it was in the act of rescuing him with a rope that John Milligan Mactier, son of the May Farm tenant, was also drawn into the icy water.

Those spring days have lived long in my memory. Not only cycling with my father to check the lambing ewes on the back hills and then back to the farm for breakfast before continuing the shepherds' watch in our inbye fields but also more relaxed cycling expeditions. On many week-end mornings I would cycle to collect our newspaper from the wife of the local blacksmith at the Loch Head near Elrig village. After collecting the paper I would briefly delay my return to the farm by watching Tommy Thomson, the blacksmith, hammer horse shoes into shape – a giant Clydesdale beside him standing calm and motionless despite the noise of the hammer and the roar of the forge fire. All this was years before I had been introduced to the poem *The Village Blacksmith* but despite the absence of a spreading chestnut tree, reading Longfellow's verses in the years since reminds me of Tommy Thomson.

Then came the leisurely cycle homewards along hedges full of white hawthorn blossom and past the newly sown fields alive with ground-nesting birds; the peewits putting on their mesmerising aerobatic displays in defence of eggs or newly-hatched young while in the surrounding moorland the curlews, or whaups as we called them in Galloway, reprised their mournful cries as they landed to be hidden from sight among the gently waving acres of cotton grass.

And then it was back to work in the lambing fields. It is a feature of any lambing season in any part of the country that there will be orphan lambs. These are invariably the result of a young ewe getting such a shock at giving birth that her natural maternal instincts are put on hold or a ewe having two lambs and walking away with the stronger of the pair at her side leaving the weaker lamb to await help from a conscientious shepherd or a speedy despatch from a passing fox.

To those outside the farming industry the idea of rearing pet lambs may seem to hold a certain rustic attractiveness. If you're involved at the sharp end of farming, however, orphan lambs are always more trouble than they're worth. With luck and good timing they can be twinned onto other ewes that have lost their own lambs but often that luck is absent and for many weeks farmers and shepherds are committed to a bottle-feeding regime.

17

And no matter how conscientiously orphan lambs are bottle-fed, they seldom grow and develop as well as lambs reared with their natural mothers. Instead, the usual end result is a motley collection of bleating pot-bellied creatures that from April to autumn slavishly pursue any human being they think might be concealing a bottle of milk with all the zeal of rats pursuing the Pied Piper of Hamelin.

For all that, every lamb that wasn't born dead represented potential income and no efforts were spared to try and rear as many lambs for the autumn sales as possible. And that included the Tommy Noddies. When I asked my father what a Tommy Noddy was, he simply explained: *Tommy Noddy – all head and no body.*

Of course, it was an exaggeration. What he was describing was what was most usually referred to as a "hung lamb" – a lamb that was not properly presented at the point of birth; instead of nose and two small hooves showing beneath the ewe's tail, there would be only a nose. Usually this presented no major problems when caught in time but if a ewe attempted to give birth in the night when no shepherd was around what could happen was that the lamb's head emerged then nothing else with the result that growing pressure around the lamb's neck made the head swell alarmingly. Even then, prompt action would save the lamb; without prompt action the lamb would die – and occasionally the ewe as well.

During the lambing season, a farmhouse kitchen often becomes the nerve centre for the halt and the lame. Weakly lambs left without mothers or exposed to spring blizzards can quickly succumb but even those on the apparent point of death can respond remarkably quickly when they exchange the worst that mother nature can throw at them for the warmth of a cardboard shoebox in the bottom oven of a farmhouse kitchen cooker.

But this emergency procedure can present traps for the unwary. For some years as a youngster I bred Aylesbury ducks. White of feather and gregarious of nature they were my pride and joy although when numbers began to exceed twenty my father took a different view as they increasingly developed the same habits as the orphan lambs when they suspected a passing human might conceal some food about their person.

After one hatching my mother and I noticed that two of the ducklings were very weak and lacked the robust qualities of their siblings. As in time-honoured fashion with weakly lambs, the two tiny yellow ducklings - the white feathers came with maturity - were immediately brought inside, placed in a small tin biscuit box with a duster as a snug bed and gently inserted into the warm embrace of the bottom oven.

To this day we don't know what happened next. It may have been a telephone call, the arrival of a visitor's car or the distraction of some report on the wireless. In any event, the door of the bottom oven was accidentally closed – and nobody noticed. In the best tradition of out of sight out of mind, the ducklings passed from our consciousness until, two days later, they were discovered – cooked to a crisp. Duck breeding immediately began to lose its attraction.

Although our farm was primarily a livestock unit, each year my father and mother grew a few fields of oats and while the dairy cows and the sheep proved an abiding interest for me, the cycle of seedtime and harvest also held undoubted attractions.

As the bluebells, primrose and hawthorn blossom of spring gave way to a profusion of red campion along the hedgerows of Galloway it was a sign that one part of the farming cycle was over and another, the annual harvest, was in prospect. And when the green oats finally turned golden at the end of summer it was a time of frenzied activity at which a youngster like me had little constructive part to play. Yet when I was around eleven or twelve years old I felt I had taken one giant step towards become a responsible adult when my father asked me to sit on the binder and handle the controls. This was at a time when only the biggest and most sophisticated farms – and the better-off farmers – could lay claim to a combine harvester. For most, like my father, a simple binder was the order of the day.

The first binders were horse drawn but ours was the next step along the road to what seemed to be technical perfection. It was driven by horsepower of a different sort - the ubiquitous small grey "Fergie". Developed by Ulsterman Harry Ferguson, the son of a dairy farmer, the seed of his idea for the Ferguson tractor was sown during the First World War when there was a demand to boost food production with the consequent pressure to move from horsepower to tractors. His invention went into mass production in 1936 and the key to its worldwide success was its three-point linkage that enabled it to handle a variety of farming implements. Within a few short years it was a familiar sight on farms from Scandinavia to Africa.

At harvest time, sitting on the binder and operating the controls was a little like patting your head and rubbing your stomach at the same time. Synchronisation was all. Or so it seemed to me with all my attention given over to ensuring one lever controlling the flails to draw the crop of oats towards the cutter bar harmonised with the other lever which controlled the level and the height of the cutter bar itself. At the same time it was important to keep an eye on the binder twine holder – forgetting to stop the tractor to refill the twine holder was a major sin in my father's eyes when the consequence of missing the end of a roll of twine saw loose unknotted sheaves thrown out by the buncher to be painstakingly gathered up by hand and brought back to be laid on the straw table of the binder.

Failing to keep my eye on the binder twine holder was not the first time I found myself on the receiving end of a fierce verbal assault by my father – what the family called a good *guldering*. It was not to be the last.

The golden days of summer harvests as a boy were in sharp contrast to the advent of the modern leviathan combine harvesters that today can achieve in one pass that which used to take months for a previous generation.

After the binder had done its work and thrown the sheaves – hopefully all properly tied and knotted – to the ground, came the stooking when every available and able-bodied man or woman or child was called on to pick up the single sheaves and built them into upright groups for drying. These small groups of sheaves were called stooks and old photographs of country life invariably show stooks formed from eight sheaves. In our part of Galloway, however, stooks were formed from only six sheaves - presumably in the belief that in a high rainfall area like ours the fewer the number of sheaves in the stook the faster the oats would dry.

Stooking could be an enjoyable experience if the sun was on your back or sheer hell if the rain was falling in sheets, a purgatory made even worse if the section you were stooking was full of thistles which could see the day's work end with tiny prickles embedded from finger-tip to elbow.

After a week – or several weeks depending on the weather – the stooks were considered sufficiently dry for the leading-in to begin. Once again it was all hands on deck with tractor and trailer slowly travelling up and down the field while two workers with pitchforks would toss the sheaves into the trailer where they were painstakingly built into seemingly top-heavy loads ready for transport to the stack-yard at the farm steading. With special rails at the front and end of the trailer to increase the number of sheaves that could be carried, the load often seemed to reach diz-zying heights – particularly if you were on top of the load – and more than once even a gentle undulation would see a full load slip off the trailer and create another perfect opportunity for a major *guldering* from father.

Building the stacks was an art form. Whether they were round or the larger rectangular type known as sow stacks they were built with care and pride by men who had been undertaking this task all their working lives. Starting with a base of stones to insulate the first layers of sheaves from the bare earth the stacks slowly took shape until they were finally topped with a sloping roof-like finish resembling a selection of giant loaves.

Depending on the weather, the stacks would be built between August and September and to protect their comparatively valuable contents from the elements the top of each stack was carefully covered with a thick layer of rashes cut earlier by scythe from a wet area of the farm where rashes could always be depended on to grow in abundance.

The covering of rashes over the grain was then securely pinned to the stack by an intricate latticework of sisal ropes the trailing ends of which were left dangling down the face of the stack and weighted down with small rocks.

If time and inclination permitted – and the second was invariably predetermined by the first – a corn dolly designed to ward off birds and evil spirits topped the stack, a tradition going back generations.

The May will live forever in the affections of our family but it was a hard farm to work with its small acreage of thin and stony inbye land that offered little depth of topsoil for crop production. If we could have harvested stones for a profit the family would have been as rich as Croesus. Being tenant farmers didn't help either because that meant we had no collateral to help negotiate bank loans.

As it was the farm relied on the monthly milk cheque from our 29 dairy cows and the income from one or two annual lamb sales. Although I was too young to appreciate the struggle my mother and father had to make a living, their financial position could have been little other than precarious. In fact, I remember my father relishing the prospect of an approaching Sunday. Not that he was religious and looking forward to a visit to church but because Sunday meant no Post Office delivery and therefore no letters requesting payment from the bank or various farm suppliers.

One of the highlights of the farming year for a youngster was "mill day" – a day of noise, colour, dust, laughter and frenetic activity. Our nearest contractors were the Wright Brothers, local dairy farmers and contractors who would travel the small roads of our corner of Galloway with what appeared like a kind of magical travelling circus – a caravan of high technology of the age preceded by a giant green Field Marshal tractor pulling a Ransomes threshing mill. In its wake came a straw baler and, occasionally, a large vehicle like a railway guard's van or caboose that offered overnight accommodation and basic cooking facilities for the contractors if their duties took them far from home.

Once the machines were placed in position beside the stacks to be threshed, the Field Marshall would be turned round to face the threshing mill and a broad canvas belt connected to the mill would be placed on a flywheel on the tractor. Once in motion this provided the power required and the rest of the day was given over to the job in hand.

The day of the travelling threshing mill was a time of incessant noise with shouted conversations between workers trying to compete with roaring machinery and with exposed flywheels and belts that would make today's health and safety specialists either roll their eyes in despair or seek alternative employment.

From breakfast to dusk the mill threshed the golden sheaves of that autumn's harvest with 168lb bags of oats manhandled and carried up the steep granite stairs to the grain loft – all of this long before the days of forklift trucks. Little wonder that many farm workers of that generation ended their days with a pronounced stoop and bad knees.

Lunch represented the one break in the day for the mill workers. By tradition this was made and served by the farmer's wife – my mother. A fine cook at any time, she excelled herself on mill day – not so much on quality as on quantity. With a rag tag army of up to twenty workers and hangers-on to feed, she invariably fell back on tried and tested vote winners like leek and potato soup followed by mince and potatoes with apple crumble and custard to complete the mid-day energy boost. Within less than an hour, the mill workers rose from the table and resumed their stations at the threshing mill. How they were able to work having consumed the amount of food they had seemed to defy the law of natural physics.

Whether by design or coincidence, an occasional visitor during mill day lunches was Galloway's resident tramp, Snib Scott. How he came by his name is unknown but while no doubt benign in character, his long dark coat, great grey beard and shuffling gait used to strike fear into the hearts of local youngsters.

Snib Scott's questionable reputation was given further impetus by the fact that he was reputed to live in a cave on the Ayrshire coast near Ballantrae which it was said had once been inhabited by Sawney Bean, allegedly the last-known cannibal in Britain who used to waylay unwary travellers. After robbing them he and his family of brigands then killed and ate them.

While there was no suggestion of any direct link between Snib Scott and Sawney Bean, nonetheless the very threat to a recalcitrant youngster that Snib might get them was enough to strike terror into the child breast.

His reputation to adults was more prosaic – he seemed to have an uncanny knack of knowing when and where the travelling mill was going about its business and he made it his business for the two to coincide, especially at lunchtime. While he may have shared a hunger with the mill workers, there was one quality they did not have in common – Snib would not work.

One tale concerns the arrival of Snib begging for food at the farmhouse door just before the mill workers broke for lunch. The young farmer said he would give Snib lunch - but only if he was prepared to work.

The vagrant considered the prospect and said he would indeed work but could not possibly consider any physical effort while his stomach was empty. Consequently the farmer invited him in and fed him the same generous three-course meal destined for the mill workers.

Eventually Snib rose from his feast and made to leave only for the young farmer to protest that he had promised to work. The tramp looked him in the eye and said simply:

Sorry – I canna work when I'm empty and I canna work when I'm full.

With that, he put his pack on his back and walked down the farm road.

Who Snib was and how he became a vagrant is unknown. It is thought that his real name was Henry Ewing Torbet, a banker who had fallen on hard times.

Fearsome he may have appeared to children but someone must have had a soft spot in their heart for him because a memorial cairn to him stands on the Ayrshire coast near the cave he is reputed to have called home for many years. This memorial to Snib, describing him as "Respected and Independent", records the bald fact that he was born in 1912 and died in 1983.

If Snib Scott made occasional appearances seeking food on mill days, the annual threshing could be guaranteed to produce a frisson of excitement of a quite different sort.

As the sheaves from each straw stack were forked into the great maw of the threshing machine, the level of the stack naturally fell. And as it fell it was also the signal for the rats and mice that had made the stack their home to descend to a lower level and seek shelter from the noise and disturbance above their heads.

As the stack level fell, so too did anticipation rise of things to come for men and dogs. Every available collie dog or terrier and farm worker or spare mill hand holding shovels would wait as the last rows of sheaves were forked into the mill then leap into action as the rats and mice, now with nowhere else to descend to, made a desperate bid for sanctuary. They seldom found it. In these situations a dog is faster than a man wielding the back of a shovel and with this pattern repeated each time a stack was completed mill days would sound the death knell for dozens of rodents.

But even here there could be distractions. On one occasion, one of the farm staff, wielding the back of his shovel with more enthusiasm than technical merit, struck one passing rat a glancing blow which succeeded only in diverting the rat from its chosen exit route to the only alternative it could find – right up my father's trouser leg! With great presence of mind and uncommon speed my father firmly grasped his upper thigh with both hands in time to stop the wounded rat from inflicting untold damage to a part of his anatomy it would no doubt have encountered had it been allowed further upward passage.

As farm workers and an assortment of expectant dogs formed a circle round my father, he maintained his grasp round his upper leg and then proceeded to slowly but firmly push the unseen but squirming and squealing rat down to his knee and then a further onward descent to his ankle. At this point the rat emerged to its more familiar environment only to be speedily despatched by the back of a shovel.

The fact that the swift and purposeful downward motion of the shovel not only connected with the rat but also my father's foot did not in any way improve his demeanour. For the rest of the day family and farm staff kept our distance from the boss. Nobody wanted to be on the receiving end of a *guldering*.

Threshing days could clearly be stressful for my father and it was never my intention that I should add to his concerns – but I did. One of the by-products of the threshing process was a large

25

pile of chaff and once the great caravan of machines had moved to the next farm this great heap of chaff was usually the only visible sign of threshing having taken place. The chaff was no good for man or beast and usually had to be disposed of by burning.

After one mill day when I was about nine years old I decided that I would surprise my father by burning the chaff for him. Despite the liberal uses of matches stolen from the kitchen mantelpiece, I quickly realised that chaff is not easy to set alight. I then hit on the idea of hastening the process by adding paraffin from the main fuel tank used to supply the tractor.

With no jam jar to be found, a galvanised bucket was brought into play and a large amount of paraffin was drawn from the main tank and added to the pile of chaff. Slowly the fire took hold. My solution had worked and like any child with a fascination for bonfires, I stood entranced as I watched the flames.

Perhaps it was youthful enthusiasm getting in the way of commonsense or maybe just bad luck. What I do know is that after maybe thirty minutes of warming myself in front of the fire, I heard a roar behind me – a sound not unlike a wounded buffalo that I'd come to recognise from cowboy movies at the local cinema.

When I turned to try and identify the noise I saw my father approaching me with a face contorted with anger. Why, I wondered, could he possibly be upset when I had clearly shown my initiative in doing him a good turn by burning the chaff.

Seeing his face, however, indicated that it might be pointless to pose that question to him. Instead I took to my heels across the field but within a few strides he had caught me and upturned me over his knee and, despite my wriggles, proceeded to thrash me vigorously on my backside – a painful procedure punctuated only by his words of justification:

You silly wee bugger... you forgot......to turn off.....the tap.....on the paraffin tank.....

Despite my pain I looked behind him as he continued to administer his own brand of punishment and I could see a large puddle of fuel around the main tank. My supposed good deed had cost my father around 100 gallons of paraffin oil and for me it brought a whole new meaning to threshing day.

In today's politically-correct times when even a harsh word by a parent to a child can bring with it the threat of official sanction, more than half a century ago matters were more clear cut. You transgressed - you got walloped. Simple.

Unpleasant although my thrashing was when I wasted the precious fuel as a youngster, the experience of corporal punishment was not new. My first encounter with my father's strong right hand on my backside had come some years earlier when I was about four or five years old.

At that time we were in the transition stage between horse and tractor. We had our little grey Fergie but we still occasionally called on real horsepower in the form of Mary, a wonderfully benign Clydesdale mare. In those far off days the worth of a farm was measured by the number of pairs of Clydesdale horses that the farmer had. We didn't even have one pair. But we had Mary, a huge gentle brown beast that was at that time the largest animal I had ever seen in my young life. One of my childhood pleasures was to go with one of the farm staff to the field and tempt Mary with a bucket of bruised oats so that she could be haltered and led to the courtyard – with me on her broad back - to take on whatever task had been earmarked for her.

One day I missed the call to collect Mary from the field and when I realised this I found her with full harness tied to the front gate of the farmhouse ready to begin her equine duties. Childishly, and cruelly, I vented my anger on the poor horse by throwing small pebbles at her. Within moments my father noticed what I was doing and told me in no uncertain manner to depart the scene.

Still feeling thwarted at missing out on my horseback ride from the field, I ran into an adjacent field where my mother and father kept around 200 hens in a shed constructed painstakingly by my father – and known for years as *The House that Jack Built*.

The number of hens was too small even in those days to be commercially viable yet the eggs they produced were of vital importance to my mother and father as barter.

These were the days of the travelling grocer, butcher and general merchant and each week a succession of vans would call on farms throughout the county bringing with them all a rural family would need to sustain body and soul. The eggs the hens produced were used as a form of barter with the travelling retailers. Once a price had been agreed, it was a simple equation to work out how many dozen eggs equalled so much bread, bacon or tobacco. Being a dairy farm there was never any need to buy milk or butter. In this manner, weeks might pass without any hard cash exchanging hands.

Even as a five year old I realised the importance of the eggs to my mother and father. But I was still angry about not collecting Mary the horse. When I reached the henhouse my father had built I found my tiny hands were not strong enough to open the main door. However, I *was* small enough to gain access by using the same small entry-exit hole that the hens used. Once inside I gathered a small pyramid of freshly laid eggs, perhaps twenty or thirty, and then began to hurl them, one by one, out of the same small hole through which I had gained entry to the henhouse. As each egg struck the ground outside the henhouse, it broke and bright yellow yolk spread across the brown earth. It is a strange fact that a hen will not touch her own newly laid egg but present her with a broken yolk and she thinks Christmas has come early.

Within minutes there was an avian stampede as the hens realised what was happening and this may have gone on for long enough had I not become aware of what was to become a familiar human bellow above the noise of the frantic yolk-sated hens.

I looked out of the small hole to see my father running down the field shouting and gesticulating wildly. It seems that he had chanced to look towards the henhouse to see eggs mysteriously hurtling into the open air. Wise enough to know that such an achievement was beyond the capacity of even a flatulent hen he had put two and two together and guessed it was his errant son.

I managed to extricate myself from the henhouse in the same way as I had gained access and took to my heels across the field with startled hens flying in all directions. It was a forlorn hope that I might outrun my father. An angry five year-old pitted against an even angrier 45 year-old who believes his son and heir is destined to ruin his business is no match at all. Within moments he had caught me and administered my first real taste of corporal punishment. It hurt like hell.

The third and final thrashing at the hands of my father took place around the same time when I inadvertently almost set alight my grandmother's hair. By now both grandmothers lived at the farm. My mother's mother, she who was prone to curtail bedtime frolics by banging on the ceiling with her walking stick, was called Big Granny and my father's mother, a sweet-natured diminutive lady was appropriately named Wee Granny.

Despite parental controls on these sorts of things I had somehow got my hands on a box of matches. They were not normal matches but had an unusually bulbous end which, when lit, flared vividly with an orange burst of flame. I was at the top of the stairs on the landing looking down on the hall below and idly fiddling with one of the matches, rubbing it gently against the ignition paper when suddenly it burst into flame.

Startled, I threw the match away and saw it fall over the staircase down towards the downstairs hall at the precise moment that Wee Granny walked below. To my horror I saw the match fall on her head but before it could set light to her hair it was instantly plucked from her head by my father who fortunately was following his mother along the hall. He looked up and saw me and began to climb the stairs towards me. For the third time in my young life I was to feel his heavy hand on my backside.

Yet while my father had stern Victorian principles, not least claiming his inalienable right to chastise as he saw fit, it would be wrong to portray him as a rigid disciplinarian devoid of any sense of humour and I recall a lot more laughter than anger in my young life.

Most Fridays mother would drive to Newton Stewart and, having deposited father for his weekly sojourn in the pub, she and I would make for the nearby farm of Skaith, the home of my mother's elder sister, my auntie Mary Littlejohn and her husband Percy, his bachelor brother Jim – always smiling despite a lifetime of disablement - and a clutch of my gregarious Littlejohn cousins,

Maureen, Pat, Perry, Anne and Fiona. Two memories of these regular visits to Skaith remain with me still – the excitement of working my childhood way through the many sections, especially comics, of the latest delivery of an American newspaper regularly sent from the USA to Uncle Percy and his brother Jim from Wyoming where the Littlejohn family had had their childhood home. The second memory is of the small flock of guinea fowl that provided a splash of exotic colour around the Skaith farm buildings. As darkness fell, however, the birds would seek sanctuary in the branches of trees near the house and give vent to a prolonged and strident screeching that might well have been heard in Africa from where the birds originated.

It is the memory of various individuals that colours the images of my farming childhood. Two such were Sonny Jardine, son of Bob the shepherd, and Andy Brolls. Countrymen to their bootstraps they were used to everything daily farming life could throw at them with one exception – Andy didn't like mice. Andy was considerably older than the youthful Sonny but the two shared a strong working bond and however their working duties would separate them on any given day, they would invariably meet every lunchtime in the farm courtyard to share each other's company during their lunch break.

It may have been the heat of the summer's day beating down or the consequence of his hard morning's work but I recall one occasion when Andy went sound asleep with his head resting on a bale of straw.

With an indication to me that I should keep quiet, Sonny then produced a dead mouse from one of his pockets and gently lowered it into the dark recesses of the front of Andy's shirt. In due course Andy awoke and Sonny and I watched as he slowly became aware of some alien object on his person. On discovering the dead mouse he gave vent to words that were new to my young ears and suggested a fate worse than death should the luckless Sonny ever try such a stunt again. Whether it had anything to do with the dead mouse or not, Andy shortly afterwards decided that a new job pulling pints of beer in the bar of the Monreith Arms Hotel in Port William offered a less stressful life.

Although mechanisation was increasing in those post-war years, farming still relied heavily on manual labour. This was especially true at busy times of the year like harvest time. Like many farmers in Scotland, my father and mother took advantage of the tail-end of the emigration from Ireland that for generations since the famine of 1846-47 had brought thousands across the Irish Sea to the west of Scotland in search of temporary work on the grain and potato harvests.

For a few weeks every year we employed two of these Irish stalwarts, Allan and Patrick. Whether it was part of their contract or my parent's generosity I do not know but these two hard-working and hard-living Irishmen stayed in our spare bedroom. What sticks in the mind from my childhood was my mother and father's exasperation that they would not use our toilet facilities during the night. Should a call of nature beckon, they preferred instead to use the chanty, or chamber-pot, under the bed. Whether this was due to an innate laziness or the fact that they had no bathroom in their own homes in Ireland we never discovered. Be that as it may, more than once in the middle of the night we awoke to a rich Irish brogue urgently calling: *Allan! Bring Paper Allan! Paper!*

Another character forever etched in my memory was the formidable Cleekit Meg, a second cousin of my mother, who came on holiday to the farm at least twice a year. Married to a retired white-collar worker from the giant Colvilles steel-making company in Motherwell near Glasgow, her proper name was Margaret Sutherland but she was universally known throughout the family – and behind her back – as Cleekit Meg. Look up any Scots dictionary and you will find various meanings of *Cleekit* ranging from the shape of a hook to having arms intertwined. But our Cleekit Meg did not conform to any of these descriptions. In our parlance, Cleekit had darker connotations.

She was upright, God-fearing – and fearsome. Her pure white hair was tightly wound up in a bun at the back of her head but the white hair that sprouted from her chin was less manageable, however, and when faced with a dreaded goodnight kiss, Cleekit

Meg's chin carried with it all the attractions of making close contact with an animated and aggressive porcupine.

A retired schoolteacher, Cleekit Meg had another quality beyond her hairy chin. She was mean. To suggest meanness in the normal sense would be inaccurate. She made parsimony look like profligacy. After dinner on the first night of arriving at the farmhouse she would produce a large tin of sweets. She would allow my father, mother and myself to take one sweet – and one only – after which the lid was firmly replaced and the tin taken back to her bedroom. If we were lucky the tin might make a further appearance a few nights later – but one sweet each was still the ration. She had no desire, she emphasised, to spoil us.

Cleekit Meg's husband James also stays sharp in the memory. A quiet man who preferred to let his loquacious wife talk for both of them, his preference after dinner was reading the paper rather than join in any conversation. In fact, the only sound to come from the direction of James was that of passing wind. What he had had to eat on that or any other evening made no difference. Each night was the same. He sat on the sofa and farted - loudly, long and frequently. His technique was always the same. Without preamble he would slightly ease one cheek or the other an inch or two off the couch before his next bout of flatulence. Sometimes it was alternate legs, sometimes not. Eventually, it became something of a game to guess if he would begin an evening's performance with two lefts followed by a right or vice versa. This virtuoso flatulence was worthy of the traditions of Joseph Pujol the 19th Century Frenchman known as Le Petomane and whose unique capacity for public farting endeared him to Paris theatre audiences for years. He even had a street named after him in his native Marseilles.

If James Sutherland unwittingly entertained us, Cleekit Meg also made a contribution with her frequent renditions of obscure poetry. One or her party pieces was a poem set in the Boer War in which her brother Col. John McEwan took an active part. This particular ode concerned a child born in South Africa at the end of the Boer War and was christened in rhyme with all names reflecting an officer or battle during the conflict.

The poem ran for many verses and I remember sitting spellbound as Cleekit Meg's warmed to her theme – her eyes rolling in theatrical over-acting and her animated hairy chin taking on a life of its own.

Another enduring character of my boyhood days was uncle Peter Skimming, my mother's only brother, who farmed a few miles away at Airyolland near the small fishing village of Port William. Tall, dark and handsome, he cut a dashing figure to my boyhood eyes when he came to visit – first in a converted military ambulance but later, as his farming business prospered, in a succession of exciting Jaguars.

When I was about six years old, uncle Peter's wife, Jean, died suddenly and while uncle Peter re-assessed his personal and farming future, his son Peter came to live at the May Farm while his daughters Dorothy and Frances stayed with relatives and close friends. Because cousin Peter and I were the same age – he was born 23 hours before me – we went to Mochrum School near Port William and became close pals over the year we spent together before the Skimming family were reunited for a new life on a large arable farm near Anstruther in the East Neuk of Fife.

Because of young Peter, we saw a lot of uncle Peter in that year and I remember admiring this dashing debonair farmer racing up our small farm road in his large shiny Jaguar.

Not surprisingly, put two six-year-old boys together on a farm – or anywhere – and mischief is bound to figure in their agenda. On one occasion uncle Peter stayed at our farmhouse while my mother and father went to Edinburgh for a rare long weekend. One evening, as uncle Peter did his best to look after two boisterous youngsters supposedly sleeping in separate rooms, young Peter and I decided that the top of the landing was a perfect command post to position ourselves to see which one of us could pee furthest over the banister and into the hall below. Just as two small jets of pee began to fall into the void, by cruel chance uncle Peter passed below and received a direct hit on his head from me. With an angry roar uncle Peter leapt up the stairs as we sprinted for our respective beds. To my eternal shame, it was young Peter's backside that was smacked as I, the real guilty party, lay in the next room quivering in mortal terror under the bedclothes. But if uncle Peter knew who the real culprit had been he never said and the incident was never mentioned again.

Soon afterwards young Peter left the May to join his sisters Dorothy and Frances and his father at Airdrie Farm in Fife. Despite being separated by more than 200 miles, occasional visits to Airdrie became a treat to look forward to. Here, in the fertile east coast were crops that I never saw at home – great broad fields of wheat and barley, potatoes and sugar beet. One long thin field between the public road and Airdrie farmhouse was known as "the strip", almost a mile long and later to boast the longest sugar beet drills of any farm in Scotland.

At Airdrie there was talk of a secret tunnel from the garden to the distant coast that had been used by smugglers in days gone by but for young Peter and me the compelling attraction was the secret Ministry of Defence radar station which adjoined part of the farm. Soon it was to occupy a vital role in the British defence system as one of a small network of bunkers throughout the UK where political and military top brass could operate deep underground in comparative safety in the event of nuclear war with Russia.

Now open to the public, it was then a firm no-go area. How we did it I do not know but one afternoon cousin Peter and I managed to find a gap in the security fence and crept through into the military installation. I dimly recall many buildings but few personnel and as it was years before CCTV cameras our presence was not detected for what seemed like hours before two shamefaced eight year olds were frogmarched back to Airdrie by a uniformed guard and returned to our worried but grateful parents.

These youthful adventures and pleasures in the East Neuk of Fife are treasured memories. For my cousin Peter there were to be all too few of them. He was killed in a car accident near Airdrie Farm when he was 18 years old.

Cars have always held a special place in my affections – particularly the memory of large motors in post war austerity Scotland. Quite apart from Uncle Peter in his various Jaguars, one of the higher profile drivers in rural Galloway in those early days was Dr Gavin Brown our local GP based in Port William. He had a Humber Super Snipe. It was black, long and massive. Its petrol consumption must have been astronomical but perhaps fuel in those post-war days was so cheap it didn't have the relevance it has today. Dr Gavin Brown was quite unlike today's GPs. Today it is almost impossible to have a GP make a house call. Then it was different. For Dr Gavin Brown, the motto seemed to be: *Have Car Will Travel.* I recall my mother or father often phoning him in the morning and suggesting he call for a coffee and, if he happened to be passing Jimmy Dewar's, the local grocer, could he possibly bring some sugar and tobacco. Shortly after morning surgery the doctor's glistening black limousine with its long torpedo-shaped bonnet would glide up the farm road and Dr Gavin Brown would alight. In one hand was his doctor's bag, in the other a brown paper bag containing sugar and tobacco as requested. After a convivial coffee break, he would then depart for his next port of call with a contribution from the farm – home baking or butter and eggs.

Another car to live long in the memory was my first school transport – a Ford V8 Pilot. Launched in 1947, a local transport contractor managed to get his hands on one in time for my first journeys to primary school in Mochrum village in 1949. Built like a tank, it sounded like one as well. One of the features of the V8 was a column change gearbox with only three forward gears. With its great bulk and deafening engine roar, it seemed indestructible.

However, one car that was certainly not indestructible was the one and only brand new car that my mother and father ever owned – a Jowett Javelin, Registration OS 8056. This was Britain's first all-new car following the Second World War. It was racy, fast and streamlined and this groundbreaking vehicle sold 24,000 between 1947 and 1953 and won many high profile races including the 1953 Tulip International Rally.

Our Jowett Javelin cost around £1250 – a princely sum in the early 1950s. How my mother and father could afford this with the income from 29 Ayrshire dairy cows is beyond my understanding but I clearly recall the arrival on the farm of this wondrous exotic shiny black limousine. To sit inside and smell the brand new leather was an excitement beyond compare.

As my father did not drive – I guess after 25 years of safely guiding thousands of tons of shipping through the oceans of the world a mere automobile was beneath his dignity – my mother carefully parked the brand new Jowett Javelin in the garage in readiness for its first real trip on the open roads of Galloway later that day. However, after lunch, father decided that as he had written the cheque for payment of the vehicle he should at least have the honour of taking it out of the garage before handing it over to the safe hands of my mother. Despite my mother's pleas for him to be careful, he jumped into the driver's seat and, after several unsuccessful attempts, finally found reverse gear on the column change. He released the clutch all too quickly, the car shot back out of the garage like a lightning bolt accompanied by a harsh grating noise and into the sunshine of the afternoon. I looked at the car. Something was missing from the front of the vehicle. I peered into the garage. There, lying on the floor where it had been untimely torn from the bodywork was the front bumper that father's incautious driving had ripped off on the garage wall. That was the first and only time I ever saw my father behind the wheel of a car. He never drove again.

To live on a farm then and now was fraught with danger – but as a child you never noticed the perils lurking around every corner. Farming is one of the highest risk businesses in the country. Familiarity breeds contempt and every year the agricultural industry records a grim catalogue of fatalities whether caused by being crushed with livestock or falling into the moving parts of powerful machines. As a youngster I realised that to that list could be added the prospect of being burned to a crisp.

One of the exciting interludes in my young life was just before springtime – burning season. This was when landowners and tenant farmers like my father were given permission to burn dead grass to help make way for new growth to feed their livestock. Our main moorland area was a low-lying flat expanse covering around 800 acres and it was important that the burning was carried out before the main egg laying and hatching season for moorland birds like the curlew or lapwing.

When conditions for burning were right and the fire was set correctly the end result was extremely productive in destroying dead vegetation. When conditions were wrong or the fire-raising was in the wrong hands the result could be devastating.

The method employed to set the moor alight was simple. A hessian sack was wrapped into a tight bundle and held together with wire. A long wire handle of about six feet was then attached and the bundle immersed overnight in a bucket of paraffin.

The following morning, if wind and weather conditions were right, the hessian bundles – now totally saturated with paraffin – were taken to the point where the fire was to start. They were set alight and the burning bundle was then dragged at walking speed across the rough ground bouncing through the dead grass igniting clumps every few feet. Within a short time a great front of fire had built up. The trick was to ensure that you burned against the wind. Burning with the wind was almost valueless as then the fire would sweep over the surface of the vegetation and miss much of the dead material it was designed to destroy.

Burning against the wind, however, was highly effective. Here, the fire crept along slowly burning all the dead grass and heather in its path leaving ample scope for the later emergence of the green shoots of new growth to provide nourishment for the Blackface ewes and their single lambs which would be put out on the moor after the lambing season was over. Ewes and twin lambs, however, were always kept on the better in-bye fields nearer the farm courtyard.

Helping my father with the annual burning was a youthful pleasure. Seeing the tightly bundled paraffin-soaked hessian bag bouncing behind me setting light to dead grass every time it landed filled with me with excitement. Father and I would begin in the centre of the outside edge of the area to be burned then he would go one way and I the other. The first time we tried this I began confidently enough. But as I looked over my shoulder and saw my father disappearing slowly into the gathering smoke I felt a growing sense of unease.

Soon I lost sight of my father and very quickly I also lost sight of the dry-stone dyke at the edge of the moor that represented a point of reference. I continued walking but soon the smoke enveloped me and I lost any sense of direction. Panicking a little I continued walking but clearly had no idea where I was. All too soon I stopped. In front of me was a wall of fire. I realised I had been walking in a circle and had hemmed myself into a circle of flame. It was a dry day and the dead vegetation was burning fiercely. Scared out of my wits, I was debating whether I should make a dash directly for the weakest point of the fire in the hope of bursting through the flames to safety when suddenly I saw a ghostly shape in the smoke. As it approached I realised it was my father who had returned to see that all was well with my end of the burning line. How well I recall my little hand slipping inside his giant fist as he led me out of the line of fire and into safety.

Growing up on a farm was never dull. The rhythm of the changing seasons brought its own special attractions and delights for a young boy be it moor burning and lambing in the spring, sheep shearing and harvest in summer or the autumn lamb sales in markets like Newton Stewart or Castle Douglas. After each farmer's batch of lambs were sold in lots of 50 or 100 there was occasionally time for "the boy's lamb", a father's reward in lieu of pocket money for the myriad of errands completed over the year as well as an introduction into the ways of traditional livestock trading.

This single lamb was paraded round the sawdust ring with the boy – me – standing beside his father below the auctioneer's rostrum. A sea of faces surrounded the ringside and the tiered seating that stretched upwards to the roof and I can hear still the cacophony of noise of clanging gates being opened and shut as thousands of lambs were brought to and from the ring. The auction of the "boy's lamb" lasted only a few seconds but the thrill of being a small part of this annual pageant never diminished and the money for my lamb – on one occasion it reached the dizzying amount of £5 – seemed like a king's ransom to an impecunious little boy.

Even winter brought its special memories, especially plucking turkeys. For many years my mother and father reared turkeys for the Christmas trade. It was never a huge operation and the most we ever produced in any year was about a hundred. To earn as much as possible we used to sell the turkeys as oven ready – in other words, gutted and plucked.

Rearing the birds in the first place was the initial challenge. For some reason turkeys share with sheep a remarkable propensity to die for no apparent reason – preferably in large numbers in the case of turkeys. Careful ventilation and temperature control was vital if two young turkeys were not to huddle together for warmth encouraging the rest in the poultry shed to join them in a mass suffocation suicide pact.

Having overcome the ever-present possibilities of death and disease and brought the turkeys to Christmas maturity the next challenge was to kill them. Killing a hen by wringing its neck is easy when you know how. Killing a turkey is harder. For a start it's far bigger than a chicken and takes a lot of strength and technique. Born and bred in the countryside my mother was a past master at despatching the birds – with one exception. Occasionally even her skills were not up to the job of killing a large male turkey known as a stag. I was too young to make any contribution to this stage of the process and even my father on occasions couldn't kill the largest stags.

Necessity being the mother of invention, however, they found a way. Holding the luckless bird by the back legs by father would gently lower it until its head reached the stone floor of the plucking room in the courtyard. Then my mother would lay the shaft of the stout byre brush across the back of its head. She would then stand on the shank pinning down the poor bird with her whole weight while father then gave a sharp yank upwards on the bird's legs. Gruesome – but it worked. Well, it usually worked. On one occasion father must have exerted a little too much pressure because immediately having pulled the legs vigorously he fell backwards with the dead turkey on top of him. I remember seeing my mother look at father then down at her own feet where the turkey's head was still held fast by the brush shank under her feet. The combination of mother's weight on the brush shank and father's strength had totally removed the bird's head from its neck.

Amid this charnel house scene I seem to recall my mother trying to placate my father by mentioning something to the effect that he shouldn't worry because the turkey's head was due to be removed a little later in any case.

What I hated about the annual turkey harvest was the plucking. Plucking is easiest if done immediately after the bird's demise when the flesh is still warm. However, trying to do the job too fast you ran the risk of tearing the warm flesh and that instantly devalued the bird as a saleable product. Therefore, plucking had to be done very carefully to ensure maximum returns from the local Christmas market.

But if the feathers on occasion were all too easy to remove from the main body of the bird with the attendant risk of tearing the flesh, plucking feathers from the wings could be a long slow task. So embedded were some of the wing feathers on the stag birds that they only way they could be removed was with the help of a pair of pliers.

Yet my parents thought the effort worthwhile. The turkeys were killed to order and as we didn't deliver, the days before Christmas saw a steady procession of buyers come to the farm to take delivery of their bird. Each night for a week of the festive season that day's harvest would lie in rows on the large kitchen table and await collection. Plucked, gutted, trussed and well dusted with flour to hide any little blemishes they represented some kind of bizarre avian mortuary for the festive season.

When I was ten years old, my mother surprised me – and possibly father as well – by producing a daughter. This small bundle of humanity was duly named Monica and life took on a new element as I watched her grow and within a few years I was able to persuade her to take part in bicycle races round the farm buildings. Not a very feminine pursuit for her but character building I have no doubt. Despite my having accidentally dropped her on her head during one bout of high jinks at the local village park she developed academically as well and in due course became a senior figure in the world of speech therapy with the National Health Service in her native Dumfries and Galloway.

But Monica, too, was to show moments of devilment. Coming back from primary school one day she eagerly confided to me that she had discovered how to make a V sign. By chance we later that day accompanied mother to Port William and en route mother caught sight of Monica surreptitiously giving me the V sign. My mother asked what it meant. We lied to her and explained it was a new convivial form of greeting between friends and colleagues. Mother received this information without comment. A few minutes later we reached Port William in time to see Jimmy Dewar, the grocer, walking across the square holding a large cardboard box of provisions. We had been dealing with him for many years so mother felt obliged to blow her horn to catch his attention and give him a vigorous V sign – thus, she believed, sharing with him this latest form of warm human communication. If my memory serves me right, Jimmy Dewar didn't actually drop his box of groceries but a strange look of hurt and puzzlement came over his face...

Edinburgh

But all that was in the past. Farming may have been bred in the bone but my future lay elsewhere. Late September 1961 saw me enrol at Skerry's Commercial College in Edinburgh's Nicolson Square for a course learning my way around an Underwood typewriter keyboard and doing my best to unravel the intricacies of Pitman's shorthand. Both were to help equip me for a career in newspapers although other aspects of the course I was taking were less likely to be beneficial – like mastering the language of Bills of Lading and import-export mysteries. Somehow, my mother and father found the £71 5s 6d for the tuition fees. Little did I think I would leave the college within less than two months.

Thanks to the connections of a former district nurse from Galloway who had her roots in Edinburgh, I was staying in digs in Polwarth Gardens near Tollcross, sharing a room with one of the sons of Mrs McClements, the widow of a Church of Scotland minister. She looked after me royally – doing my washing with that of her own family, feeding me breakfast and lunch and all for the princely sum of £3 a week. But it was still £3 a week my parents could ill afford as with no income of my own, I still leaned on them for some support – and looked forward eagerly to the pink ten shilling note that would occasionally drop through the letterbox and thus help keep body and soul together.

In those early days I also learned that the way to learn about interesting sights in a new city was not to take a bus – but to walk. However, in my case one of the most interesting sights did not even require a walk. My bedroom at Polwarth Gardens overlooked a small cobbled lane called Merchiston Mews, home to the legendary motor racing team of Ecurie Ecosse, founded in the 1950s by local businessman and racing driver David Murray. By the time I reached Edinburgh in 1961 the racing team's fame was known the world over as a result of their star driver Ron Flockhart winning Le Mans in a D type Jaguar in 1956 and 1957. And so it was I whiled away many boyhood hours watching the blue Jaguars in this little cobbled street beside my digs. But of their star driver who had twice won Le Mans there was no sign. Ron Flockhart was killed in an air crash near Melbourne, Australia, in the spring of 1962.

In the early morning the cobbled streets of this part of Edinburgh used to resound to the clip-clop of horses' hooves from the nearby Fountainbridge stables of St. Cuthberts, the Edinburgh-co-operative store which seemed to have a monopoly of both the sale of milk to the local population and the attendant result of ensuring no-one was late for work – horses' hooves on cobbled streets are better than any modern alarm clock. I was also about to discover that one of the former St. Cuthberts' milkmen was about to hit the world stage as a major Hollywood star – he was Sean Connery who became the first James Bond with the release of Dr No in 1962.

While my commercial course at Skerry's College was due to run for a year, the need within me to find a job quickly was strong. I began to put my new typewriting skills to good use by writing to virtually every leading newspaper in Britain seeking employment. Many did not reply; those who did offered little by way of encouragement.

Surprisingly, perhaps, one of the last letters I wrote was to the newspaper that was nearest – *The Scotsman* in Edinburgh. Within two days I had a reply from the News Editor of Scotland's national newspaper. Would I attend an interview as there might be an opening? You bet I would.

In those days the headquarters of *The Scotsman* were at 20 North Bridge, surely one of the most imposing buildings in Edinburgh with its commanding views over Princes Street, the New Town, the Firth of Forth and the Kingdom of Fife beyond.

But as I walked down the old steps of Fleshmarket Close to the back entrance of the newspaper for my interview, I was in a different Edinburgh. This side of the building was part of the Old Town with its ancient closes and dark alleyways where on dark winter evenings it was all too easy to imagine you had stepped back in time.

The interview with Stuart Brown, the news editor, must have gone well. I recall a friendly man who had started his reporting career in Berwick-in-Tweed but who had his life interrupted by the Second World War and five years as a prisoner of war before resuming his time in newspapers. I cannot recall the detail of what he asked me – only that at the end of our short meeting, he offered me a job as a copy boy at the princely sum of £2 17s 6d a week. Was I interested? I accepted on the spot. The fact that my digs were costing more than my weekly wage did not deter me. Mr Micawber's clear distinction between happiness and misery may have been appropriate in the circumstances but somehow it didn't matter - I had a job in a newspaper office and nothing in my young world seemed more important than that.

And so it was that on the afternoon of November 12th 1961, Remembrance Sunday, I began my duties as a copy boy. Knowing nothing about anything, or *ten per cent of bugger all* as my father often described my early grasp of the human condition, my first task was to distribute the previous day's mail that had arrived when the offices were silent and empty. Helping me to make sense of the vast pile of letters and envelopes that first afternoon was a tall friendly youngster who had just graduated from being a copy boy to more responsible duties in the newsroom along the corridor. He was Chris Baur, soon to become a good friend and who was later to rise through the ranks and after spells on *The Financial Times* and the *BBC* was to return to his first newspaper and become Editor of *The Scotsman*. Helping me to sort out the mail that Sunday afternoon was not the only time I had cause to be grateful to Chris. Some time later he helped me out of a motoring dilemma of which more later.

In today's hi-tech journalism, there is not the same need for copy boys but traditionally they were a vital part of the newspaper world. Based in the sub-editor's room, the copy boys were also known as tube boys because a central part of their role was manning the pneumatic tubes that connected the sub-editor's domain to the wire room and the case-room. The wire-room – an entire room full of chattering printers - served as the point of intake for foreign stories from sources like Associated Press or Reuters or domestic UK news from the Press Association.

The case-room was two floors below and was the point at which all edited stories were set up in hot metal.

I had discovered the case-room on my second afternoon. While I was sorting out the mail, a pleasant man in an immaculate pinstriped suit appeared in the subs' room and gave me an envelope to take to the case-room. I had no idea where he meant and my hesitancy must have been obvious to him.

"*You must be new,*" he said. "*Come with me son and I'll show you where the case-room is.*" As he led me down the stone steps he added: "*Actually, a case-room in a newspaper is usually simple to find – you just follow the smell of burnt toffee.*" And so it proved – part of the hot metal process did indeed carry the slight aroma of overdone confectionery.

Later, back in the subs room, I asked a colleague who my personal guide had been. "*That,*" he said, "*was the Editor!*" It was my first sight of Alastair MacTavish Dunnett, one of the most respected newspaper editors of his generation who was to go on and become a pioneering figure in the developing North Sea oil industry in his capacity as Chairman of Thomson Oil and end his business career with a Knighthood.

And so my voyage of discovery continued. Whether receiving and sorting incoming copy or ensuring edited stories were carefully rolled and secured in their little cylinders before being sent to the case-room, the "swoosh" of compressed air as the tubes were opened and closed every few minutes became a constant part of my daily life.

One of the celebrated figures of *The Scotsman* was Wilfred Taylor who, for more than 30 years, wrote *A Scotsman's Log*, a daily column written in the third person. By coincidence, within a couple of weeks of my beginning work as a copy boy, he had happened to walk through the subs' room on a deserted Saturday and, seeking inspiration for his Monday column, noticed various humorous newspaper cuttings we had pinned to our work station area. As a result, he chose to write about us thus:

"*The tube nexus in the middle of the room is to the copy boys what a barrel of apple-jack is to the elderly gossips*

*of New England. The copy boys tend these compressed
air orifices when they aren't serving coffee, washing-up or
discharging their myriad errands. The laden tubes are the
insistent social centre of their oppressed lives.*

*"Tube boys are the lowliest form of editorial life.
Compared with them the handmaidens of the Muses are
pampered parasites. They are the beck-and-call boys, the
little slaves of the night. We always try to treat them with
grave courtesy because you never know when one of them
will shoot, like one of the cylindrical carriers, right up to the
top and become your boss!"*

Wilfred Taylor reckoned that the copy boys put Ganymede in
his place as a pouting loafer and imagined that carrying cups of
wine to the gods was an idle, eupeptic job compared to serving a
dyspeptic sub-editor. Seeking ideas for his column, the celebrated
diarist, standing alone that Saturday afternoon in the darkened
subs' room, reckoned the office was full of the ghosts of dauntless
copy boys who, ground to pieces by their daily chores, had faced
extinction itself with good cheer before their shrunken remains
had been callously stuffed into a carrier tube and sent to one of
those bournes from which no traveller returns.

As *The Scotsman* was a morning newspaper, the sub-editors
did not begin work until the afternoon and so consequently the
pattern of my daily life changed in parallel. Within weeks, I had
abandoned my course at Skerrys commercial college and adopted
a schedule that saw me sleep late and enjoy lunch before walking
through the city to begin work at 3pm.

There were four copy boys and in addition to handling the
key role of receiving and despatching copy, one of our main
tasks was to ensure that the sub-editors' every dietary whim was
catered for. With a healthy diet and lifestyle enjoying less of a high
profile than today it was not unusual to find myself, around 8pm,
staggering down the High Street from the Mocambo Grill towards
Fleshmarket Close with an armful of eleven fish suppers, three with
brown sauce and eight with salt and vinegar, four pie suppers, and
a range of hamburgers and haggis.

Any spare capacity I might have had was usually absorbed by small packs of tobacco for the hand-rollers or packets of Capstan Full Strength and Players Navy Cut.

One dark winter evening a mixture of too much haste and a slippery step saw me miss six feet of Fleshmarket Close on my return bearing my bounty of cholesterol-laden fuel. Pies, chips and battered haddock went flying down the several steep stone steps towards Waverley Railway Station. By the time I had done my best to retrieve the situation, my copious tears of fear and embarrassment had mixed with spilt vinegar and brown sauce. But if any of the hungry subs detected any foreign bodies in their meal that night, they were too busy or kind-hearted to mention it.

Despite a common taste for eating their evening meal out of yesterday's newspaper, the subs were a disparate bunch. There was Pat Gaffney, the genial Irishman with a fondness for Guinness who planned the blockbuster novel but never quite completed it; Jeremy Bruce-Watt, the aspiring playwright who smoked cheroots and to whose flat I was once despatched to awaken him after he overslept beyond 4pm; Gordon Anderson, the gruff but friendly pipe-smoking chief sub, whose nightly order never varied – tea without milk in a tannin-stained red plastic cup, a Tunnock caramel biscuit, an ounce of pipe tobacco and a box of Swan Vestas; A.D.Fraser, taciturn and pipe-smoking and in charge of the Letters to the Editor columns and who wore the most perfectly polished black shoes I had ever seen; and Stewart Boyd the kindly assistant Art Editor and another pipe-smoker whose presence was usually preceded by voluminous clouds of smoke. When I was uncertain about how my career was progressing, Stewart Boyd, just a little older than myself, showed an understanding and a kindly support for which I was always grateful.

Well-known names, too, were to pass through the subs room – like Gus Macdonald who was to go on to carve a distinguished career as a television presenter and executive before securing a peerage and a ministerial role in Tony Blair's government.

The subs were an amiable and amenable bunch, working far into the night, usually under pressure, always wreathed in tobacco smoke. Many had an impish sense of humour. One such was John Campbell who had previously been a Town Clerk on the west coast of Scotland before he turned to journalism. When he wanted me to take copy to one of the paper's leader writers who went by the unlikely but genuine name of Arthur J. Arthur, he would delight in shouting: *"Take this to Arthur Arthur Arthur!"* This was the only time a lowly copy boy like me was to hear his Christian name. By tradition we reacted to the single command: *"Boy!"*

Still, it was a good grounding in the basics of newspaper production. And, if you showed enthusiasm, opportunities were given to the copy boys to try their hand at basic sub-editing. These would be simple, virtually formulaic contributions, like the radio and television schedules, horse racing returns, the weather forecast or movements of shipping. Within weeks, I became sufficiently well versed in the movements of Ben Line steamers plying their trade between Yokohama and Cobh in the Irish Republic, that I even impressed my father when I mentioned it in a telephone call to the farm.

A tube boy's last duty of the night was one I eagerly looked forward to – waiting until the mighty printing presses rolled into action then following that thunderous sound to its source in the bowels of the building. There I would collect thirty or so copies of the first edition to distribute to the subs and the late duty reporters. The printing presses pounded like the engine room of a great liner and I used to tremble with excitement listening to the roar of the machines as they spewed out thousands of copies of the next morning's newspaper. I can hear them still.

Once the first editions were delivered to the waiting subs, my day was over and I would welcome the fresh air as I walked the one mile or so back to my digs in Polwarth Gardens near Tollcross. It was another chance to have a couple of fags before I entered the no-smoking environment of my landlady's house. Usually at that time of night I had Edinburgh more or less to myself. One evening, however, I became conscious of a patter of feet following me. I stopped but was afraid to look behind me. The footsteps also stopped. I continued for a hundred yards and once again the footsteps followed. I stopped again. The footsteps stopped. I whirled around, terrified out of my wits. There, a few paces behind me, looking at me plaintively stood a forlorn Beagle. Within moments we had become friends and the dog dutifully followed me back to my digs.

There, with the benefit of some decent lighting, I could see he had a telephone number on a collar tag. We rang the number and a pleasant sounding man expressed his gratitude for finding his lost dog. He would be round in 15 minutes to collect it. The dog's owner duly appeared. It was Sir John Greig Dunbar, then the Lord Provost of Edinburgh. He took charge of his dog, thanked me profusely and pressed five shillings into my eager hand. I considered that it had been a good day.

After some 15 months of manning the tubes, I was assigned a new role among the phone clerks, more usually known as copytakers. This job was part of the newsroom. Gone were the sound of the compressed air tubes and the constant cries of "Boy!" In their place were the clatter of typewriter keyboards and the incessant demands of ringing telephones.

The task here for the members of the small team of copytakers was to wait until a light flashed above one of six small booths about the size of a telephone box. We would then answer the call that might come from one of the newspaper's staff reporters in the field or, more usually, from one of the large network of freelance correspondents spread throughout the country – occasionally sporting stars who had turned their hand to journalism like Australian cricketers Jack Fingleton and Richie Benaud or an athletics hero like Harold Abrahams who, long before he turned to journalism, had won the gold medal in the 100 metres for Britain in the Paris Olympics of 1924 and, with Eric Liddell, inspired the film *Chariots of Fire*.

As the reporter at the other end dictated his or her story word-by-word and phrase-by-phrase, our task was to type it as fast and accurately as possible before passing to the sub-editors. Variety was the rule rather than the exception. Who knew what story might be presaged by the red flashing light – fish prices from Peterhead, a murder in Perth or industrial unrest in Paisley.

Accuracy was vital – and the world of copy taking produced its own language and style accepted and understood throughout the newspaper industry. To differentiate between *Miss* and *Mrs* down a poor telephone line, the reporter would invariably add "married lady" after *Mrs*. Equally, it was important to establish whether names like *Thomson* had a "p" in the middle or whether names like Mackenzie were indeed *Mackenzie, McKenzie or MacKenzie*. To help ensure maximum speed, certain words were also abbreviated in a style that was understood by sub-editor and compositor alike. The word *committee* would appear as *cttee*, while *that* would be shorted to *tt* and *the* would simply become *t*.

The code quickly became second nature. Once these stories reached the sub-editors' desks, however, these abbreviations were carefully circled to ensure that the printers would translate the abbreviation to the word that would mean something to the next morning's readers of *The Scotsman*. Little did I know it, but many of these abbreviations were to become commonplace decades later when texting became one of life's principal tools of communication. I may have mastered those abbreviations as a copytaker in the 1960s but texting in the 21st century I chose to leave to the next generation.

Yet no matter how fast our typing, the process of reading stories over the telephone to be transcribed at the other end could often be a laborious if not tedious operation. Not surprisingly, some correspondents could be less patient than others.

One such was Frank Moran, the paper's golf correspondent, respected and admired throughout sports journalism and the world of golf for the knowledge, authority and style he brought to his work. Patience with fledgling copy-takers, however, was not one of his virtues. He would insist that as each page was typed, it was read back to him and any sins of omission or commission were forcefully pointed out to the unfortunate copy-taker. As far as Frank Moran's copy was concerned, my weakness was maintaining consistency of style and remembering when and where to use numbers rather than letters when referring to the type of club, the hole being played and the number of strokes taken. When I got it wrong, Frank Moran let me know in no uncertain manner. Little did I know it then but years later when I became a BBC producer I was to work closely with a fine writer and farmer-historian named Tom Barry who turned out to be Frank Moran's son in law.

Another occasionally irascible correspondent was Ian Morrison, the assistant agricultural editor, and a master of the reporter's craft. Years later he was to become a close colleague but my first contact with him in my rôle as phone-clerk did not begin well.

He had been reporting from the annual sale of Galloway cattle at Castle Douglas in South West Scotland. This was the heartland of this black or dun curly-coated hardy cattle and the big February sale was the highlight of the breeders' year.

Ian had no doubt had a long and tiring day and his final act before a well-earned beer and dinner was to telephone his copy. A simple enough task, perhaps, but he hadn't reckoned on my total inability to understand the subtle nuances of how place names and the pronunciation of them can vary widely.

From far away down a crackly telephone line, Ian's voice intoned: "*Top price of the day went to the four-year-old bull Stalwart of Cholmondeley....*" His voice tailed off. "*Did you get that?*" he asked.

"*Which bit?*"

"*All of it dammit.*"

"*I think so sir, but can I just check that the spelling is C-H-U-M-L-Y?*"

One hundred and fifty miles down the telephone line came the sound of what I took to be an apoplectic explosion. Clearly, he was less than happy.

"*Good God boy, if you don't you know how to spell the well known Cheshire name of CHOLMONDELEY get me a copy-taker who can or this is going to take all night!*"

I persevered but it was a comprehensive and detailed report and I fear that Ian's evening meal that evening was long delayed.

The constant pounding of the typewriter keys soon helped increase my typing speed – and not only as a result of my professional labours. My landlady, the Minister's widow, gently insisted that I accompany her family to Church on Sunday mornings. It was a well-meant form of blackmail. Before I could enjoy my

Sunday lunch, I had a special duty to perform – taking down the morning sermon in my faltering shorthand. The moment it was over, I would steal out during the start of the last hymn, catch a No 27 bus to the High Street, make a mad dash to my small corner of the copy-takers' room and begin transcribing as fast as I dared using as many "blacks" as I could – our term for carbon papers. Using thin airmail-type paper, I could usually manage about twelve copies although it has to be said that the final copy would have tested the sharpest of eyes.

Then it was back on the No 27 bus for lunch clutching my twelve copies of the sermon. The Minister would distribute them later that day to the aged and infirm of the congregation who had missed the morning service - whether they wanted them or not. Whether it improved my shorthand skills is open to debate. What is not in question is the edge it put on my appetite.

Modern newspaper technology has now rendered the work of the copy-taker virtually obsolete but at the time it was another good experience of the basics of newspaper life.

And so my nocturnal life on *The Scotsman* continued. It began to develop a routine of its own – bed by midnight or 1am followed by a long sleep. The day began for me about lunchtime followed by frequent visits to Edinburgh cinemas in the afternoon to while away a couple of hours before it was time to begin my shift on the paper. My favourite picture house was The Playhouse at the top of Leith Street. It was a vast cavernous place offering a brief respite from the realities of life outside in the grey streets of the capital. The seduction began in the foyer that welcomed the bored and the lonely with a constant musical theme in the form of Percy Faith's *A Summer Place*. I may have been a regular customer but that conveyed no special favours from the management - on one occasion I was politely asked to leave the premises when the rich aroma of fish and chips wrapped in brown paper under my coat was detected by the usherette showing me to my seat in the darkened stalls.

Copy taking was interesting enough yet it was not what I wanted to do for the rest of my life. I wanted to write. And I wanted to earn more money. Both opportunities were to come more quickly than I had dared hope.

In those distant days one of the most important routes to learning the newspaper craft from the bottom up was wanting to do it. If you showed enthusiasm then somehow somewhere some kind-hearted senior reporter or sub-editor who had probably started at the bottom of the ladder like you would give you a break. And so it was for me.

In addition to my daily duties on *The Scotsman* I began extra work on a Saturday for the green sporting edition of our sister paper *The Evening Dispatch*. The Sports Editor was Bill Heeps who was later to become one of the Thomson Organisation's senior UK executives. His deputy was the kindly and highly respected Bill Cairns who doubled up as the paper's boxing correspondent. My duties on a Saturday were simple: sit in a booth at a predetermined time with a pair of earphones clamped on top of my head and listen for the Press Association feed from London of the English and Scottish league football results. Woe betide me if I failed to hear any score because it would not be repeated. For all I knew I was one of dozens of other youngsters throughout the UK doing precisely the same job for a few extra shillings to see them through the weekend. After each Saturday shift on the *Dispatch* I always felt a little glow of pleasure as Bill Cairns pressed two half crowns into my eager young hand. I guess he would claim it back on his expenses under a heading like "casual labour."

Later, Bill Cairns entrusted me with small reporting tasks like schools cricket and sports in the summer and schools rugby in the winter months. I was paid a pittance for these freelance activities but I loved it. When added to my weekly wage as a phone clerk I could now be sure of two things – I had enough extra to pay for my fags and, perhaps more importantly, I could pay my way in the world – without ringing up my mother or father to see if they could slip a pink ten shilling note into an envelope.

And this sporting freelance activity was to expand slightly one floor up when *The Scotsman* began to entrust me with small freelance assignments. John Rafferty, the doyen of Scottish sports writers at that time, was the football and boxing specialist par excellence but when his duties took him elsewhere I was asked to cover events like the East of Scotland Amateur Boxing Association championships held in the Music Hall in Edinburgh's George Street. There I would witness the early career of a future world champion called Ken Buchanan, a gifted young boxer who joined Leith Sparta club when he was eight years old. He turned professional in 1965 and went on to become the world lightweight champion in 1970 and in due course the first living Scot to enter the International Hall of Boxing Fame in New York.

Having listened spellbound on the radio as a youngster to the heavyweight bout between world champion Rocky Marciano and the Essex pig farmer Don Cockell I had become enthralled with boxing and was further captivated when I listened late at night in my friend Chris Baur's Great King Street flat to Eamonn Andrews' commentary of the world championship fight when a young and gifted 22-year-old athlete called Cassius Clay beat Sonny Liston on February 25th, 1964.

It was to be a special moment in the sporting history of the 20th century. Sitting in the flat in Great King Street drinking coffee, smoking and eating Swiss lackerli biscuits, it was also to be the last time that Cassius Marcellus Clay ever fought under his family slave name. From that point on he became Muhammad Ali.

For all that, boxing began to pall. Having a front row seat as a reporter seemed a privilege at the time but it also opened my eyes to other aspects of the fight game. Sitting at the press table directly under the ropes at the amateur championships in Edinburgh's Music Hall, I began to grow weary of the fathers, uncles, trainers, and hangers-on - often with beer-bellies to shame a sumo wrestler - shout and seek to drive the youngsters in the ring above me to greater efforts. Although amateur boxing with its strict rules is much safer than the professional game it is not immune from some of the worst excesses when two human beings are brought together to see which one can inflict the most physical damage on the other. From time to time, lips and eyebrows would be cut and noses would bleed copiously, often splattering my reporter's notebook in the process. On more than one occasion I looked up from my notebook to see young boxers' tears mix with the blood.

Athletics seemed altogether more wholesome. As my love affair with boxing began to pall, so an enthusiasm I had had for athletics as a schoolboy found a new lease of life. Having been recommended as a good "runner" by one freelance reporter for whom I had worked covering football matches in the Edinburgh area, I found myself on weekends working with Brian Meek, the athletics correspondent for the *Evening Dispatch*. A fine reporter who in later years was to become the Conservative leader on Edinburgh City Council, Brian and I spent three seasons together covering all the principal athletics events in Scotland. It was a time when Menzies Campbell, the UK record holder at 100 metres from 1967-1974 and a competitor in the 1964 Olympics was in weekly competition with a brilliant athlete called Mike Hildrey known as the Balfron Bullet. Hit the fast forward button of life and Menzies Campbell is now Lord Menzies Campbell and a former leader of the Liberal Democrats while Mike Hildrey became an award-winning investigative journalist in Glasgow.

My thirst for writing – and extra cash - was still insatiable. I covered cross- country running fixtures and basketball for *The Scotsman* and I even began early morning shifts as a copy taker for the *Edinburgh Evening News* that had recently taken over the *Evening Dispatch*.

I also added a little extra cash during winter Saturday afternoons by working as a runner for Jack Drummond, a compositor on the *Evening Dispatch* by day but on Saturdays boosted his own income by covering Scottish junior league football matches for the paper. As so it was that on frosty winter afternoons I could be found at exotic locations like Arniston Rangers at Gorebridge, Armadale, Newtongrange, Tranent or Pumpherston. None of these villages near Edinburgh exuded much charm but they all had their own character born of a common heritage of coal mining. In those far off days of the early 1960s the main leisure activities for the locals were racing pigeons, greyhound racing – and football. The pigeons and greyhounds were a closed book as far as I was concerned but I was grateful for the football games that helped put a few extra shillings in my pocket for fags or a chip supper.

But I had to earn the cash first and it was energetic work sprinting between the press bench and the nearest telephone with progress reports as the match unfolded. I recall I had two priorities – first, to find a public phone box that hadn't been vandalised or used as a public urinal and second, to decipher Jack's tortuous hand-writing as I waited for a connection to an available copy-taker in the North Bridge newsroom.

But there was one other type of writing I also made a stab at - fiction. In those distant days the *Evening Dispatch* ran a feature called Today's Short Story. This was never destined to be a contender for the Pulitzer Prize but it was at least open to anyone to submit a piece of fiction. Never longer than about a thousand words it could have a love angle to rival Mills and Boon, a murder mystery or a ghost story of improbable provenance. Time after time I tried to compose a suitable contribution. Week after week I submitted one. They were all rejected. The fact that H.G. Wells is said to have papered his wall with rejection slips before his first piece of work was accepted was little consolation to me.

At last I hit the jackpot. *The Dispatch* accepted one of my stories. It was called *Thanks to Bob*, a ghost story about a dead shepherd mysteriously appearing to stop a car going over a bridge destroyed in a storm. Well, let's leave it there because that's all I can remember.

But here's the best bit. It produced a handsome reward of £3 for my efforts, the equivalent of a week's salary – a king's ransom indeed.

I celebrated by taking a girl to the pictures for the first time. Her name was Liz. She had red hair, the date was October 18th 1963 and the movie at the Edinburgh Playhouse was *Tom Jones* starring Albert Finney.

It was to be a momentous evening by the standards of those far-off innocent days. We went for a meal afterwards in a new type of catering establishment called a Chinese restaurant. While Liz tucked into something suitably oriental I contented myself with something more conservative - liver, bacon and chips - before I saw her to her bus stop. The last of the great romantics.

Liz and I went out a couple of times more but if I was found lacking as a suitor it wasn't before she had given me a lock of her

red hair which I tucked behind the band of a little pork pie hat
I used to wear. I didn't think I was a teenage geek but I must have
looked like one. For a few weeks, I proudly wore the hat with
the lock of red hair until one weekend I took the train south to
Galloway to help mother and father with the lambing and left my
hat on the train when I alighted at Dunragit near Stranraer. I've
never worn a pork pie hat since. Truth to tell, I've never been
given a lock of red hair since then either.

It occurred to me that perhaps my attraction as a young
romeo might be greatly heightened if I could roar up to a girl's
home and whisk them off to the cinema in my own car instead of
walking to the nearest bus stop. By chance an opportunity quickly
arose. I heard that A.D Fraser, the man in charge of the *Scotsman's*
hallowed Letters to the Editor columns was wanting to get rid of
his old car, a 1935 Austin 12, registration WG 3186. I approached
him tentatively. We made a deal on the spot – for £10. With pride
I walked around my new purchase parked on Cockburn Street
and filled my young head with the prospect of romantic drives in
and around Edinburgh. I had the car. Now I needed to find the
girl. And then realisation dawned. I couldn't drive. I had never
had any lessons and had never taken a driving test.

Panic. What to do – I could hardly leave the car parked in an
Edinburgh street for weeks or months until I had passed a driving
test. Luckily, Chris Baur and his girlfriend Jackie, soon to become
his wife, came to the rescue. Within 24 hours of my spontaneous
and ill-advised purchase, Chris and Jackie agreed to take it off my
hands for the same price I had paid for it. At least they could
legally drive.

In years to come Chris and Jackie wrote to me with vivid
memories of their first car – and mine:

*"It had blinds on the windows, a single wiper on the front
windscreen, indicators that flipped out like miniature
railway signals, foot-rests in the back and plaited tassels
for the alarmed passengers to hold on to when going round
corners at speeds greater than 15mph. It ate petrol and its*

choke was held with a clothes peg and there was a slightly disturbing area of the front floor through which you could clearly see the road whizzing past underneath you."

But while my daily life was filled, and more or less fulfilling, it lacked one central feature – I was not yet a full-time reporter, a job I had my heart set on. And so while I continued my work as a phone clerk together with my various freelance activities I also set about trying to secure a suitable permanent journalistic berth.

Writing to a wide variety of newspaper organisations for a wide variety of jobs for which I believed I might be suited, there followed a bizarre turn of events which left a youngster like me with a heady choice. In the space of three short weeks and following interviews in Edinburgh and London, I was offered jobs as a reporter with the *Bury Free Press* in Bury St Edmunds in Suffolk, the *Sunday Post* in Nairobi, the *Zambia Times* in Lusaka and *The Scottish Farmer* in Glasgow.

For the record it should be noted that during the same short period I was turned down for a job as a sports reporter with the Reg Hayter News Agency in Shoe Lane off London's Fleet Street. I reckon that some close questioning during my interview about the sporting prowess of various football stars playing for Spurs, Arsenal, West Ham, Fulham and Chelsea exposed a grievous lack of knowledge to compete successfully in that area of journalism.

Despite that, it seemed that after a long time knocking my head against a brick wall it seemed someone wanted my services. The two positions in Africa may have seemed tempting but with my farming roots, the prospect of joining the *Scottish Farmer* - for generations the bible for the Scottish farming industry - seemed like a good bet. I went to Glasgow.

A Reporter at last

And so it was I began my first full-time job as a reporter at the beginning of January 1965. Having found digs with a British Transport police sergeant and his wife opposite Queens Park in Pollockshaws on the south side of the city I soon began to discover Glasgow in the same way that I had found my way around Edinburgh – by walking. Over the years I have found that, if time permits, the best way to lock in the geography of new surroundings is to go on foot. Glasgow was no exception and each morning I would leave time to walk the one and a half miles from my digs down Pollockshaws Road into Eglinton Street, along Bridge Street, cross the River Clyde onto Jamaica Street then a sharp left at Argyle Street would find me in the offices of the *Scottish Farmer* in York Street just off the famous Broomielaw which ran parallel to the Clyde. It could be a long walk in bad weather but I reasoned that what I saved on bus fares could go towards another packet of cigarettes.

Although declining in importance by the 1960s, the Broomielaw had served as Glasgow's harbour since the end of the 17th Century and in 1812 was the departure point for the first European commercial steamer service in the shape of Henry Bell's Comet. Later, in the early part of the 20th century it was the departure point for steamers taking thousands of families *doon the watter* on their annual holidays to west of Scotland resorts like Gourock, Dunoon and Rothesay.

I soon settled into life as an agricultural reporter and enjoyed the camaraderie of my fellow scribes – Ross Muir, soon to head east for a post as assistant agricultural editor of *The Scotsman*, Allan Wright, many years later to become a colleague in the BBC and Douglas MacSkimming who, apart from a couple of brief spells on other papers, was to stay as one of the *Scottish Farmer's* most loyal reporters for more than 40 years.

Journalism is seldom class conscious, at least among those in a newsroom even if the paper's editorial stance may take on a different perspective. But there are exceptions. I first became aware of this when I realised that my colleagues Ross Muir and Allan Wright were paid monthly while I received my wage each week. Later I was to discover that both Ross and Allan had secured diplomas in agriculture from colleges in Aberdeen and Ayr and were therefore deemed eligible for monthly salaried employment. Having joined the paper with only experience of being a copy boy and phone clerk, however, I was clearly not so highly rated and therefore received a weekly wage. Even so - at £10 4s 6d a week, then the National Union of Journalists minimum for a 21-year-old, I was still earning almost double what I had been earning on *The Scotsman*.

Truth to tell, my duties at the *Scottish Farmer* were far from arduous. Being a weekly paper, life settled into a pattern of frenzied activity at the beginning of the week leading to the paper's Wednesday lunchtime deadline then tailing off into what could pass for indolence towards the end of the week.

Lunch breaks tended to be long and leisurely. They too, took on a pattern that seldom varied – chicken fried rice and a portion of curry sauce at the local Chinese restaurant in Hope Street followed by a recuperative snooker competition when the only side betting allowed was to play for the 20p stake which would buy lighting for the snooker table for around 15 minutes.

While we tended to be more or less attentive to our journalistic duties, one day the white-hot heat of competition over the snooker table made us forget about the time and Allan, Dougie and I arrived back at the newsroom well after three o'clock in the afternoon. It was the only time I had ever witnessed the paper's Deputy Editor Angus MacDonald – normally a gentle and mild-mannered son of the Western Isles – to be apoplectic with fury. There must have been strength in numbers. He could have fired any one of us but firing all three would have emptied the newsroom. We heard no more about the incident but we began to ration our snooker tournaments.

This leisurely work schedule was only broken during the summer show season when all hands were on call to travel the length and breadth of Scotland to document in fine detail the successes of the country's breeders of pedigree dairy cattle, beef cattle, sheep, pigs and Clydesdale horses.

Like their fathers and grandfathers before them this was Scottish livestock breeding at its most traditional, part of farming endeavour that has remained unchanged for generations. There may be fewer local shows now but the drive towards producing what they perceive to be excellence on four legs still dominates livestock breeders' attention around the country.

Central to the editorial work on The Scottish Farmer was the work of the livestock photographer. This was a real specialist area of photojournalism like no other I had ever experienced. Apart from being expert technicians with a camera, the livestock photographer is an expert in knowing how a pedigree animal should stand before its image is captured for posterity. Forget the quick snapshot, this was something entirely different. I used to marvel at the patience of the photographer in his ability – it was always *him* in those days – to wait until the animal was standing in an ideal stance – head in the correct position, four feet clearly displayed, and a perfect back-line – before gently squeezing the shutter.

One of the masters of the craft was David Todd, the senior photographer on the *Scottish Farmer*. There were other staff photographers who followed, also expert in their special field – Douglas Low, John Fraser, Niall Robertson and freelances like Sandy Cowper of Perth and his colleague Louis Flood who was to later take over Sandy's Perth-based business and put his own stamp of professional mastery in this specialist field. Louis was a fine photographer who became a good friend and in years to come we were to share many laughs on far-flung assignments for *Farmers Weekly*.

In today's world of digital photography, a few deft strokes on the computer can create enhancements that can transform any image. That wasn't possible in the 1960s but that is not to suppose that some photographers could not create a little enhancement of their own making once in the sanctuary of the darkroom. It has been suggested that the champion dairy cow that might not have had a perfect back-line or a perfect udder in the show-ring could well appear as perfection itself when her picture appeared in the paper.

One anecdote concerned one paper with an ultra sensitive proprietor. When it was noticed that a report of a major bull sale included an accompanying photograph of the champion animal with a majestic pair of testicles it was demanded, allegedly, in the interests of the tender sensibilities of the non-specialist readers, the testicles be removed by sleight of hand in the darkroom. They were - but afterwards, the bull's owner, allegedly once more, sought redress for having aspersions cast as to the breeding ability of the champion animal.

Perhaps not surprisingly, testicles are part and parcel of life in the lexicon of an agricultural magazine. One of our female colleagues, an able and intelligent young writer, had helped to cover the annual show of Clydesdales in Glasgow's Kelvin Hall.

On her return she was pounding the keys of her typewriter when she noticed the editor passing through the newsroom.

Excuse me sir, she asked nervously, *what's the difference between a gelding and a stallion?*

He paused and his face became a little flushed. It was long before the days of sexual equality and he clearly did not want to embarrass her or himself.

Let's just say, he said as he opened the newsroom door in readiness for a quick escape into his private office, *a gelding is two stones lighter than a stallion.*

As she looked into the middle distance trying to absorb this piece of information, we didn't dare ask her if she had grasped the significance of the gelding having been castrated.

While I enjoyed my time on the staff of the *Scottish Farmer*, I didn't see it as a job for life. I didn't feel stretched and I wanted to try my hand in other areas of the trade.

By chance I heard there was a vacancy for a young sub-editor on the *Glasgow Herald*, a daily newspaper which commanded the same levels of affection and respect in the west of Scotland that *The Scotsman* enjoyed in the east. I applied at once.

I was called for interview and interrogated, briefly and gently, by the editor Alastair Warren. Two days later I received a letter from his deputy, George M. Fraser, telling me I had been successful and that I should report for duty to the Chief Sub Editor Allan Munro on Monday June 13th, 1966. While I had every reason to be grateful for my time on the reporting staff of *The Scottish Farmer* I felt that by becoming a sub editor on the *Glasgow Herald*, a national institution, I was on my way at last – but on my way to what?

I was only on the subs' table of the *Glasgow Herald* for a year – but what a year. I loved every minute of it. Officially, I had nothing to do with the paper's agricultural page – in those far off days many of the quality UK broadsheets, including the *Glasgow Herald,* carried many columns devoted to farming and rural life and with that rolling commitment came a full-time agricultural sub-editor. Instead, I was a general sub for four days a week handling whatever was given me by the Chief Sub or his deputy, known as the Copy Taster. One night I could be on foreign news, another evening parliamentary reports and a third on home news from all over Scotland. On Sundays, however, I was given the task of page layout and subbing the agricultural columns when the long serving full-time farming sub, Jimmy Stables, had a day off. I loved the challenge, not least when I had a chance to join the stone sub, Len Bell, an old friend from my Edinburgh days, in the case-room which in the *Glasgow Herald's* building was one floor above the editorial area compared with *The Scotsman* where it lay two floors below.

Here in the case-room with Len's help I partially learned the art – and I suppose it is an art that I would be hard pressed to repeat today – of proof reading the page once it had been set in hot metal. Only this was reading of a different and very challenging sort – upside down and backside foremost. If it was good enough for the print pioneers like William Caxton then it was good enough for me.

When my old friend Len arrived in Glasgow from Edinburgh it was time to leave my digs in Pollockshaws Road and move into a flat together in Nithsdale Road, still on the south side of the river.

We weren't there long. It was something less than salubrious. The roof leaked and settlement over many years meant we could place an old style threepenny bit with all its straight edges at one end of the kitchen floor and it would happily roll across the linoleum at increasing speed until it hit the opposite wall.

So we moved to the other side of the river to the upmarket Woodcroft Avenue into a tall red sandstone block near Anniesland Cross. We loved it. It had style, possibly due in small part to the fact that the flat was owned by the grandson of former Prime Minister Harold Macmillan and who was working as a journalist in East Africa at the time. What Len loved about it most was the grand piano.

An accomplished musician, Len departed each weekend for Edinburgh where family duties saw him play the organ in his mother's local church. To keep his hand in, he played the grand piano in the flat during the working week. Grieg's Piano Concerto was a special favourite.

The problem was we didn't finish our sub-editing duties on the *Glasgow Herald* until close to midnight. By the time we had returned to the flat, made coffee and Len had settled at the piano it was into the wee small hours and despite his talents not even the most ardent music lover necessarily enjoys a classical rendition at that time of night – or morning.

It was either the music or the coalman's horse that led to our undoing. Being night shift workers, each morning was ours to do with what we would. In those days, most flats and houses burned coal and in our area of Anniesland the regular supply would be delivered door to door by horse and cart.

Once or twice a week, the same horse and cart, with the same soot-blackened driver would make their way up the street looking for sales. The man's sales pitch was simple: *Coal! Coal! Coal!* shouted at the top of his voice.

Each time he shouted *Coal!* he left a gap of about four seconds – just enough time for Len and I in the flat far above to yell in unison:

What do you feed your horse on?

Back would come the response: *Coal!*

He never failed us.

Whether it was the mid morning shouted enquiries about equine dietary habits or late night music I will never know but our lease was not renewed. After six months we left seeking new a new roof over our heads.

We found one – a splendid ramshackle floor of an old building in Belmont Street beside Kelvinbridge that in turn had been split into three flats. One apartment was shared by three girls while the flat along the corridor had four girls in residence. Parties became frequent and memorable.

Meantime our work at the *Glasgow Herald* continued – but for me on one of my Sunday shifts in charge of the farming page I feared that my time on the paper was to be cruelly cut short.

Just as I began my stint I received a telephone call from Alex Yeaman, the highly respected Agricultural Editor. He advised me in unequivocal terms that he had a major exclusive coming my way – the chair of agriculture at Glasgow University was threatened by cost cutting and his story on the matter would run to at least one whole column. I noted the point.

Some time later, the ebullient and extrovert Chief Sub, Aubrey McDowall, a native of Galloway but who had spent several years cutting his journalistic teeth in Bulawayo, then Southern Rhodesian and now Zimbabwe, asked his page subs how much space they required for the next morning's edition.

Adding my Alex Yeaman special to the normal demands, I asked for four columns. Aubrey McDowall, looked up sharply.

How much?

Four columns please Mr McDowall, I asked timidly.

You can have two and a half.

But Alex Yeaman has this special story and it's going to run to at least a column on its own.

I don't give a damn – cut it and cut everything else. You've got two and a half columns tonight and that's all.

Chastened, I crept back to my desk and began the evening's work. When Alex Yeaman's copy arrived at my desk I began to cut it so that it would, together with the other farming stories that night, fit the finite space set by Aubrey McDowall.

My shift ended. I went back to my flat and slept fitfully because I knew there would be a reckoning. I was not to be disappointed. It came the following afternoon when I was midway through subbing an article of overseas news.

Suddenly, the door of the subs room burst open. I looked up. Looking directly at me was Alex Yeaman, suffused with rage. Beside him was George M. Fraser, the Deputy editor.

Who was it Alex? I could hear George Fraser ask.

Him! Alex Yeaman was pointing directly at my trembling figure trying to make myself invisible behind a spike of rejected copy.

I was sure that my last days on the *Glasgow Herald* were about to unfold. In fact, I heard nothing more about the incident.

Whether George Fraser prevailed upon Alex Yeaman's good nature not to press the point I do not know. Maybe the exalted farming editor was not used to having his copy savaged by a callow youth but I was just following orders.

In any event, it was almost the last I saw of George M. Fraser. Very soon afterwards he left the *Glasgow Herald* in double quick time for a more kindly tax environment on the Isle of Man when he hit the publishing jackpot with the first of his *Flashman* novels. From that point on he was not simply George M. Fraser – he was George MacDonald Fraser who over the next thirty or so years was to carve out a lucrative career as a writer of best-selling novels. George MacDonald Fraser and Alex Yeaman are now dead and I don't imagine that in their ageing years they would ever remember that Monday afternoon when a young sub editor thought his career, recently begun, was about to end abruptly. For my part, I will never forget it.

While sub-editing and reporting are two branches of the same tree, they can often find themselves in opposite corners of the editorial arena. A reporter who gives his or her all to a story does not take kindly to seeing it cut in half or disappear altogether when the morning edition of the paper hits the streets.

This was amply demonstrated in my early days on *The Scotsman* when one freelance brought into the subs room on a Sunday evening about 40 pages of a closely hand-written report on some obscure week-end event. He handed it to the Chief Sub who looked through it rapidly.

For God's sake Archie, this is far too long. Go and cut it in half.

Thus instructed, the freelance came across to the copy boys' table and began to go through the report page by page ending by dividing his long report into two equal halves. He returned to the Chief Sub's desk:

Here you are, said Archie, *Which half do you want?*

In the meantime, subbing on the *Glasgow Herald* continued. I was enjoying my life both professionally and personally. Regular parties with the girls in Belmont Street were punctuated by dancing at the Plaza at Eglinton Toll with its famous fountain in the centre of the foyer and also the Locarno in Sauchiehall Street. At neither venue did I ever meet the love of my life but I do recall one of the constant fascinations at the Locarno was a band leader who was missing his left hand, the result of an accident in his youth. Undeterred by this significant drawback to his musical future he would make his own contribution to the band's output by banging a tambourine on his stump. The image has lived through the years.

By this time Len Bell and I had been joined in our Belmont Street flat by another old colleague from our Edinburgh days, Alistair McNeill, who was now working as a reporter on the *Glasgow Herald*.

If Len's musical prowess at our previous flat, with my complete endorsement, was instrumental in having our lease terminated, it seemed we hadn't learned our lesson. Len and I were still on night shift but Alistair was on day duty with the result that when we arrived back at our Belmont Street flat after midnight, Alistair would be sound asleep in readiness for the next morning's early start in the newsroom.

Despite the lateness of the hour we felt it incumbent on ourselves to treat ourselves to a bowl of cornflakes and enter his bedroom, sit on the bed and try and involve him in some serious discussion about our life and times. Seldom did he participate with the enthusiasm we had hoped for.

It was even worse for poor Alistair on a Monday when he returned from a weekend at his parents' home in Tranent, East Lothian. Between his departure on a Friday evening and his return there would inevitably have been a party in one of the three flats, all or part of which may well have spilled over into our flat and even perhaps into Alistair's bedroom. On his return on a Monday he would walk round his bedroom looking at the bed suspiciously and sniffing the air like a gundog. His opening gambit never varied:

Who's been sleeping in my bed at the weekend?

We always professed complete innocence. I don't think he ever believed us.

And so my short time on the *Glasgow Herald* followed a memorable pattern with my journeys to the office punctuated with occasional chats with a local Polish landlord who had three fingers of his hand torn off by an Alsatian guard dog in a Russian prison camp or passing the local shop with the owner's cat lying spread-eagled on the heated tray of salted peanuts. Picking the cat hairs out of the hot peanuts it was then a mad dash down the Kelvinbridge steps to the Underground station and thence to Buchanan Street where on dark winter afternoons it was wise to raise an umbrella for the short distance to the *Glasgow Herald* building to protect yourself from the blizzard of droppings from hundreds of thousands of starlings that found their nightly perches on the wires and windowsills of Glasgow city centre.

Life continued thus until one night on the subs' break in Ross's Bar in Mitchell Lane I happened to meet Ross Muir. I had first encountered Ross nearly three years earlier when I joined the *Scottish Farmer* and who shortly afterwards had decamped for a higher profile post on *The Scotsman* taking over from Ian Morrison who in turn had moved north to become Farming Editor of the Press & Journal in Aberdeen.

Ross told me he was leaving Edinburgh to try his hand at public relations in London.

Who was getting his job on *The Scotsman,* I asked.

He said he didn't know but why didn't I try. I thought I would have no chance but over another couple of half pints Ross persuaded me to throw my hat into the ring. After all, he argued logically, the worst that could happen was that I would be turned down.

So I applied to return to *The Scotsman.* I was interviewed by Bob Urquhart, the Agricultural Editor who commanded the same high profile in his field in the east of Scotland as Alex Yeaman of the *Glasgow Herald* did in the west.

To my surprise and delight I got the job as Assistant Agricultural Editor on a salary of £1000 a year. Years later I was to discover that had I negotiated a little harder I could have got more because Ross Muir's departing salary was £1250. Never mind. I was back on *The Scotsman* where I had begun my newspaper life as a copy boy. But this time I was a reporter and I wouldn't have called the king my cousin.

Uswayford Farm, Northumberland, where my great great grandfather George Anderson and five of his sons worked as shepherds in the middle of the 19th Century.

The May Farm in Galloway - A lonely white house but with happy childhood memories in every stone and in every acre. It has been home to the Andersons and the McTurks for almost 80 years.

Jeannie Skimming with her four children – Mary on the left; Jean on the right and my mother Frances in front with their brother Peter beside her.

Almost a lifetime later – my mother Frances on the left, her brother Peter with sisters Mary Littlejohn and Jean Bicketts.

Within a few days of our first date, by coincidence Andrea's photograph appeared in "The Scotsman" on Christmas Eve, 1969. She was then a nurse at the Royal Hospital for Sick Children in Edinburgh.

Wedding Day in Inverness – Saturday, April 24th, 1971.

Four wonderful rapscallions

– Left to right:

Ailsa, Andrew, Angus and Anna

A medley of cousins from the Skimming side of the family – Pat Strang, Anne Littlejohn, Perry Littlejohn, Frances Black, Fiona Littlejohn, me and my sister Monica McTurk.

A gathering of Anderson cousins –

Muriel Timlett, Jennifer and her husband Peter Anderson and Helen Smith.

Pretending to direct a shot on the Murray River, Australia, in 2000. With me are two of the stalwarts of BBC Scotland's *Landward* programme, cameraman Ken Gow and presenter Lindsay Cannon.

Ross Muir and me in the Central Highlands of Papua New Guinea. Over the years Ross was the main presenter of *Landward* and his contributions to the programme were much respected by Scotland's farming and rural communities.

On the windswept moors of the Western Isles with the late Fyfe Robertson, known affectionately throughout the UK as Robbie. A joy to work with, he celebrated his 80th birthday while shooting this programme, which turned out to be his last documentary.

A Capital Return

There followed a memorable two and a half years of my life travelling Scotland, learning my trade and getting to know the leaders of the food and farming industry in Scotland. My boss, Bob Urquhart, was a native of Banff in North-east Scotland who had seen war service as a Squadron Leader in the RAF Bomber and Coastal Command. He had been involved with the bomber group that attacked Gestapo HQ and broke the walls of Amiens prison in February 1944 to allow Resistance and Allied POWs to escape. Shot down over the Mediterranean near Gibraltar, he spent the rest of his days with a piece of stray shrapnel in his backside and arthritis in his left arm, a condition apparently eased by the wearing of a rigid protective leather shield. His painful arm didn't stop him pounding a typewriter but the manner of so doing occasionally somehow gave his left arm a life of its own, from time to time drifting away from the keyboard and held erect and motionless – no doubt to give some respite from the constant discomfort - while the right hand continued on its own solitary creative path.

Bob and I shared a small glass panelled office with two other specialist writers. Conrad Wilson was the distinguished music critic who barely spoke – at least to us. Perhaps he felt that as his working life ranged from opera houses to music salons he had little in common with sons of the soil who were likely to be more at home in auction markets. Then there was the sports writer Jack Dunn. In his day Jack Dunn had been the doyen of rugby and cricket scribes but was coming towards the end of his working life and while his writing was still sharp the image of him that stays etched in my memory is down to three things – his raincoat, his pipe and the perpetual drip at the end of his nose. Occasionally, he didn't wear his coat. Very occasionally I saw him without his pipe. But afternoon or evening, summer or winter, some things never varied. The drip at the end of Jack's nose was always there. As the comedian Chic Murray might have observed – maybe it ran in his family.

Bob Urquhart was a good boss, particularly if you happened to be an enthusiastic youngster. It seemed to me and previous assistants like Robin Crearie, Ian Morrison and Ross Muir, that if you were willing to do the work, Bob would let you do it – even most of it.

For all that, he was a fine writer and while he would happily let his enthusiastic assistant of the day drive from the south of Scotland to the north to pursue stories, he would occasionally turn his hand to the bigger picture and had a habit of writing award-winning features on food and farming which brought him well-deserved kudos throughout his peer group in the UK.

For my part, I was happy to beaver away and never more so than when Bob Urquhart would take off on his travels and leave me in charge of the farming page. I did it all eagerly and gladly and only once felt the pressure of responsibility weigh heavily on my young shoulders. Bob had accepted an invitation to visit an old friend, Jim Lingle, who ran the Wye herd of Aberdeen Angus cattle in Maryland in the United States, and had left me to cover in his absence – a period that included the Price Review, the annual government announcement of farm prices for the year ahead. Whether it contained good news or bad news for British farmers was not the point at issue. It was always big news and involved not only writing several columns for the agricultural page but a column for the front page of *The Scotsman,* a rare occasion when general readers might be permitted an insight into the complexities of the farming industry.

Despite the pressure of the day when I felt the world weigh heavily on me, I nervously ploughed through the work and felt great relief when the first editions tumbled off the printing presses to find my by-lined front page story securing the second lead spot. That at least, was the general reader taken care of. All I had to cross my fingers for now was that the sharp and discerning specialist farming reader would not see anything amiss in my coverage and interpretation of the Price Review in the several columns my report occupied on the farming page.

I must have acquitted myself reasonably because there were no phone calls of query or complaint. Moreover, Bob Urquhart returned from the USA and as I slipped away to Galloway for a week's leave to help my mother and father with the annual lambing I was heartened to receive a generous commendation for my work by Bob in his weekly round-up of the previous week's news. He was a kind and supportive boss and I thoroughly enjoyed my time with him.

Life on *The Scotsman* the second time round was good. I was enjoying my work even though at first glance much of it might have seemed a repeat of my time on *The Scottish Farmer* given the dominance in our weekly diary of pedigree sales of cattle and sheep.

The difference now was that with only two of us on the farming desk of *The Scotsman* many of the best jobs invariably landed on my desk with Bob Urquhart taking top billing for the main set pieces of the year – the pedigree Bull Sales at Perth in February, the Royal Highland Show in Edinburgh in June, the Royal Show in Warwickshire in July, the London Dairy Show at Olympia in October and the Royal Smithfield Show at London's Earls Court in December.

These were possibly the peak years for agricultural journalism in the British press. In addition to Bob Urquhart and his chief opposition Alex Yeaman of the *Glasgow Herald*, the southbound contingent to the big London events would include a chain–smoking Bert Clark of the *Dundee Courier*, Ian Morrison of the *Press & Journal* in Aberdeen, Sandy Hogg of the *Scottish Daily Express* and Roy Gregor of the *Scottish Daily Mail*. All the national dailies in those days also had full-time agricultural correspondents – John Winterbottom of the *Daily Mail* (although his abbreviated byline of Winter was easier to fit into a single column) and his deputy Peter Bullen, Alex Kenworthy of the *Daily Express*, Stanley Baker of the *Guardian*, Len Amey of *The Times*, Jimmy James of the East Midland Allied Press and Tommy (the Bishop) Thomas of the *Daily Telegraph* who was later succeeded by fellow Scot David Brown.

The only time Bob Urquhart and I travelled together to these major events was the Royal Show in Warwickshire when we would leave Edinburgh early on a Sunday morning with the aim of reaching our hotel in Leamington Spa in time for dinner. The pattern of our journey never varied. Bob would drive as far as Scotch Corner where he would enjoy a pint of warm beer and then his assistant would take over for the rest of the road south.

That suited me down to the ground. I was glad to take over the driving, not because Bob had enjoyed a pint of beer but because I found part of his driving technique slightly disconcerting. This was especially true when he braked. Every time he put his foot on the brake pedal he simultaneously pulled back on the steering wheel with a strange upward motion as if he was trying to lift the nose of one of his wartime bombers. Clearly aviation was ever present in his thoughts because each time we arrived in the bar in Leamington Spa he would be asked by some of his pals what kind of journey south he'd had. I was to find out later that no matter who his assistant of the time might have been, his answer never varied:

What a speed he drove from Scotch Corner, Bob would say. *Nothing on the clock but the maker's name. If we'd had wings we'd have flown.*

Part and parcel of coverage of these principal annual events was the vast coverage given to the detailed results in the show-ring. It was not unusual in the 1960s for the introductory report to run to little more than three quarters of a column followed by up to two columns of results in small type. Needless to say, Bob Urquhart wrote the words and I dealt with the detailed statistics. I used to think that these occasions bore more relation to a clerking job than journalism.

Bob Urquhart and Alex Yeaman were fierce journalistic competitors – with the Glasgow man arguably the better reporter but my boss the more natural writer.

For all their competitive nature, however, Bob and Alex were at least civil to one another unlike in earlier times when there was bitter rivalry between Archibald McNeilage, editor of the *Scottish Farmer* magazine and his nemesis, David Young, editor of the *North British Agriculturist*. Writing a brief history of Scotland's Farming Press in 1953, the late William Adair of the *Glasgow*

Herald wrote: *Neither* (Young nor McNeilage) *would condescend to recognise the other, even with a passing greeting, let alone enter into conversation.*

But these old animosities did not extend down to the next generation. Allan Wright, my erstwhile colleague from the *Scottish Farmer* and now my opposite number on the *Glasgow Herald*, would share the task of sourcing and delivering the vast volume of results from these London events for the next morning's editions of both the Scottish broadsheets. Six or seven hours of solid typing in the press rooms of Earls Court or Olympia in London did nothing for the good of our health. Almost to a man in those days we were smokers and being virtually a captive for those long hours of compiling statistics meant our consumption rose sharply. It was the custom on those days for *The Scotsman* and *Glasgow Herald* to work in a loose co-operative way so while Bob Urquhart and Alex Yeaman would compete for the best stories, Allan Wright and I would routinely buy 100 cigarettes each morning and we would chain-smoke our way through all five packets before our day's duties of compiling results were completed.

In reality we would probably smoke little more than half of the cigarettes because as our fingers flew over the typewriter keys our fags would inevitably smoulder away untouched in the ashtrays beside us.

In my time with Bob Urquhart, the boot was on the other foot when it came to telephoning my reports to the *Scotsman*. After two years as a copytaker during my first stint on the paper I was now the reporter dictating phrase by phrase my report down the line from wherever I might be. Invariably the copy-takers at the other end were an amiable bunch. But on these long stints of phoning results from Olympia or Earls Court, I was always a little discomfited when a copy-taker would ask nervously:

Is there much more of this to come?

There was one other occasion when the farming desks of *The Scotsman* and the *Glasgow Herald* would unite in common purpose – the Kelso Ram Sales. This was the annual historic event on the banks of the River Tweed at Springwood Park in the Border town where hundreds of farmers from all over the UK would sell thousands of breeding rams.

There were usually nine or ten different auctioneering companies at work and all the rams representing all the many different low-ground breeds in the country were sold, usually singly, in a dozen or more open-air rings. This was a pattern that had remained unchanged for generations. The day began with the ringing of a bell before all auctioneering hell broke loose and the day reverberated with the cacophony attending Britain's biggest one-day sale of breeding rams.

Where *The Scotsman* and the *Glasgow Herald* united in coverage of this event was in the joint hire of a comptometer and operator with the two newspapers paying the cost on alternate years. The comptometer was first developed in the USA around 1900 and was a forerunner of the hand-held calculator. The size and weight of a standard typewriter, it had the advantage of being able to multiply and subtract quickly.

We used it to calculate the total revenues and average prices that would flow each minute into the pressroom delivered by runners working for the various auction companies. Given the volume of statistics involved it would have been impossible to manually calculate the details on pieces of paper. With the mechanical comptometer in the hands of a skilled operator, however, we more or less stayed abreast of the action.

But that often depended on daylight. Because of the sheer volume of rams to be sold, very often the Kelso Ram Sales did not end before darkness fell. As there was no electricity in those days in the press tent at Springwood Park, candles were issued by the event organisers to we weary scribes. It became something of a contradiction in terms that very often our days in Kelso would end with our skilled comptometer technician trying to see the results of her labours surrounded by a semi-circles of reporters each holding a flickering candle to offer a semblance of illumination. Somehow, we won the day.

Other ram sales were less of a hard slog. Chief among them were the Blackface ram sales at Lanark each October. The

Blackface is a hill breed and unlike many of the low-ground breeds sold at Kelso which could boast strong genetic information about their technical breeding qualities, Blackface were assessed – and purchased – on visual merit alone.

It always seemed to we mere reporting mortals something of a contradiction in terms that one day we might be reporting from a press conference where the nation's hill farmers were bemoaning their lot and how they hardly were able to make ends meet. The following day could find us reporting the news that a Blackface ram had made £40,000 or more. It didn't help us clarify the merits of such a purchase when we were told by the buyer that he felt compelled to pay such a heady amount because he liked it's fine head or how good a back-line it had. The succeeding decades have not changed this strange rural ritual.

Blackface breeders did not like to be closely questioned on the black art of Blackface ram trading. When approached by one colleague to explain why he had just spent the best part of £30,000 on a ram, one breeder famously said:

"I don't know – and if I did I wouldn't tell you."

The auctioneers, too, were not averse to a little gentle arm-twisting which we tried to resist. This invariably concerned the final averages for the day's event or an individual breeder's sale receipts. The higher the figures the better it looked for the auctioneers.

It was not unusual for a seller to be unhappy with the bids for a ram and it would be turned out of the ring unsold. These facts were clearly documented on the auction slips that were passed into the pressroom. Very often, however, we would be approached later by one of the auctioneering staff and told that such and such a ram that had been unsold at auction had been subsequently bought privately for such and such a sum.

Many a raised voice was heard in the pressroom as we steadfastly refused to include in the official averages any deal that was later done privately and on the basis of hearsay. Unless the deal had been done at public auction, we argued, we would not include it in the averages. The auctioneers never saw matters from our point of view.

Many of these auctioneering companies were not above a little gentle persuasion to have the farming press on their side. Most were quick to issue lunch vouchers to all working reporters at the big sales. In one or two cases where we knew the network of contacts in the local pubs and cafes the vouchers could be exchanged for two packets of cigarettes. Another company used to give us two-dozen eggs instead of luncheon vouchers. Oh yes - we managed to exchange the eggs too. A lungful of smoke while we scribbled in our notebooks seemed a fair exchange for a bellyful of food.

There were other more pleasurable aspects to covering the Blackface ram sales at Lanark. The first was getting there from Edinburgh. The best route was on the A70 road known as the Lang Whang (Long Way in old Scots) via Currie and Balerno then skirting the edge of the Pentland hills to Tarbrax and thence to Carnwath and Lanark. For the most part this route went through wild moorland scenery and what made it memorable was first, the distinctive red tarmac used in that part of Lanarkshire and second, that it represented a natural race track for boy racers like myself and Robin Crearie, in earlier days Bob Urquhart's assistant before Ian Morrison who had left to become a press officer for the British Egg Marketing Board in London. Having tired of metropolitan life, Robin had recently returned north of the Border as a reporter on the *Scottish Farmer*.

Robin and I would meet at a pre-arranged spot near the outskirts of Edinburgh, he in his Ford Anglia and I in *The Scotsman's* Hillman Minx drawn from the paper's car pool. We would then race each other to Lanark, the side bet being that the one who lost would buy the other a bowl of oxtail soup, a staple of the Lanark auction mart café that had stood the test of time over the years and was almost *de rigueur* even at 10am. Locals reckoned it would put hairs on your chest as thick as joiners' pencils.

In truth our races along the Lang Whang were more of a procession. The road twisted and turned and by judicious drifting into the centre - in those days traffic was much lighter than today - it meant that whichever driver managed to get ahead at the start would very likely stay there until the Lanark auction market hove into view.

Opening his mail one morning Bob Urquhart casually asked if I would like to go to Czechoslovakia. It was 1968, the year of the Prague Spring, when Alexander Dubcek, the head of the country's Communist Party was in the forefront of political reform for an eastern bloc nation stifled politically, economically and democratically since the end of the Second World War. Plans were made for open elections, free trade and economic reform – Czechoslovakia was on course to become the world's most liberal Communist state.

But mother Russia had other ideas. On August 21st, 1968, the tanks rolled in and the fledgling democracy of Dubcek was over. Eight weeks later Bob Urquhart received an invitation from Zetor tractors, then a subsidiary of Skoda cars, to visit Prague and Brno to see the manufacture of Zetor tractors which were then trying to gain a foothold in the agricultural markets of Western Europe. Bob decided the invitation should be passed to me.

I leaped at the chance of going and so in November 1968 I found myself in Prague. If I imagined I was in the front seat for some historic occasion I was disappointed. The main Soviet armies had pulled back two weeks earlier and by the time I found myself in Prague the only Soviet presence I could see were Russian sentries in Wenceslas Square.

There were six or seven British journalists on that visit to Prague and Brno, including Ian Mather the well-known journalist from the *Daily Mail*, but only two from Scotland. My fellow Scot who I met on the night train from Edinburgh to London before our flight east was a friendly and engaging young man in a beige duffle coat called Pat Chalmers, then an Edinburgh-based BBC radio producer responsible for a daily programme called *Farm Journal*.

As the two Scots on the facility trip, Pat and I shared a room. One evening, after the usual tour of press conferences and factory visits in Prague we were taken to what was allegedly the only nightclub in Eastern Europe – I doubt for a moment that that was true. What was true was that there was a stripper dancing desultorily to recorded music who eventually removed her overcoat - and nothing else. It was a cold night after all. What was also true was that there was a considerable amount of Czechoslovakian black beer consumed that evening and I suspect that I had enjoyed more than my fair share. In any event Pat Chalmers had to help my stumbling figure from the nightclub back to our hotel, passing though Wenceslas Square on the way and he maintains that in the course of the journey I swore loudly at every Russian soldier I saw. The fact that I reached my bed safely at all is in part due to Pat's help and the Russians' inability to comprehend a rather tipsy Scot.

It was the first time I had cause to be grateful to Pat Chalmers but not the last as years later he was to become a central figure in my career with the BBC. In the event, shortly after my visit to Prague, an Edinburgh colleague of Pat Chalmers called Robin Hicks asked me to record a short piece for the daily farming radio programme he was producing. Nervous as I was, I welcomed the challenge and welcomed the £5 fee even more. Somewhere within me I knew then that a seed had been sown about a future in broadcasting.

However, I had no intention of moving from *The Scotsman*. I was back where I started and I loved the job I was doing. That was, until I went out to Gorgie auction mart to pick up my boss Bob Urquhart.

Gorgie Auction mart was within the city of Edinburgh, a complex of an abattoir and three auction company facilities. Managing Director of one of the companies, Oliver & Son, was the rotund figure of Bertie Bryden, one of the larger than life characters of British agriculture.

Bertie was always immaculately dressed. Like all good auctioneers he could sell anything but Bertie's speciality was pedigree pigs. And when he sold pigs he was especially well dressed – highly polished black brogue shoes, pinstripe suit, bowler hat – and a red carnation in his buttonhole. Thus attired he would sell pedigree pigs from dawn to dusk. *Full of pigs and profit* was his opening gambit as each in-pig gilt entered the sawdust ring below his rostrum.

Once his stint was over, however, Bertie would lay down his gavel and retire to his office and take the cork out of a bottle of malt whisky and offer hospitality to whomsoever happened to be passing by. Surprisingly often, it was Bob Urquhart.

I had gone out to collect Bob from one such celebratory session when I met Alastair Strathearn the Scottish Correspondent of the Fleet Street-based Farmers Weekly. Over a coffee, he asked if I would be interested in taking over from him as the paper's man in Scotland as he was about to be promoted to a new role within the organisation.

I had much preferred the daily challenge of reporting for *The Scotsman* compared with my earlier experiences on the *Scottish Farmer* and had no wish to reprise the role. However, *Farmers Weekly* was different. For a start it had a huge profile within the farming industry not just in Scotland but throughout the whole of Britain. And while it allocated its share of column inches in the livestock section to many of the traditional events, it was not a paper for the traditional pedigree breeder. *Farmers Weekly* was, and still is, a paper for the arable farmer.

The idea appealed to me. There was a little more money involved and the clincher – a staff car of my very own. And so the deal was done. I left *The Scotsman* and joined *Farmers Weekly*.

There followed four very happy years, once again travelling the length and breadth of Scotland and occasionally being called south of the Border to help bolster the editorial team at the main UK events.

While all these events over the years tend to merge one with the other, there is one occasion that stands out in my memory – covering the Great Yorkshire Show at Harrogate.

I had been called south because of illness in the paper's North of England office and the evening before this prestige event I found myself in the company of fellow journalists in a bar in the Yorkshire Dales.

Ordering a round at the bar, I was overheard by a man beside me, a large Yorkshire farmer.

Where are you from lad? he enquired

Edinburgh, I replied.

Is that an Edinburgh accent?

I explained that I didn't really have an accent and that although I worked in Edinburgh I was originally from a Galloway farming background.

He said: *Years ago I used to go out with a lass from Galloway. She was a farmer's daughter. I wonder if you'd know her?*

I said it was unlikely because I had gone away to school before I was twelve years old and had seldom been back other than to help on the farm during weekends and at lambing time.

Just out of interest though, I ventured, *what was her name?*

Frances Skimming, he said. *Does the name mean anything to you?*

Just a bit, I replied. *She's my mother.*

You should have seen his face. More than that, you should have heard my mother's startled exclamation later that evening when I rang to tell her of my encounter. Not for the first time I was to realise that the world of farming can be a small one indeed.

It was during my tenure as Scottish Correspondent of *Farmers Weekly* that the broadcasting seed that had been sown near the end of my time on *The Scotsman* was to take root.

During my time on *The Scotsman* I became friendly with a young reporter called Fordyce Maxwell, then working for *Farming News,* a weekly newspaper based in Perth which was a competitor of *The Scottish Farmer.* A farmer's son from North Northumberland, Fordyce and I had much in common because of my own links with Northumberland through my father.

During my final weeks on *The Scotsman* before beginning a fresh challenge with *Farmers Weekly* I suggested to Bob Urquhart that he could do worse than see if Fordyce might be interested in taking over my berth as his assistant. I was delighted when in due course Fordyce was appointed to *The Scotsman* and especially pleased in later years to see him take over from Bob as Agricultural Editor and continue a long career as one of the country's most distinguished and respected writers and commentators of the farming and rural scene. Nearly 50 years on, Fordyce and his wife Liz, also a successful journalist, have remained stalwart friends.

It was also at this time that my personal life was about to take on new meaning. I met a girl called Andrea. She was the cousin of Leslie Fraser, a colleague on *The Scotsman* who introduced us in a bar called the Golf Tavern on Edinburgh's Bruntsfield Links.

I was immediately impressed, not least by the fact that this girl who came out of nowhere into my life was clad in sexy red leather.

She had been a nurse at the prestigious Officers' Nursing Home in the West End of Edinburgh but had moved to The Royal Hospital for Sick Children. We seemed to get along - within six weeks I had proposed and we shortly afterwards became formally engaged with a wedding planned for April 1971.

Suddenly, life had taken on a new and enjoyable but uncharted course.

In truth, our relationship was nearly over before it began. Shortly after we met I was invited to her Inverness home to meet her parents. Because of conflicting work commitments she had gone ahead of me by train and I was to drive north. It was mid winter and the first flurries of snow had begun to fall as I reached Perth. But I felt insulated against the elements as I enjoyed the comfort of driving north in my powerful six-cylinder Vauxhall Cresta. The remaining 100 miles would soon pass I imagined. However, the snow gradually became heavier until by Carrbridge the road was virtually impassable. Anyone with a little wisdom would have pulled over and found a bed and breakfast for the night. But I had a girl to see and began to inch my way ever northwards using a heavy goods vehicle ahead of me as something of a trailblazer. Determinedly I tried to follow the lorry's tracks in the deep snow. For a mile or two I succeeded but the snowfall grew heavier and heavier and the lorry's greater weight saw it gradually pull away from me. As I watched its tail-lights disappear into the swirling flakes, I realised I was on my own and could go no further.

An optimist at heart, I presumed a snowplough would soon come to my rescue. But no such help was to be forthcoming. The snowfall that night was widespread and the road clearing services were stretched to breaking point.

At least, I comforted myself with the knowledge I had a full tank of petrol which meant I could keep the engine running and benefit from the car's heater. That turned out to be a major mistake because, warmed by the heater and drowsy from the mesmeric effects of the snowflakes falling on the windscreen, I fell asleep.

I was awakened with a loud banging. It was daylight and I became conscious of an intensive headache the like of which I had never experienced before or since. The engine had cut out and I was freezing. Beside the car were police and the AA. The snow had stopped and I could see that the snowdrifts had arrested my progress north at a section of the A9 called Slochd Summit. Once in the fresh air, I slowly recovered although my headache was to remain for most of the day. The police and AA officers reckoned that the heavy snow had built up around my rear exhaust pipe and somehow had channelled the poisonous carbon monoxide fumes along the side of the vehicle and in through the driver's quarter light which I had left slightly ajar. Eventually the snowfall around the exhaust had caused the engine to cut out. Had it not done so I may not have lived through that long winter night. It would have been an undignified end to a life not yet fully lived but lady luck had been on my side.

Journeys to and from Inverness with Andrea proved to be memorable – not least with the saga of a wild goose that Andrea and I encountered on our return to Edinburgh one New Year morning. We had gone north to spend Hogmanay with her mother and father – a convivial occasion with a regular procession of friends and neighbours ensuring the festivities ran far into the night.

Driving south the next day we were just north of Perth when we heard the sounds of a shooting party in nearby fields. As if on cue, a goose crash-landed on the main road about 50 yards ahead of the car.

I stopped. The goose was quite dead but of the shooters there were distant sounds but no sign. What could I do. I threw the goose into the boot and drove on to Edinburgh.

Nobody in our flat in Newington's Findhorn Place had the enthusiasm or the facilities to deal with the goose and as Andrea had a phobia about feathers getting her to deal with the bird was out. I contacted my old boss Bob Urquhart to see if he wanted an unscheduled New Year treat. He didn't.

Meantime the goose stayed in the boot of my car and life went on. I forgot about the goose. It was a mild start to January that year and by around the middle of the month I became aware of a certain sharp pungency whenever I opened the door of my car. It was then I remembered the unfortunate bird.

Clearly it had to be disposed of – but how? I didn't dare put it in our dustbin. Had I done so, castration or defenestration by flatmates or neighbours would be the least of what I could have looked forward to.

Instead, that night I waited until well after midnight before going to my car and extricated the decomposing and stinking goose and wrap it as best I could in newspaper. I then quietly and quickly walked 200 yards into Causewayside, one of Edinburgh's busiest commuter routes and stuffed the poor bird head first into a wire-mesh waste paper container attached to the lamp standard beside a deserted bus stop. Sadly, it was a very small waste paper basket and was never designed to contain a goose, albeit one that was in such an advanced stage of decomposition that it would eventually no doubt have fallen through the wire-mesh. There I left it, filling the whole of the small container with only its back-side and its legs pointing vertically into the night sky. I can only imagine how the following morning's commuters waiting for their bus might have speculated about the flight path of such a goose that could have led it to such a final destination.

With marriage in the offing, it was time to give up the relaxed lifestyle of flat dwelling and try and find a home to begin married life. But we simply couldn't afford one. We did look at one three-bedroom house in a village south of Edinburgh. It was priced at £6000 yet despite adding Andrea's salary to my own it was beyond our reach.

In the event, we found a farm cottage to rent halfway between Edinburgh and Glasgow near the village of Breich, known locally, and with good reason, as dreich Breich. This was generally a depressed area of central Scotland and our small bungalow was beside the triangle of Bathgate, Fauldhouse and Whitburn. The area had been built on coal mining but now the two local pits at Polkemmet and Whitrigg were closed and on a wet winter's day an air of dereliction and neglect hung over the whole area. Our rented bungalow didn't fall into the luxury class but it was to represent a reasonably comfortable start to married life.

In the meantime my frantic driving around Scotland on behalf of *Farmers Weekly* continued. One morning I was about to leave my office to drive to Paisley to interview William Young, the well-known chairman of the Scottish Milk Marketing Board who was just about to import the first Simmental cattle from the continent into the UK. For a nation like the UK that used to pride itself on being the breeding stock capital of the world, here were industry leaders prepared to spend large amounts of money on importing cattle that they thought would improve the national beef herd. By any standard, it was a big story.

The telephone rang. It was Roy Gregor, the BBC radio producer who in recent years had moved from his *Daily Mail* duties to produce and present BBC Radio's daily *Farm Journal* from the capital's Queen Street studios. Roy had heard I was going to interview William Young. Would I be prepared to take along a BBC tape recorder and record an interview with him for radio?

I said I would love to but hadn't a clue how to work a tape recorder. Come in and we'll give you a 10-minute course, Roy offered. I did - I was hooked.

All that remained was a telephone call for clearance to *Farmers Weekly* in Fleet Street. Travers Legge, my editor, agreed – with one proviso. If my name was mentioned on BBC radio as the reporter, my association with *Farmers Weekly* had to be included. I agreed readily. Thankfully, so did the BBC.

And so my first interview was duly broadcast on *Farm Journal* the following lunchtime. My mother was bowled over by hearing my name and my voice on the radio. I was much more impressed by the contract that arrived a few days later offering me £6 for recording the interview.

There followed a steady and growing pattern of radio reports recorded in tandem with my duties for Farmers Weekly. My broadcasting activities were wholly supported by the paper with that early proviso remaining constant – that the paper's name was always mentioned with my own.

Farmers Weekly took the not unreasonable view that as the BBC *Farm Journal* daily programme was almost compulsory listening for the farming and rural community in Scotland then the paper's profile was equally heightened every time I appeared on air. It suited them. It certainly suited me to the point that I began to wonder if I could make a career out of this broadcasting business.

Over the next three years I began to apply for BBC producer posts. Usually I got a polite rejection slip saying I had not been called for interview. Once, I was even asked to attend a BBC board – then as now the organisation's term for a formal interview. At one time there could be up to six BBC managers on a producer board. Today they manage to get by with about four. In the event, I didn't get the job.

Throughout this period I was still supplementing my income from *Farmers Weekly* by doing two or three radio interviews every week. Wherever my *Farmers Weekly* diary led me, I invariably had a BBC tape recorder in the back of the car.

The extra money was handy because by now Andrea and I were married – a grand Inverness affair on April 24th, 1971 in the West Parish Church beside the River Ness. It was to prove a joyous coming together of the Highlands and the Lowlands – fortunately without any ethnic animosities or incidents other than when the wayward action of my new father-in-law during a Strip the Willow sent our diminutive Church of Scotland Minister, the Rev Samuel Devlin, hurtling horizontally across the dance floor like some evangelical missile.

As Andrea's mother and father generously funded the reception in the Drumossie Hotel overlooking the Moray Firth I have no idea what it cost. However, as an exercise in how money values have changed over the years it is worth recalling some of the sums involved during this landmark week in my life. My full kilt outfit, a wedding present from Andrea, costs £70.50 from Duncan Chisholm, the famous kilt outfitter in Castle Street, Inverness; the wedding photographs, taken by my freelance friend John Wilkie, amounted to £37; the first night of our honeymoon, in the Strathspey Hotel in Aviemore, totalled £8.08 – and that included a pot of tea and a round of sandwiches; and the cost of registering the marriage (Inverness Registry No. 19800) was a princely 50p. This roller-coaster of extravagance was to continue during our honeymoon week. Driving south to Luton airport, Andrea and I broke our journey at the King's Head Hotel in Barnard Castle where dinner, bed and breakfast came to £6.20 and the following night in the Red Lion at Luton saw a bill of £8.28. As for the honeymoon itself, a week in Hammamet, Tunisia, cost £41 each – plus a 35p daily supplement for the provision of shower and toilet facilities.

But back to work. Journalism, of any sort, tends to be an eye opener to life more than most trades or professions. Travelling and meeting a broad church of people as part of your daily round can open minds as well as eyes. One of the great privileges of journalism can be the opportunity to travel overseas and working abroad, even if only for a few days in any one location, can offer greater insights than any package holiday ever could.

Sometimes, these insights into the lives of others must be learned the hard way. One colleague found himself in Paris covering one of Europe's biggest food and farming fairs. He had never been to France before and had been booked into a small hotel near the centre of the city. On checking his room he discovered in the bathroom a piece of equipment that was new to him. It was a bidet. Later he described his discovery to a colleague who then outlined what a bidet was and how the French used it to best effect.

Thus armed with new information, the daring reporter decided that he should put the bidet to the test. Dropping his trousers he sat on it and began experimenting with the seemingly complex levers and taps beside him. Whether it was a fault with the plumbing or his confusion with the French word for hot and cold we never discovered. What matters is that, on pressing one lever, a jet of scalding water at full force went straight up his backside and, he alleges, out again somewhere near the top of his spine. He claims to this day that there's a bathroom in a small hotel somewhere in central Paris that will still have claw marks down the wall from which he had eventually slid to the floor. Whatever thoughts passed through his mind at that point, you could be sure that despite his farming lineage it wasn't the melody of *How ya gonna keep 'em down on the farm after they've seen Paree*......

To continue the slightly scatological theme, I had my own cross to bear on an early visit to the Royal Smithfield Show in London. After the day's work was over I had arranged to meet a pal in the hotel bar before going out for a meal.

In those days I was submitting myself to what might be seen as an excessive exercise regime which included running every day plus games of squash. As a result I was treating myself for two small inconveniences – athletes' foot and piles. Hardly major handicaps, and both could be suitably subdued with the application of lotions bought over the counter in my local chemist.

After my shower I had duly applied both unguents, dressed, and was heading down to the lobby in a packed hotel lift when I was suddenly struck with an intensive pain in my backside akin to what I imagined the insertion of a red hot poker might involve. But this was possibly worse than that - as if someone was applying a welder's torch to my nether regions. I began to sweat and whimper slightly to the obvious discomfiture of the other hotel guests in the lift. Instead of getting out of the lift when it reached the hotel lobby, I immediately sent it racing back up the sixth floor followed by a mad dash for my bedroom and the removal of my trousers prior to a dive into the shower and a liberal hosing with cold water.

By now you've guessed – in my haste to get to the bar I had inadvertently rubbed the athlete's foot cream on my backside. By a process of elimination I realised I must also have applied the pile cream to my feet. It was a form of medication I would not recommend but as the years have rolled on I must confess to no longer having problems with either athlete's foot or piles.

If my painful experience was confined to the relative privacy of a London hotel lift, another colleague suffered a much more public embarrassment. Having moved from the north to a senior position in the newspaper's Fleet Street offices, he had only recently found a new home in the home counties about one hour's drive from his office.

One day while at work he was struck down with a stomach bug that occasioned frequent visits to the loo. After work he began his drive to home and bed. It was mid winter and dark and once out of the main metropolitan area the discomfort in his stomach began to impinge on his recall of the geographical direction to his new home. He got lost.

By now the need to make a call of nature became overpowering. He turned off a main road into what he believed was a quiet country lane with no traffic whereupon he leapt out of the car, dropped his trousers and squatted down in front of his vehicle to let nature take its inevitable course. In the midst of this, he heard engines approaching. Unknown to him there had been road works and a long line of cars had been held up by a red light. In the midst of his unscheduled comfort stop, the light had turned to green and the cars, with headlights on, came round a corner to find my luckless colleague with his pants at his ankles. Some tooted and many others wound down their windows and cheered him on. It was the living embodiment of the saying – you may run but you can't hide.

My first visit to the Royal Smithfield Show at Earls Court for *Farmers Weekly* coincided with the closure by the British Sugar Corporation of their only factory in Scotland – at Cupar in Fife – and my first encounter with an enraged Cabinet Minister. For farmers on the east coast of Scotland who supplied the factory with this important break crop, it was a bitter blow. What made the closure all the more contentious was the fact that the British Sugar Corporation was part-owned by the British government yet who vigorously maintained that they could not interfere in a commercial decision taken by the BSC.

It was a live issue in agricultural politics for many weeks and while it concerned farmers in Scotland rather than England, I decided to raise the matter at a press conference given at Earls Court by Jim Prior, the Minister of Agriculture. Evidently, he had not been briefed that this was a subject likely to be raised; no doubt he had been expecting matters relevant to the Smithfield Show taking place around him. He tried to fob me off as politicians do but I persisted in my question to the point that many of the English journalists watched bemused as one of their kilted colleagues – I occasionally wore my kilt in those days – continued close questioning Jim Prior about why the government were prepared to sit on their hands while an important source of revenue was being lost to Scottish arable farmers.

Jim Prior grew redder in the face and angrier with each passing question. After some muttered irate asides to his worried-looking minders, the press conference came to an early end and Jim Prior stalked out of the room. It was the only time in my life when my performance was quoted in the *Guardian, Times, Telegraph, Daily Mail* and *Daily Express*. Maybe it was the kilt that did it.

No doubt Jim Prior felt like kicking my backside for the dogged way I pursued a subject he had little interest in. Fortunately for me, he didn't. Shortly after this incident I also escaped without my backside being kicked by a major Hollywood star.

It was 1971 and I had been in Oban in Argyll with a freelance photographer Sandy Cowper covering the annual bull sales of the Luing breed of cattle and we were returning towards Perth when we decided on a brief pit stop at a hotel beside Loch Awe.

What we didn't know was that the hotel was the base for some of the movie stars taking part in a film called *Catch Me A Spy* being shot in the area.

While we were at the bar I decided to visit the gents that, unusually, were on the first floor. In those days I was young and fit and generally ran up stairs three steps at a time. Sprinting headlong up the dimly lit stairs I accidentally collided with someone racing down. He fell to the ground and I helped him to his feet.

We apologised to each other and in the dim light I could see that the man I had caused to tumble was Kirk Douglas the star of the film and a celebrated celluloid tough guy. I was amused to note that he was actually fairly short in stature. For all that I had seen his rippling muscles in *The Vikings* and *Spartacus* and I wasn't about to press any issues. Sandy and I finished our beer and left.

Andrea had left Edinburgh's Royal Hospital for Sick Children just before we married and had returned to the Officers' Nursing Home in the city's West End where she enjoyed looking after her "old boys". One of her patients was Lord Reith, the first Director General of the BBC, underlining the fact that Andrea's official links with the BBC came before my own. Although Lord

Reith has been held up over the generations as one of the dominant figures in BBC history, I was surprised to learn from Andrea that in the last few weeks of his life he had very few visitors apart from his family. One of his only callers was Malcolm Muggeridge, a well-known journalist and broadcaster of his time.

Andrea was dedicated to the officers and gentlemen under her charge in the nursing home and it was because of them that she came close to ending our engagement..

I had been covering the annual meeting of the National Farmers Union on the island of Bute and after dinner had found myself engrossed in a late-night snooker tournament with some of my reporter colleagues. Andrea was on night duty and at 1am I realised I had not made my nightly call to my girl. When she answered, she gave me short shrift for telephoning so late and waking up her patients. The call was quickly terminated. Subdued and chastened I returned to the snooker match and brooded over how to make amends. Two hours later, fortified with a little more Dutch courage, I rang her to apologise for my earlier call – and woke her old boys again. I was not spoken to for several days.

After our marriage, Andrea continued her work with her patients but in due course we had high-profile responsibilities of our own when Andrea gave birth to Anna in Edinburgh's Queen Mary Nursing Home on May 12th, 1972 – by coincidence the same birthday as my mother. Becoming a parent was clearly a watershed in our lives and we adored the little girl that now came to dominate our lives. Little did we know then that as the years were to roll inexorably onwards, our Anna would grow to adulthood and marry a fine young man called Keith in Stonehaven near Aberdeen who lived next door to the house where Lord Reith had been born in 1889.

Meantime, my freelance broadcasting activities were continuing and I was still keen to get into radio full-time if I got the chance. But having been turned down for interview on more than one occasion and having failed a BBC board I was not optimistic.

And then I noticed an advertisement for a news producer on a new local radio station due to be set up by the BBC in Carlisle. What they wanted, the advert indicated, was someone who could handle local news stories but also with an interest in and knowledge of farming. I thought it would suit me down to the ground. I applied immediately.

I was called for interview on June 22nd, 1973 at the BBC's small office in St Mary's Gate, Carlisle. Despite BBC local radio's well-earned reputation for achieving on a shoestring the same amount of work that cost an arm and a leg in other area of the corporation's work, I was surprised to find that there were five people on my board. In addition to Tim Pitt, the Station Manager, John Pickles, the Programme Organiser and Stuart Campbell, the News Editor, the board was chaired by a senior figure from the Appointments Department in London and a colleague from what was then known as Personnel but now termed Human Resources.

Prior to my interview I was given the task of selecting five items from a ten pieces of copy and construct them into a short bulletin for broadcast. I was then required to read this bulletin on air followed by which I had to read two record requests. Having stumbled my way through this I then had three minutes to prepare to interview a member of the Carlisle Fabian Society.

For more than a week I was on tenterhooks. I desperately wanted the job but had no idea how well or badly I had performed at my board. On July 3rd I received a letter saying that they would offer me the post at £2700 per annum. I was delighted and disappointed. Delighted that I had been successful in my application but bitterly disappointed at the salary offered. The advertisement for the post had mentioned a salary ranging from £2700 to £3700 and in my ignorance had hoped that, if successful, I would join the BBC nearer the top of the scale rather than at the bottom because of my knowledge of farming. I was quickly to learn that in those days virtually everyone began at the bottom of a grade and then worked their way to the top by a series of annual increments.

It was with heavy heart that I wrote to the BBC and turned down their offer. With a wife and little Anna to support, the offer of £2700 was the same as I was earning on Farmers Weekly – and I would be saying goodbye to a staff car. Joining the BBC by then had been a cherished ambition but I had to say no.

I expected to hear no more about it but on July 17th, 1973, I received a further letter from the BBC indicating their disappointment at my rejection of their first offer. They understood about my reluctance to come south on the same income as I was earning but if I would reconsider my position they would be able to offer me an interest-free car loan of £500 repayable over two years. Was I still interested? I was. I accepted the post and a new chapter of my life was about to begin.

Heading South

I was 28 years old when I joined the BBC in Carlisle. Being part of a young team starting to build a following for a local radio station from scratch was to become one of the most satisfying periods of my working life.

In truth, there were only three of us on the editorial side who were complete newcomers to the BBC. The rest of the production team had already served their time with BBC Radio Durham, a VHF station, which closed when the broadcast footprint of other stations in North East England swamped the output from Durham.

One of the Durham team who decided to go south to the BBC in Bristol rather than move across to Carlisle was Kate Adie whose role at Durham had been to mix news and farming programmes. Effectively, it was her role I was trying to fill. Katie Adie went on to become a respected news correspondent for BBC Television both at home and overseas and although I have never met her I feel I owe her a drink for creating an opening in local radio for me.

Before we went on air, the BBC reckoned that it would be prudent to send me on a three-week radio course in London. In those days the BBC's radio training unit was based at The Langham directly across from BBC Broadcasting House. Today The Langham is a five-star hotel; then it was a vast sprawling mix of corridors and rooms with young men and women either walking around distractedly talking to one another with a microphone between them or running like hell with bits of quarter inch sound tape round their shoulders trying not to spill the ever ubiquitous coffees in polystyrene cups without which it seemed to me the BBC would grind to a halt.

One of our tasks on the training course was to team off in pairs sharing a tape recorder and go to a London landmark and, having composed ourselves for a few minutes, then deliver as live into the microphone appropriate commentary about what we saw in front of us.

I was paired with a young producer from BBC Radio Birmingham. A jovial chap, he thought a walk along the Embankment would be a good idea and then, on finding a suitable spot, we would sit and describe what was happening on the Thames. We tried it. Somehow the words wouldn't flow, largely because there wasn't anything happening on the river when we wanted to talk about it.

I don't know if it was he or me but one of us spotted a tourist vessel tied to the Embankment that was open to visitors. More than that, it had a bar. Maybe it was the time of day – mid morning – or maybe it was our surroundings but we thought the best option would be a small sherry to whet our creative appetites. On second thoughts, we felt it may as well be a schooner of sherry.

When we had downed our second schooner we repaired a little unsteadily across the gangplank back to the comparative safety of the Embankment and found a seat and switched on our tape recorder. Whether there actually was anything happening on the river or not by then I cannot recall. What I do remember is that we waxed eloquently as if there had been. Back at BBC training HQ our taped contribution was warmly praised although there were some raised eyebrows at our occasional lapses into barely controlled laughter for no apparent reason.

During the course of our training we also had to pull together a 20-minute report on the subject of our choice. Because of some current issue about immigration I chose race relations and was able to interview Mark Bonham-Carter, the first Chairman of the Race Relations Board. But on that occasion I felt it wise not to begin my duties with a schooner of sherry.

At the end of the training course and before heading north for Carlisle I managed a couple of hours to myself and was strolling along Knightsbridge when I spied a small cruet set in the window of a small jewellers'. It would make a splendid gift for Andrea. There was no price visible – which usually means expensive – but despite my impecunious situation I thought I would at least enquire within. When I tried to enter the shop the door was firmly barred with a small notice on the glass indicating I should ring the bell if I wished to venture inside. I rang the bell.

The door opened and I was ushered in. There was one other customer present who had his back to me examining some objects on the counter. I asked if I could see the cruet set and was busy wondering if I could afford it when I felt a tap on my shoulder.

I turned round. It was the other customer – David Tomlinson, the well-known British character actor who used to describe himself as a "dim-witted upper class twit" who had been taken to the hearts of the nation with two memorable film performances in Mary Poppins and Bedknobs and Broomsticks.

I say, he said, *would you mind helping me young man?*

I asked why.

He led me to the shop counter where two beautiful large silver salvers were displayed.

Well, he said, *I want to buy one of these but I can't choose which one. Which one do you like?*

A little startled and confused by this sudden turn of events, I looked at both and eventually pointed at the one I preferred.

Thank you young man, said David Tomlinson, *then that's the one I'll have.*

He paid for his salver and left.

For the record, I also bought the cruet set for Andrea.

Being part of a newsroom in local radio was far removed from my previous broadcasting experience of recording the occasional interview for BBC radio in Scotland. While I believed I had always worked under a fair degree of pressure for newspapers and magazines, working in the BBC newsroom in Carlisle seemed to double the daily intensity of meeting on-air deadlines.

For most of us, 80 or 90-hour weeks were not uncommon. Some of our journalistic colleagues outside local radio suggested that our youth and enthusiasm were being taken advantage of. We didn't agree. We felt we were part of something new, something special; a team creating a radio station for the local population with the emphasis on public service. For their part, the audience took us to their hearts and we were offered enormous support and encouragement from the beginning.

Our patch was North Cumbria, centred on Carlisle. We went as far north as the Scottish border and as far south as Keswick.

In the west we took in Workington and Whitehaven and on rare occasions would make contact with Appleby in the east. More than thirty years on, the station has now grown to include the whole of Cumbria including Barrow in Furness.

The working pace of our young lives was frantic – but we loved it. My duties were strictly defined. Two days a week I was a news producer and three days a week a farming producer. In reality one merged with the other and a supposed five-day week became six long days at least.

Virtually all of us in the newsroom were heavy smokers – par for the course in those faraway days. One of the reporters was Bob Dickson, a fellow Scot from Edinburgh, who didn't just begin work every day with a packet of fags. He also brought his dog Misty as well who stayed throughout the working day in a small wicker basket below Bob's feet. She was a "Westie", a West Highland Terrier. Like others of her breed she was pure white. The wonder is that after a couple of years in the Carlisle news-room her constant exposure to nicotine didn't turn her a deep shade of brown - or perhaps deaf from the constant pounding of the stone-age typewriters that dominated every reporter's desk.

BBC Carlisle had one white Ford Escort pool car with a distinctive livery emblazoned on both sides and its use was encouraged by Stuart Campbell our supportive and energetic News Editor for two understandable reasons. First, he liked to know the station's profile was enhanced when the car would be seen driven through the many villages of our patch. Secondly using the BBC car was cheaper than paying me a mileage rate when I used my own.

My farming duties were straightforward. During my three-day specialist stint I had to produce 10-minute evening bulletins that were a mix of news and market prices plus a weekly half-hour magazine programme broadcast on a Saturday morning and repeated on a Sunday. It was a marvellous job and I loved meeting the friendly farming families in North Cumbria from the arable farmers in the fertile Eden Valley between Carlisle and Penrith to the milk producers in the Whitehaven area and the hill men around Ullswater.

My news producer duties were markedly different. The prime objective here was to ride shotgun in the newsroom as the following morning's flagship breakfast programme was being pulled together. The programme, AM in Cumbria, was on air from 0700 until 0930 and the main news content was between 0745 and 0815. Some public service tapes were supplied like a weekly contribution on transport or road safety from the AA but most of the rest was generated by the newsroom staff and a couple of local freelances.

This editorial side of the breakfast programme was usually complete by early evening – if you had a clear run. Very often, it seemed I did not and found myself often completing the running order for the following morning as late as 9pm.

Then came the hard bit – the music. Each morning show required the selection of about 26 record tracks and these had to be chosen to reflect specific categories of music be it country and western, light opera or music from the shows. Once selected, the discs had to be timed if the duration was not contained on the record sleeve and the instrumental opening also timed and noted so that the following morning's presenter could be briefed on how long he could speak before the vocal began.

Some of my fellow producers had a natural affinity with all of this. I didn't. It took me many hours. What was worse was that the producer who found himself or herself on duty setting up the programme also had the task of producing it live on air the following morning by reading the half hourly news and sports bulletins and newspaper reviews.

By the time I had finished finding and timing my music selections it was often 0200 in the morning – occasionally later. As I then had to be back in the station by 0500 I was terrified I would sleep in and miss the show. I overcame this nightmare scenario by producing my own fail-safe solution. Having completed all my work I would turn the loudspeaker for local output to full volume. At that time of night the station took a feed from Radio 2 but Radio 2 in those days went off air at 0200. All I could hear was silence. I then tried to make myself as comfortable as possible on two chairs pulled together in the centre of the BBC Reception area. Having positioned myself directly in line of the loudspeaker I was thus assured that when Radio 2 began with a fanfare at 0500, I was awake and alert. Well, awake at least.

Being alert was also a requirement of being the early morning producer. While the presenter of the day was left to get on with linking all the items and music live on air, it was the producer's job to keep abreast of a steady stream of national and local news bulletins plus a sports report and a newspaper review.

The national news and sports bulletins came up the line from London and a system called Rip 'n Read. It meant simply that. Once the teleprinter had stopped spewing out the latest update in the corner of the newsroom, all the producer had to do was rip it off, take it through to the studio and read it when cued to do so.

I was usually on top of all this – or thought I was – until one morning I found myself having broadcast the newspaper review and was then sitting in the studio absorbed in a salacious tale in the Mirror of a defrocked vicar or suchlike when I heard the presenter John Jefferson announce:

It's 0725, time now for the latest sports headlines. Over to Arthur Anderson.

I looked up like a startled rabbit and realised that I had left the sports bulletin beside my typewriter in the newsroom. All I could think of saying was simply:

Sorry John – not quite ready yet. Come back to me in a minute or two.....

Professional to his bootstraps, John carried on as if nothing had gone amiss. In the meantime, I scurried out of the studio to collect the missing bulletin and get back on schedule.

If my working life at BBC Carlisle was enjoyable, my domestic life was less ordered. Having bitten the bullet and decided to head south for Carlisle, Andrea and I felt it was time we got a foot on the housing ladder and put our name down for a three bedroom detached house off the Wigton road and agreed to pay – over the next 25 or so years – the princely sum of £9250. It was more than we could afford but we had little option. Pricey though it was I recall standing with Andrea in front of our first home one evening and looking up the hill where more upmarket four-bedroom detached homes were going on sale for £13,000. Then, it seemed that affording a £13,000 home represented riches beyond the dreams of avarice.

The problem was our house was behind schedule. This meant that when my duties at Carlisle began, I had to spend the first two months in an appalling flat in the village of Eastriggs just over the Border in Scotland and about half an hour's drive from my work. Andrea and little Anna meantime stayed at the May Farm with my mother and father.

Eastriggs was built between 1916 and 1918, originally comprising mostly wooden huts to house workers employed in the huge explosives factory at nearby Gretna. Street names in the village were drawn from around the Empire – Durban Road, Delhi Road, Ottawa Road and Melbourne Road - to reflect the nationalities of the thousands of workers at the explosives plant.

Whatever the history of Eastriggs, I hated it – or at least that part of it that contained the fairly squalid flat I was renting. Two windows were cracked, the roof leaked, the main door lock was suspect and there was constant smell of gas in the kitchen. As soon as my lease would allow, I left and found myself a pleasant room in Carlisle in a house run by an Indian couple. I enjoyed their company and they just about tolerated my smoking.

Most Saturday mornings I would leave Carlisle about 7am and drive for an hour until my weekly half-hour farming magazine programme came on air. I would then pull into a lay-by on the A75 overlooking the Solway Firth and listen to what my previous week's work had produced before heading on for the May Farm and a brief reunion with Andrea and Anna and my parents. Whether it was the content of the programme or the restful and reassuring strains of Beethoven's 6th Symphony – *The Pastoral* – that served as the programme's signature music I know not but that regular half-hour tended to be one of peace and relaxation. Thus fortified, I would start the ignition of my ageing Ford Escort that I had purchased with my £500 interest-free loan and drive west to see the family at the May Farm.

Happily, this regular Saturday commuting between Cumbria and Galloway was not to last forever. Six months into my job at Carlisle we were able to move into our new home. We were together as a family once more.

But if domestic life had improved and my daily radio tasks for BBC Carlisle were hard work but enjoyable, there were occasions when broadcasting life could deliver hard little knocks along the way.

Part of the duty news producer's tasks on a Sunday evening was to sit behind the main broadcasting control desk with all its switches and sliding faders. Technology and I have never been easy bed fellows and I dreaded the Sundays when I had to take control of the station's output – albeit for only a few minutes.

For anyone who was at ease with the situation it was simplicity itself. At that time on a Sunday afternoon, we took a feed from Radio 2 broadcasting *Charlie Chester's Sunday Soapbox*.

At the close of his programme, we went live on air and broadcast our own local news with and occasional taped inserts played in from the machines at our right-hand side. While this was going on, it was vital to listen on earphones to what is known in the business as pre-fade – hearing another station but without broadcasting it. In our case, the idea was that after our local news bulletin we would then opt back into the network. But not Radio 2. That would have been too easy. We had to opt into Radio 1 broadcasting *Tom Brown's Top Twenty*.

For me all this was complicated and demanding co-ordination of hand, eye and brain. Perhaps I could have managed two out of the three but not all at the same time. In the event, I opted out of Radio 2 reasonably enough. I then began our local bulletin in fairly confident matter but began to feel a cold panic while I simultaneously searched for the proper button to press to pre-fade Radio 1. I eventually found it but felt my voice was quivering with tension as I continued to read the short bulletin. At what I thought was the appropriate moment, I announced to an unseen audience that we were now going over to *Tom Brown's Top*

Twenty. I will never know how I achieved it but Tom Brown duly came on air while from some other source a completely different selection of music was playing in tandem. Added to this I had forgotten to close my own microphone fader..........

I knew I had screwed up but didn't know how to unscrew it. As luck would have it, a production colleague called Chris Rogers was in the next door studio preparing for his presentation stint on the daily two-hour Cumbria Here and There slot. He looked up, saw a fellow producer clearly in despair and distress and came straight into the cubicle, immediately identified the problem and fixed it in five seconds flat.

Our studios were on the top level of a small multi-storey office block and back in the newsroom I looked down at the cars parked below and briefly contemplated suicide until I realised that such an action might leave Andrea with a baby daughter to support and a mortgage to pay with no income. So I had a fag instead and reckoned that if I kept my head down none of my bosses would have heard my gaffe.

As for Chris Rogers, I owed him a drink but duties interfered that evening and I never bought him one. Now retired as one of the BBC political correspondents in South West England, I still owe him my thanks and that drink.

Clearly I was better suited to the great outdoors than sliding faders and driving a broadcasting desk and fortunately that's where I spent most of my time - recording interviews on location most of the day then coming back to the studio to edit short packaged reports for the breakfast programme or longer items to form part of my weekly half-hour magazine edition.

From time to time my boss and my budget allowed me to venture outside Cumbria and cover local angles at national events like the Royal Smithfield Show, the Royal Show in Warwickshire and the Royal Highland Show in Edinburgh.

It was a welcome change to the normal routine and I particularly enjoyed covering the Cumbrian angle at these national events – with one exception. The first year I attended the Royal Show near Coventry coincided with two of the wettest days in the history of the event. The showground turned to a quagmire and both man and beast were sodden and down in the mouth.

In these situations all a reporter can do is get on with the job as best you can. Make the weather work for you. Forget the stories about how unseasonal high temperatures meant the sensitive skins of the pigs had to be hosed down. Instead, concentrate on how the monsoon-like conditions were affecting man and beast. One way or another, a programme has to be filled.

The main problem for me came during the editing session I had booked with the BBC's Outside Broadcasting team in Birmingham. At national events like the Royal Show every man and his boy from around the BBC's empire would converge and require editing and broadcast facilities and time and space were at a premium. If you had booked two hours' editing, you had to crack on with the job or your programme would not be ready for transmission up the line later that day.

So I cracked on. The problem was that during my two-hour stint of editing, there was not one but six or seven brief power cuts. It should be underlined that in those far-off days before digital editing, our recordings were done on quarter inch tape. Wearing headphones, or cans as they're called in the broadcasting business, the tapes were played across the voice-head and careful use of a china-graph pencil indicated where you would make a cut and where you would come back into the interview. The tape would then be physically cut with a safety razor, the discarded section dropped into a waste-basket and the two remaining ends joined together with sticky tape. It was a precise but time-consuming operation.

The only problem was, as I soon discovered, that safety razors are not necessarily safe in all conditions – certainly not when a power cut comes at the instant of slicing the tape and everything around you stops and you are plunged into temporary darkness. Hard to believe, but I cut myself twice that evening and had considerable difficulty in stopping the flow of blood from my knuckles dripping onto the edited taped interviews.

For the most part working as a producer for BBC Radio Carlisle was public service at its best - serving the local community. Our daily round saw us interview the great and the good and the ordinary man and woman in the street or in my case, on the land. Budgets were tight – ridiculously low even by other BBC standards of the time. In my case I had £9 a week to spend on any freelance help that I thought I could afford. In reality even hard-up freelances wouldn't work for what my budget could pay them although I did find one vet, Tom Barr in nearby Penrith, who began a long series of highly successful advisory pieces which he prepared and broadcast once a fortnight. I paid him £6 a time. He continued this work long after I left and I only hope his fee increased over the years.

Occasionally, however, even farming producers like me brushed shoulders with the great and the good. One of the local Conservative MPs was Willie Whitelaw who lived near Penrith and had a prize-winning herd of Charolais cattle. He also used to hold his political surgery in Carlisle and, like all MPs in opposition, was only too happy to be door-stepped from time to time by a local radio reporter. I always found him to be a gentle and kindly man and I don't suppose his basic nature changed even when he later found himself in Government serving as Deputy Prime Minister to Margaret Thatcher. He was a loyal and trusted second in command for, as Margaret Thatcher once famously remarked:

Everyone needs a Willie.

Another genial political soul was Fred Peart, Labour MP for Workington. By dint of good fortune – for me at least - he was also Minister of Agriculture in Jim Callaghan's government during my time at Radio Carlisle.

Coming north on the night train on a Friday, Fred Peart always made it a point of principle to maintain his links with his working class voters and most Saturday mornings would find him in the Workington Working Men's Club. From time to time he would agree to an interview and I was happy to give up part of my Saturday to head to West Cumbria instead of Galloway to secure what was usually a strong story for Monday morning's programme.

Whether he felt more relaxed with me or his surroundings compared with London I do not know but very often he would reveal more about the comings and goings of political events to me than when in London. As a result, most of the interviews I did with Fred Peart were also broadcast on BBC Radio Scotland and on *Farming Today* on Radio 4.

One of Fred Peart's simple pleasures in the Workington Working Men's Club was a pint of beer and a game of snooker and he deigned to let me play a frame with him on one memorable occasion. He won but in that situation I felt it would have been a little less than diplomatic for me to suggest his victory might have had anything to do with a misspent youth.

The story is told of Fred that during his time as Minister for Agriculture he was summoned to 10 Downing Street by Jim Callaghan who said:

Fred, I'm going to move you upstairs because I require your seat in the Cabinet for a younger member.

Fred said: *But Jim, you're older than I am* to which Jim Callaghan replied:

Yes but I'm the Prime Minister.

In fact, during his long career in politics Fred Peart was Leader of both the House of Commons and later, as Lord Peart, the House of Lords - the first politician since Disraeli to be leader of both Houses of Parliament.

While we interviewed our fair share of politicians, when it came to stars of stage or screen it might be stating a self-evident truth if I suggest that Radio Carlisle seemed to come at the fag end in this department. Not surprisingly, Shaftsbury Avenue took precedence over Botchergate, Carlisle's main street that led directly to our new studios at Hilltop Heights.

I remember dealing with a couple though – David Whitfield, a big star in the 50s and 60s with his fine tenor voice belting out hits like *Cara Mia* and *From Rags to Riches*. Sadly, he was no longer a big star when he dropped by our studios and he failed to take the station or its small audience by storm.

A more contemporary star at the time was George Melly, the Jazz singer. Andrea and I saw him perform at a hotel one evening in the Carlisle area and I persuaded him to come on air the next morning. I recall collecting him from his hotel and walking with him the short distance to the studio. Seeing an extrovert George Melly in his flamboyant patterned suit and pink fedora hat was not a sight the good citizens of Carlisle were used to of a weekday morning.

There is one particular aspect of my work that will live long in the memory – the Lamb Bank. In a rich agricultural area where livestock production was central to the rural economy the annual lambing season was a highlight of the year – as I knew only too well from my own background at the May Farm in Galloway.

And like any farming community anywhere in the country, lambing time held its own share of problems for the good rural folk of Cumbria. Despite the highest standards of husbandry and years of experience, things can and do go wrong.

Ewes with plenty of milk can give birth to dead lambs. Ewes can die during lambing leaving healthy lambs without mothers. Both can represent an expensive headache for the farmer.

I wondered if local radio could offer a service here that would be impossible in other sections of the media. Could we, for example, offer a special service during lambing time when, several times a day at specific times, we would broadcast details of farmers who had lambs without mothers and of other farmers who had ewes without lambs. We would broadcast the names of the farmers involved and give out on air their telephone numbers. It would then be up to the farming community to contact each other and come to their own private commercial agreements.

My bosses agreed that we should try it. I was delighted. It began slowly at first but as word spread through the farming community the numbers of calls into the station multiplied rapidly. By the end of the lambing season the Cumbria Farming Lamb Bank was judged to have been a success and a shining example of the kind of beneficial public service broadcasting that local radio can do so well.

News of the Lamb Bank spread to the wider media. Articles were carried in the local papers, the *Newcastle Journal*, and the northern editions of the *Daily Mail* and the *Daily Express*. One morning, shortly after finishing my shift on the breakfast programme, my News Editor Stuart Campbell asked if I would phone the BBC in Newcastle who wanted a word.

The call turned out to be from a Newcastle-based researcher for *Nationwide*, the early evening news and current affairs programme broadcast from London presented by Frank Bough. Would I, the researcher asked, be prepared to go through to Newcastle and be interviewed live by Frank Bough about the Lamb Bank, its origins and its success?

I agreed in an instant – not only would it be great publicity for BBC Radio Carlisle, it would be worth a few brownie points within the family for me to be seen on national television.

At lunchtime I rushed home, showered, changed into my best suit and left Andrea to phone around our relations in Scotland to ensure that they would be tuned to *Nationwide* that night.

I then went back to the radio station to collect the pool car to drive to Newcastle to find an urgent message waiting for me. Very sorry but a stronger story had come up, it said. They would get back to me another time. They never did. My debut on television would have to be put on hold.

Yet while BBC Television left me in the lurch – at least on that occasion – editorial policy at Radio Carlisle was made of sterner stuff. The Lamb Bank became a regular part of the station's programme schedule and more than 40 years later is still broadcasting its important service to the rural communities of the region.

Truth to tell, while working hours at BBC Radio Carlisle were long and intensive, there was time for some light relief. I have never been a football fan but my father-in-law from Inverness, Ken MacKenzie, most certainly was.

He certainly hit lucky during my time in Carlisle because it was during the 1974-75 season that Carlisle United played in League Division 1 and under the guidance of their manager Alan Ashman they even topped the league for a heady few weeks thanks to star players like Chris Balderstone who was not only a local hero to the football fraternity but during the summer also played first class cricket for Leicestershire. Twice my father-in-law came south for the weekend with his wife Beth and he and I would head out to Brunton Park to watch Carlisle United take on teams like Liverpool and Spurs. Ken would have liked to be in the stand for Manchester United games as well, but that wasn't possible – that season Manchester United had been relegated to Division 2.

After two years at BBC Radio Carlisle I was still enjoying my work immensely – and working as long hours as at the start, as indeed were all my production colleagues. This kind of constant pressure became part and parcel of local radio life and we had come to accept it. Apart from anything else, there was little alternative but to keep my nose to the grindstone as domestic life had taken on a new turn with the arrival in our lives of our son Angus born in Carlisle on January 22nd, 1975.

Within weeks of the arrival of Angus into our world I began to prepare to say goodbye to my father. He had been unfit for some years but took a stroke on the evening of Friday, February 21st followed by a second the following day that lost him the power of his left arm and leg.

Although he was to rally a little over the coming days, by the middle of March it became clear that he was weakening and that his struggle for life was almost over. He died peacefully just before 11am on Thursday March 20th with mother, my sister Monica and me at his bedside.

My father had never been a fervent churchgoer and he always hated a fuss so we held a short funeral service at the May Farm. Somehow, I managed to read *Abide With Me* without breaking down.

Despite having lived a full life and done the two things he most wanted to do – sail the seven seas and be a farmer – father's funeral was naturally a sad affair although his passing brought to my mind one of his phrases from years before. I recalled that from time to time father could be seen looking into the middle distance and saying *"I must go to the other side."* The first time I heard him say it I rashly imagined he was minded to defect to Russia taking with him the accumulated wisdom of how not to make a rich living out of cattle and sheep on a small Galloway farm. Or maybe he had in mind a séance and a few sessions with an ouija board. But no – going to the other side for father simply meant making a nostalgic trip from South West Scotland to North Northumberland to seek out some old friends from his youth. Accompanied by either my mother or me he was to make that nostalgic return to his boyhood roots on three occasions in his final years. But as the strains of the final hymn faded at his funeral service on that winter's day in 1975 I knew that this time there would be no return from the other side for our Captain Jack.

Shortly after the arrival of Angus into the bosom of our Carlisle family, I received a telephone call from Pat Chalmers, the BBC radio producer who helped me some years earlier cross Wenceslas Square following my intake of too much Czechoslovakian beer.

By now Pat had moved from Edinburgh to manage the BBC studios in Aberdeen. There was, he indicated, a producer post coming up for the daily radio farming programme which had also moved from Edinburgh to Aberdeen. Would I be interested in applying and could he come down to Carlisle to see the kind of programme I was then producing and presenting?

This Aberdeen-based programme was the same one on which I had cut my teeth some time earlier as a freelance. The idea of a daily programme appealed to me and I was resolved to apply for the vacant post when it was advertised.

Despite that, we had only been in our new home for 18 months, Andrea had two youngsters to handle with Anna and Angus and while the job appealed in Aberdeen – assuming I would be successful in my application – the idea of shifting homes again was less than attractive.

In the event Pat Chalmers came down to Carlisle and having listened to the standard of the local programmes persuaded me that I should throw my hat into the ring for the Aberdeen post – but with no guarantees.

In the event I did apply and was invited to attend a BBC board in Glasgow. On the day of the interview I had just finished my early morning stint on the breakfast programme when I rushed home to change and drive to Glasgow.

Sod's Law decided it was time to intervene. Thick fog blanketed the A74 and the heavy traffic was reduced to a crawling pace. Halfway to Glasgow I realised I was going to be late for my interview and pulled off the road to phone ahead to the BBC and explain the situation as best I could. They were sympathetic. Get here as soon as you are able to, they said.

One hour late, I reached Queen Margaret Drive. The nearest parking place was several streets away and by the time I reached the BBC studio I was sweating profusely.

Don't worry, said the friendly receptionist. *Just go straight up. They're waiting for you.*

I reached the conference room on the third floor – the sanctum sanctorum of the BBC in Glasgow as I was later to discover – and knocked on the door.

Come in! I opened the door to a large room and saw five distant figures sitting behind a desk. As I fixed my eyes on the empty chair on my side of the board-room table, I failed to notice the three steps leading down from the conference room landing and fell flat on my face in front of my interrogators. How to make friends and influence people. They say first impressions count yet somehow, despite that inauspicious beginning, I got the job.

I was going back to Scotland.

BBC Radio Scotland

So began two hectic but happy years as a radio producer and reporter, retracing my earlier *Scotsman* and *Farmers Weekly* steps around Scotland but this time eschewing a notebook and pencil in favour of a Uher tape recorder. I was working with the presenter Roy Gregor, an experienced and respected colleague who I had first met years before when he had been a farming correspondent on the *Scottish Daily Mail*. The other member of our small team was Dorothy Robertson – self-styled as Daft Dotty – who was extremely efficient at her job and she and Roy did a lot to make me settle in and feel one of this new Aberdeen family. In fact the two of them proved a special team in more ways than one – they eventually got married.

However, there was one problem on the domestic front. We had sold our house in Carlisle for £9500 – in 18 months we had made the princely profit of £250. How far would that go in Aberdeen we wondered. Answer – nowhere.

At that time Aberdeen was at the beginning of the North Sea Oil boom. Walk down the city's Union Street and Americans in cowboy boots and stetson hats were a common sight. Have a bar lunch anywhere in the west end of the city and American accents were as common as the local Doric dialect.

When the oil boom came it brought money with it and with the cash came high housing prices. Coming from Carlisle, one of the cheapest areas of housing in the UK at that time to Aberdeen, one of the most expensive areas, posed a seemingly insurmountable problem.

We had sold our home in Carlisle for less than £10,000. To replace that standard in Aberdeen at that time would have cost almost £20,000. With my salary then around £4000 that was clearly well beyond our reach. We settled instead for a new end-terrace house in Stonehaven, 15 miles south of Aberdeen, for £10500. Unexciting perhaps but it was a home. Needs must as the devil drives.

While the basics of my job in Aberdeen were virtually the same as in Carlisle, the atmosphere was entirely different. Carlisle had been young and vibrant while Aberdeen was part of the old traditional BBC.

For a start, when you entered the BBC reception area in Carlisle you exchanged pleasantries with the lass behind the desk and that was it. Not so in Aberdeen where all visitors were met by a splendidly uniformed Commissionaire. Over the years there was a succession of these impeccably attired stalwarts who offered a formal but friendly welcome to staff and visitors alike – Charlie Glass who liked a bet on the horses, Alex Watson whose son played football for Glasgow Rangers, Harry Morrison, Norman Michie and Jim McKay – all former policemen.

Then there was the coffee break both morning and afternoon, a luxury unheard of in BBC local radio. There, you grabbed your coffee from a machine – if you were lucky enough to have a machine on the premises - and drank it on the hoof. Not so in Aberdeen. The morning and afternoon ritual of trooping up three flights of stairs to the small canteen beside the film cutting room was virtually compulsory. Pleasant, of course, but a waste of valuable production time and I soon found a series of excuses to bypass this time-honoured BBC practice.

While the basics of the Aberdeen job may have been the same as in local radio, the principal difference was geography. There wasn't one area of the Carlisle patch that I couldn't reach by car within the hour. Covering Scotland from Aberdeen was very different and represented all kinds of logistical difficulties – not least where you could find a far-flung studio to play in an interview if you happened to be a couple of hundred miles away from base. Occasionally you could carefully wrap your taped interview and put in on a train bound for Aberdeen but on the few occasions I tried this I found the mounting blood pressure in case it got lost was more than I could bear. In the event, I'm glad to report that no tapes ever went astray.

If the geography of Scotland occasionally posed a logistical problem for a radio producer compared with working within the narrower geographical confines of North Cumbria, the broader canvas on which I now found myself working also created opportunities previously unheard of – reporting from abroad.

The first occasion came when I was invited to be a guest of the then West German government to visit farms in Bavaria and see how many small farmers supported their rural lifestyle with a second job in a car plant near Munich. Radio 4 were also interested in taking a report from me and so with the prospect of thus getting two bites of the cherry I was given the green light to go to Germany.

The farm visits in Bavaria were straightforward enough and provided good radio material as the farmers involved operated on quite a different scale than in the UK – and it seemed that in general they had a higher standard of living.

On the second day of our visit our West German hosts from the Ministry of Agriculture notified us that later than evening we were invited as guests for a performance of Beethoven's *Fidelio* in the newly refurbished Bavarian State Opera House in Munich. Attending an opera was to be a new experience.

In the event, our farm visits ended earlier than scheduled and I was asked if there was anything particular I would like to do in the two or three hours before attending the opera.

I hesitated in case I was treading on diplomatic toes. Would it be possible, I wondered, as we were so near, if I could see Dachau?

No problem, I was assured, and I was assigned a guide who drove me the 15 or so miles from Munich to the camp, opened in 1933, and which had set the standard for the barbarism that was to follow during the years of the Second World War.

Dachau has been described as the Academy of Terror, the role model and training ground for the brutality that followed in the wake of Hitler's armies and culminating in perhaps the greatest crime in history – the Holocaust with the loss of more than six million lives.

Dachau today is a place of memory and pilgrimage. It is an ever-present reminder of the people from 34 nations who lost their lives after passing through the gate bearing the legend *Arbeit Macht Frei – Freedom Through Work*.

My guide to all of this chilling history was a young Munich lawyer whose father had been a General in a Panzer division in Northern France. While most of his time was occupied practicing his chosen profession, he explained that from time to time he would take individuals groups on tours to Dachau. I asked him why.

He beckoned me to follow him. We passed one of the original camp buildings and turned a corner and approached another wooden building in front of which was a sign. He pointed to it.

It was a quotation, in English, by George Santayana, the Spanish-born American philosopher. It said simply: *Those who do not know history are condemned to repeat it.* There was little need to say more.

It was probably only a coincidence that the opera I attended later that night was to be Beethoven's *Fidelio* that has a theme close to its composer's heart – the defeat of tyranny through man's innate desire for liberty.

The National Theatre in Munich, reminiscent of a Greek temple, ranks among the world's leading opera houses. Sad to relate, therefore, that despite my opulent surroundings and the performance before me, my day in the hills of Bavaria and the emotional experience of visiting Dachau must have combined to bring out the philistine in me. I slept throughout much of the performance.

Sometimes a radio story could take on a momentum all its own. During my time in Aberdeen I was reporting from the annual sale of Hereford bulls in Edinburgh and chanced to inter-view one buyer, Roger Snell from Hereford. The theme of the interview was not so much the qualities of the bulls he might have bought or sold that day but the fact that he was about to start a new farming life in Bolivia.

The interview was broadcast on BBC Radio Scotland and the farming programme on BBC Radio 4. A couple of days later I received a telephone call in my office in Aberdeen from a farmer in Banffshire called Alan Raven. He had heard the interview and asked if I could I help put him in touch with Roger Snell. I was happy to do so and promptly thought no more about it.

Some years later I picked up a copy of the *Sunday Telegraph* and read with growing interest a feature on a former Scottish farmer called Alan Raven ranching 4000 cattle on 86,000 acres of Bolivia. They had a home in Santa Cruz but the ranch was several days away by horseback. On their first journey overland, the article revealed that they had finished their drinking water in two days. But they had a solution. A hole was poked in oranges and the holes filled with gin. The article further revealed that his interest in Bolivia had been sparked after having heard a radio interview with Roger Snell. Could Alan Raven really have decided to quit Scotland and begin a new life as a result of my interview? I wrote to him to inquire. He answered and agreed that I had indeed been responsible for his new life in South America. The power of the media perhaps.

Apart from the occasional forays to the hills of Bavaria and the fanciful notion that I might go to Bolivia and make a programme with Alan Raven (which sadly I never did), I had ambitions to make programmes in the Middle East. It was an enthusiasm fired by stories of how farming entrepreneurs had made the desert bloom be it in the work of the Israelis in fruit and vegetable production in the Negev Desert or British pioneers with dairying in Saudi Arabia. Once again, it never happened – although I had a perfect Middle East contact in Andrea's young brother Gordon MacKenzie who was to spend virtually all his career as a leading hotelier in Jordan, Saudi Arabia, the Sudan and Qatar. From modest beginnings in Inverness, Gordon climbed the career ladder with him and his wife Margaret now living in Doha in Qatar where he is General Manager of the Radisson Blu international hotel. Gordon's hotel is owned by a Sheikh Al Thani, a member of the Qatari royal family and who has large herds of dairy cattle and flocks of sheep. Perhaps there's still time to capture that Middle East story after all.

But back to the past. Farm Journal, was broadcast live every weekday at 12.45pm. This was an ideal time – not only did it catch virtually every farming family in the country who traditionally stopped for lunch at around 12.30, it meant that a large cross section of the wider public also listened to the programme. For that reason, we saw ourselves as having a dual role – on the one hand we were a daily source of the latest news and information for the important rural sector of Scotland's community but also we believed we had a responsibility to try translate more complex technical or political material in a manner that the general public would understand.

While the programme, concentrating as it did on the news of the moment, did not specifically solicit feedback from its audience, we would receive letters – usually from the general public – on a regular basis. I came to realise that in those days at least the listener believed implicitly anything and everything that was broadcast by the BBC.

This was forcibly underlined to me on one occasion when by way of a little light relief on April 1st I wrote and recorded a short item about a genetic breakthrough in turkey breeding. This majored on the fact that consumer research had shown that the most popular part of the turkey was the drumstick and to increase economic returns from this section of the market a special strain of turkey had been bred with four legs rather than two thus at a stroke doubling the profit for the turkey producer. The problem was, my story suggested, that four-legged turkeys could run a lot faster than the two-legged variety. To overcome this, a variant of a Jack Russell was being trained to catch the birds. It was pointed out that the dogs were being bred without teeth so that they didn't harm the flesh of the turkeys when they caught them.

All utter nonsense, of course, but a little light relief for April Fools' Day. The key to a successful April 1st spoof is to deliver it seriously and straight and do not immediately reveal the joke at the end of the broadcast. As long as the report is not calculated to alarm it is best left for the listener to evaluate the information as best they can. Mind you, I doubt that such a view would hold sway in the politically correct BBC world of today.

But back to the four-legged turkeys – within five minutes of the programme coming off air, we received a phone call. The woman caller said she had heard my report and thought it fascinating. She was a teacher and wondered if I could supply her with any further information so that she could further inform her pupils. Interrupting her gently, I thanked her for her complimentary tone but asked her if she knew what day it was. She paused for what seemed an unnaturally long time, then came a loud groan. *Bloody hell,* she said, and hung up.

During my time producing the daily radio programme there was humour of a more regular kind when *Maxwell on Monday* took to the air. Fordyce Maxwell, who had succeeded me as Bob Urquhart's deputy on *The Scotsman* six years earlier, had quickly made his mark as a first class specialist on the farming and rural scene and I offered him a weekly three-minute slot on radio to either reflect or preview events in rural Scotland. In addition to his natural abilities as a writer, Fordyce turned out to be a great success as a radio broadcaster, combining his experienced eye with a touch of cynicism where necessary and a dash of humour as appropriate. The mix proved very popular and Fordyce rapidly built up a loyal following among the audience. I was particularly grateful for his contribution - his guaranteed three-minute slot every Monday morning meant it was three minutes less I had to find to fill the airwaves.

I was beginning to learn that no matter how humble I might have thought my role in the great scheme of the BBC machine might be, the very name of the organisation tended to open doors. I heard some years ago that a survey in the UK claimed that the three best known brand names in the country were the Monarchy, the National Health Service and the BBC. I didn't doubt it then and I don't doubt it now. Whether they are the three most popular brand names is quite a different matter.

No matter where I found myself pursuing a farming story in Scotland, I was always welcome – even if the welcome occasionally took on an individuality of its own.

One morning a colleague found himself, by appointment and on time, in the farm steading of a well-known woman farmer. One of her staff explained that, as a keen horsewoman, she was out riding but if my colleague cared to hang about she would soon be back.

In due course, he heard the approaching sound of a galloping horse and then witnessed his potential interviewee clear a farm gate with a style that would have won plaudits at the Horse of the Year Show.

She drew to a halt in front of him. He looked up at the large horse and the towering presence of womanhood on its back.

Lost for words, he heard himself mumble: *My goodness your horse is sweating.*

She looked down at my nervous colleague: *Young man, if you'd been between my thighs for the last two hours you'd be bloody sweating!*

And then there are the surprises that can follow a simple introduction. I found myself on the island of Mull recording a programme on rural depopulation and was in the process of doing the usual balancing act of talking to locals who had been there for countless generations and incomers – the island used to have the reputation as the Officers' Mess because of the large number of senior ex service personnel who retired there.

However, I wasn't recording the interviews with my usual enthusiasm. The people I met were fine but I wasn't. I was ill. I had 'flu and like all men with 'flu I imagined that my very life was hanging by a thread. As it was my nose ran constantly, my eyes watered and every bone in my body ached.

I was in the company of a staff member of the Highlands and Islands Development Board and we had stopped for a brief lunch at the small hotel beside the Glenforsa airstrip.

I was manfully trying to force down a bowl of soup when a local approached us. When told I was feeling unwell he offered to buy me a large malt whisky.

I declined.

I insist, he said, *a wee dram will put you back on the road to recovery.*

No, I repeated, *I have to drive from here to the ferry terminal to meet the local councillor and the last thing I want to do is meet the local bobby on the road.*

He said: *Have a large dram – I can guarantee you won't meet the local bobby.*

How can you possibly guarantee that? I asked.

Because I'm the local bobby!

And he was. We had the dram.

So continued my life in Aberdeen as a radio producer and reporter continued. I was enjoying it immensely and had no thoughts of making any immediate change in my career. In any event, I was not tempted to make any rash decisions about my future because with the arrival in the world of our second son Andrew born in Aberdeen on September 21st 1976 parental responsibilities were never far from my thoughts. With three youngsters to care for, Andrea was fully committed and with my income from the BBC just about keeping pace with the demands of the mortgage and other household bills I was not tempted to make any career moves that I might come to regret, particularly if it meant moving home again.

Nonetheless, a career move was about to drop into my lap, unsought and unexpected.

Lights, Camera, Action

In our office in Aberdeen there were two other BBC staff members who worked in an area of broadcasting that I knew nothing about – television. One was Jean Hodge, Production Assistant on the monthly television programme *Farm Forum* produced by Pat Chalmers. Jean was a farmer's daughter from Dumfries and was soon to be in the vanguard of Scottish broadcasting history when she teamed up with producer Mike Marshall to create *The Beechgrove Garden* that was to become one of the longest running television programmes in Scotland.

The other member of the *Farm Forum* production team in our office was Jock Mearns an amiable former film editor who now worked as Assistant Producer to Pat Chalmers. Jock was an able technical operator who knew every stage of the production process but by his own admission was not an expert in the business of farming.

Out of the blue, Jock Mearns decided to take early retirement and laid plans to buy a small hotel in Turriff, north of Aberdeen. While Jock was working his notice Pat Chalmers looked around for a likely candidate as a new Assistant Producer. Generously, Jock Mearns suggested me.

While I knew nothing about television production and had never even thought of television as a staging post in my BBC career, I was excited at this new possibility. Diligently I prepared myself for the prospect of another grilling by a BBC board and firmly resolved that if it was to be held in Glasgow I would not fall down the three steps of the conference room a second time.

In the event, there was no board. I had prepared several pages of story ideas for filming and this, together with my performance as a radio producer over the previous two years, appeared to have sufficiently impressed the BBC that I was offered a six months trial as Assistant Producer, Television.

One of the immediate pleasures of my new role was working with Ross Muir for the first time. Ross, whom I had first met on the *Scottish Farmer* and who nearly three years later had suggested I throw my hat into the ring to succeed him on *The Scotsman*, had by now returned from public relations work in London and was working as a freelance in Aberdeen – part of which was as on screen presenter and reporter for *Farm Forum*. While Ross provided the solid journalism on *Farm Forum* the other reporter on the programme was John Harle, manager of a local farming company who was also an economist and had a good knowledge of the technical detail of the farming industry.

While working with Ross and John was a pleasure, I had a problem. I didn't really have a clue what I was doing. That was especially true on studio day on a Thursday when my role as Assistant Producer doubled up as Director as I had the responsibility of packaging all that had been done before into one neat bundle to be piped down the line to be recorded on videotape in our Glasgow studios from where the programme would be broadcast the following Sunday.

While the responsibility for directing in the studio was mine, in the early days I leaned heavily on the greater studio experience of my Production Assistant Irene Gibbons who in later career was to become part of the religious affairs department in BBC Manchester. Maybe it was working with me that caused her to seek the path of righteousness.

Whether on location or in the studio I began my time in television by not liking my job at all. My problem was that I felt I was making no significant contribution. Up to that point my previous time as a reporter for a daily newspaper, weekly magazine, local radio or national radio had been as a one-man band.

In television, however, I was part of a team and that was new to me. For a start I was not taking the ultimate editorial decisions about what we would broadcast – quite properly Pat Chalmers, the producer, fulfilled that role. Neither was I doing the reporting – that was the job of Ross Muir or John Harle.

That left me the task picking up the decisions from my producer and seeing them safely onto the screen. But I didn't know how.

I began to wonder seriously if I had made a wrong decision to move away from radio. Apart from anything else, when my father had died four years earlier while I had been at BBC Radio Carlisle I had wondered then if I should resign and return to the family farm. However, my mother was adamant that she would do her best to run the farm alone. In any event, she argued, I had worked hard to secure my first job with the BBC and I should hang onto it with both hands.

But that had been four years before. Further thoughts of whether I should pack it all in and try my hand at farming began to surface. I shared some of these feelings with Ross Muir who wisely cautioned me against making any sudden moves that I might later come to regret. It was good advice and I have always been grateful to Ross for that.

I also confided to Pat Chalmers that I didn't feel I was earning my corn. He sympathised and managed to secure a place for me on a Director's course in Television Training in London.

For three weeks I was part of a small group of six fledgling directors who were coached intensively – directing in the television gallery, operating cameras in studio, shooting on location. They were long tough days trained by senior figures in the BBC including Colin Strong, at that time handling studio direction for the *Michael Parkinson Show*, and Mike Catherwood, a studio director on the *Panorama* programme. Slowly, imperceptibly, my confidence grew day by day. Maybe I could return to Aberdeen and make something of a useful contribution to the team after all.

On my return to the day job I was delighted to find that the pieces began to fit together. I began to look forward to it. Directing in the gallery became a special pleasure. Of course, there was always an old BBC hand to slap you down if he thought you were being a bit cocky. Before every studio session it was important to relay your technical requirements to the engineering manager well in advance so that you could be sure that all the bells and whistles were to hand when required. Shortly after my return from the London training course I put on my list of technical requirements a request for three cameras for the recording session the following day.

My telephone rang. It was the engineering manager.
I see you've asked for three cameras?
Yes please, I ventured
Look son, he said, *when you learn how to use one properly you might get two!* He hung up. I felt duly chastised.

Coincidental to my return from London Pat Chalmers had secured agreement from senior management that the output of farming and rural affairs would double. Instead of one pro-gramme a month there would now be two and the old title *Farm Forum* was abandoned in favour of *Landward* – a title that was to encompass a broader range of rural subjects.

These were the days before videotape recording on location although the final broadcast package was recorded through the Aberdeen studio down the line onto two-inch video in the BBC's Glasgow studios. In those distant days, BBC Television in Birmingham's Pebble Mill studios also did a programme called *Farming* which was broadcast throughout the UK every Sunday apart from the first and third Sundays of the month when BBC Scotland opted out with its own home-spun *Landward* programme.

The Birmingham producer John Kenyon was always open to suggestions from a keen youngster to try and get material from the national regions onto the UK network. It was a policy that made financial and editorial sense. Once an idea had been approved, Birmingham would make a financial contribution to our budget. That extra funding could go to make a more costly programme at a later date.

I suggested to Pat Chalmers that we cover the Smithfield Show in London for the UK network but in such a way that in would not be seen to be exclusively for Scottish viewers only but could enjoyed by a wider UK audience. Pat agreed and so did John Kenyon. Making the programme was to be my responsibility and I grasped the challenge eagerly.

There followed a frenetic three days of intensive filming at Earls Court with Ross Muir and John Harle followed by long nights in a film cutting room in Soho. It was hard work explain-ing to anyone that you had been working in Soho until 3am but that was the truth – in those days Soho was a major centre for freelance film editors because temporary interlopers like me from Scotland usually had to find facilities for editing outside the main BBC premises at Television Centre.

Finally, the long haul was over and we returned to Aberdeen with our edited film package from the Smithfield Show. But on this occasion we were not recording down the line to Glasgow two days prior to broadcast – we were going out live.

The arrangement was that our complete filmed programme would go out live but we had built in an "opt in" point after about one minute of the film so that Birmingham's presenter, Norfolk farmer David Richardson, could introduce the programme and maintain something of his ongoing programme identity. He could then in theory sit back and watch BBC Scotland's film go out until about five minutes from the end where we had built in an "opt out" point at which juncture the Birmingham studio would go live and end their programme with an interview with John Silkin, then the Minister of Agriculture.

Ah well......as Robert Burns said: *The best laid plans of mice and men gang aft agley...*

The rehearsal went flawlessly. The programme was good and strong and I was looking forward to seeing my first full television programme broadcast throughout the whole UK to an audience of more than a million viewers.

As was common practice, after rehearsal the film was taken off the telecine machine and cleaned by running it gently through a cloth. This was reversal film, the common stock in trade for news, current affairs and speech-based programmes like *Landward* in those days. Cheaper than negative film, it had a tendency to gather dust so ensuring it was as clean as possible before transmission was vital.

After being cleaned, the film roll was replaced on the telecine machine and "synched up" with the separate roll of film sound thus ensuring that sound and picture ran in perfect unison.

This was the job of one of the engineering staff and a young director like me took it for granted that the task would have been performed accurately and conscientiously. Sadly it was not to be.

On cue, our programme began and shortly after the opening titles and music had died down and Ross Muir appeared on film we realised something was seriously wrong. The programme was out of synch – badly.

In fact the sound was preceding the picture by several seconds. Disaster. It was my first major Network show and we had made a balls of it. Birmingham technicians and production staff were screaming down the telephone to Aberdeen but the film was running and there was nothing we could do. We had to let it run. Exasperated, Birmingham apologised to their audience and opted back to their live studio presenter and the presenter David Richardson found himself conducting a much longer than expected interview with John Silkin.

As for our own audience in Scotland, they had to endure the remainder of the programme with the sound of people talking running seconds after their lip movements. After the show, Pat Chalmers generously offered me a whisky in his office as some kind of consolation. As senior producer he too was upset and annoyed that all our hard work of the preceding week seemed for nothing although he knew the fault did not lie with me. I declined the whisky. For the second time in my BBC career, suicide seemed a realistic option. But on my drive home to the seaside town of Stonehaven for a late Sunday lunch, thoughts of suicide gave way instead to the infinitely cheerier prospect of inflicting grievous bodily injury on the hapless technician who had proved less than conscientious in his duties. Though never enacted – in any event, he was bigger than me - the mere thought of it at least sustained me for months to come. Not surprisingly, the date of what proved to be my broadcasting nightmare, Sunday December 13th, 1981, has forever been imprinted on my mind.

Despite that setback, I began to look forward to studio days and the challenge of marshalling Aberdeen's scarce television resources to make interesting television. Well, we hoped it was interesting. Our audience seemed to enjoy it although what the casual layman viewer thought of some of our items was anyone's guess.

Looking at the monitor in the television gallery it was hard to tell if the Suffolk ram was suffering a loss of dignity. He should have been. Propped up on his backside with rear legs spread-eagled, he was the star attraction in the middle of the small studio in Aberdeen. The bright television lights revealed all to the three probing cameras as John Rodger, the Perthshire vet, explained to Ross Muir at length and in precise detail the finer points of the ram's testicles.

In those days of glorious political incorrectness, we'd never heard of the nine o'clock watershed. But then we didn't need to because wasn't this *Landward*, that specialist programme about and for Scottish farmers? And the Suffolk ram's role? Well, it was nearly tupping time and what better piece of public service broadcasting could a farming programme turn its attention to than to make sure Scotland's low-ground sheep producers turned out their rams in peak breeding condition.

It was maybe excellent viewing if you were a low-ground sheep producer but a touch esoteric if you didn't fall into that specialist category. Don't worry, there was always the next programme when our deeply-researched film report on the merits of 24 reverse gears on the latest all-singing all-dancing tractor might be more to your taste!

But in the changing and challenging world of broadcasting, the instinct for survival is strong and it became increasingly apparent to me as assistant producer that the long-term future for such a specialist programme might well be called into question.

And so with the agreement and support of Pat Chalmers the programme began to paint on a broader canvas. The attractions of the latest tractor or the niceties of ram's testicles became largely eschewed in favour of a wider range of countryside topics. Our criteria for stories had been simple: if it's a good story and it's rural - it's in. In addition to the ongoing farming diary stories headlining the latest political or economic issues, *Landward* regularly featured stories on rural housing, rural employment, rural education, rural health, rural transport, the environment and wildlife. Yet in pursuing that broader editorial agenda, we tried to ensure that real farming issues remained at the heart of the programme for the simple reason that we believed family farming was the main economic engine of the Scottish countryside.

It was a policy that seemed to work. Audience figures regularly topped 250,000 and with less than 20,000 full-time farmers in Scotland, the popularity of the programme was a fair indication that, in addition to our loyal core audience of farming families, there were a lot of other people out there who liked rural affairs treated in a serious way.

And all too serious it often was. One day I took a call from a hill farmer who spoke to me movingly and articulately about the difficulties he and his fellow farmers were facing. With so many of his fellow farmers at the end of their tether, he said, would we do a special television feature on his plight? I explained that while it was a subject we had profiled more than once, if he was prepared to open his books and reveal the true extent of his own situation then we would make a film. He agreed.

But there was to be no film. When I rang his home as arranged a few weeks later to set up the shoot, I discovered he had died a few days earlier - another victim of unrelenting worry and stress. For him at least, the farming crisis was over.

But, of course, a magazine programme should have light as well as shade. Doom and gloom economic stories were part and parcel of our schedules but we believed in good human interest tales too. Like the story of the seed potato grower from the Ayrshire coast who left the business his family had been in for generations to grow hops near Tonbridge in the Weald of Kent. And so in the blazing heat of mid summer of 1983 we found ourselves filming a farming feature with a new angle - no-one north of the south of England grew hops. The sight and smell of the hops in the oast houses will live long in the memory. So too will the fond recollection of a post-shoot gin and tonic on the lawn of the farmer's new home – Spitzbrook House, a magnificent property built in 1850 by Lord Palmerston, the Prime Minister, as a wedding present for his illegitimate daughter.

Incidentally, there's a postscript to that studio session with the Suffolk ram. After the recording, the studio floor was cleaned and polished and the atmosphere returned to normal with the help of liberal amounts of aerosol spray. Despite the challenge that the nature of the interview posed, even our front man Ross Muir regained his composure. Until the following programme that is, when he held the Guinea Fowl from Inverurie just a little too close to his new jacket......

But that, as they say, is show business.

Studio Day, the all-important final packaging of the programme prior to transmission, may have been the culmination of the work of the preceding two weeks. Much though I enjoyed the challenge of directing in the studio, for me the most truly satisfying element of *Landward* grew to be directing the film items on location.

I use the word "directing" loosely because in those days, young production staff like me were very much in the hands of experienced cameraman who worked on the whole range of BBC programmes from news and current affairs to sport and from comedy shows to drama.

They were cameramen like Norman Shepherd who used to tease me with: *"Be careful son – or I'll give you the shot you're asking for"*. A jovial Yorkshireman who entered the BBC after service in the Royal Navy, he was a gifted cameraman who took the time to explain to television beginners like me the basic shots required to construct a simple sequence and the importance of the device of "cutaways" to help bridge between one shot and the next at the editing stage.

And in those days long before the use of videotape on location, deciding what to shoot, why and for how long was critical. Even the cheaper reversal film was expensive and represented by far the lion's share of the programme's cash budget. When I began in television, a roll of reversal film that rattled through the camera in a mere 10 minutes cost more than £50. By the end of my time in TV production, a 30-minute videotape costs less than £10. Yet there can be a downside in the much cheaper videotape. Because it is so much cheaper than film, there's a tendency for young directors to shoot far more material than they will ever possibly require with the result that what they might have saved compared with using expensive film is more than eaten up by less productive days on the road and expensive extra hours selecting material at the post production editing stage.

Using film on location was expensive and it was important to know how many seconds were required to give enough footage for the film editor to work and build a sequence. Programmes on small budgets like *Landward* could not afford to over-shoot.

In normal circumstances, once a young director like me had put an experienced cameraman like Norman Shepherd in a given situation you could be sure that his skill and experience would give you all that was required. Generally, you left it to the cameraman to decide when to "cut". In the early days, however, I tended to say "cut" until Norman said to me:

> *How come you have such a good idea when to tell me to cut?*

I had to confess the answer was neither genius nor gifted intuition. I just watched his right hand come round below the camera and his finger pause briefly above the start-stop button before taking my cue. I think he admired my initiative.

In the fullness of time, Norman retired and went back to his native Yorkshire. But he wasn't given much time to enjoy his retirement and died within a few short years of laying down his camera. I attended his funeral one cold Christmas Eve at Darlington Crematorium. Many of his old colleagues, and mine, from the BBC Scotland film unit were there as was the actor Robbie Coltrane who had worked with Norman on the ground-breaking *Tutti Frutti*. I was saddened to note that I appeared to be the only person from BBC production in attendance although I'm certain I was only one of many young directors who had been kept on the right path by Norman's experienced advice.

Working with film cameramen was a valuable training ground. Men like Norman Shepherd, Alex Scott, Mike Herd and Stuart Wyld. But they also had talented assistants whose main role in life (or so it seemed to me) was to spend the better part of each working day with their hands in a black bag changing film magazines so that there would never any delay when the cameraman announced "tape out" and called for fresh ammunition. Usually these assistants, like John McNeil, Tony Cowan and

Andrew Dunn went on to become talented cameraman in their own right working across a broad range of programmes. And some went on to find a new world outside the BBC – such as Andrew Dunn, now a noted Director of Photography with films to his credit like the Oscar-winning *Gosford Park*, *The Bodyguard*, *The Madness of King George* and *Lady in the Van*.

Another part of the learning experience was to try and curb your enthusiasm on the public highway. One morning early in my directing career, I raced off down the road at 60 mph with the camera car, sound recordist's car and lighting electrician's car in hot pursuit. At least I had hoped it was in hot pursuit. Soon I lost sight of them and I had to wait in a lay-by while they caught up with me.

The cameraman got out of his car and gently took me by the elbow:

Look son – I know you're keen to get to the story but we're not going to break the speed limit and lose our driving licence because of you.

Suitably chastised, I drove more slowly.

At the end of the week's shoot, I loaded the film rolls in my car, said thanks and farewell to the film crew as they loaded the last of their boxes and gear while I began the long drive back to Aberdeen.

I had driven less than a mile when I saw a flash of headlights behind me as camera car, sound car and lighting car swept past at more than 70mph.

I was learning that what might seem pragmatic on a Monday morning didn't necessarily fit when you're racing home on a Friday night.

I also learned to recognise that television programmes, unlike anything I had ever done before, was the result of a team effort. But not everyone outside or even inside the BBC saw it like that.

Filming in the Northern Isles on one occasion we were invited into a grand stately home for lunch following the morning's filming. Having washed my hands I followed my colleague Ross Muir into a beautiful and expensive dining room.

We sat down as requested and it was then I noticed that only five places had been set at table – two for Ross and myself and three for our hostess and her son and daughter. I politely inquired about the whereabouts of my missing team.

Oh – we've given them some soup in the kitchen. We didn't think you would want to share lunch with them.

Ah well. It takes all sorts. I had to buy a round in the bar that evening before the teasing ended.

On another occasion we were filming in the hills of Argyll with a landowner who had been a former Royal Navy officer. The story concerned the introduction of a pack of hounds from the Lake District as a way of reducing the local fox population that was playing havoc at lambing time.

There were no horses with this pack of hounds. Everything was done on foot and where the hounds went we tried to follow. It was a cold, wet and tiring shoot jumping swollen streams and through waist high bracken and heather. I was just carrying a notebook compared with the heavy gear carried by the cameraman and the sound recordist.

At lunchtime there was a chance for a breather. The landowner invited us all into his house to find his wife had organised a warm and tempting spread of soup and sausage rolls and sandwiches. There was even beer for those who wanted it. We fell upon the food like hungry wolves. Within seconds several plates had been cleared until someone asked where the cameraman was. Nobody knew. I went to look for him.

He was outside eating an apple and at the same time loosening the laces on his sodden walking boots.

I told him we were waiting for him and that inside the house there was warmth, company and good food a-plenty. It was the wrong thing to have said.

Don't bloody well tell me where I'm having lunch, he said hurling one walking boot into the dark recesses of his vehicle.

I'll decide what I'm going to eat and when I'm bloody eating it, he added throwing the second boot to follow the first.

I guess that was the first thing to understand about team working. We're all different and some are a bit more different than others.

After many years on the road I reckon it takes a special trait of personality to handle life on the road. At BBC bases up and down the country, staff members who never have to venture outside a centrally heated office always assume you have a great time on location. But that isn't always the case.

Norman Shepherd, full-time cameraman and occasional poet, put his finger on it when he quoted *Out Filming*:

Your alarm goes at five and no one's alive
And your wife and your children are sleeping
Your dog doesn't care when you walk down the stair
Who you are or what hours you are keeping.
And you can't find your shirt or your pants or your vest
And you can't find your passport and cheques and the rest
Of tickets and vouchers and labels and things
- But you'll have a great time on location.

Arrive in BH at a quarter to six
When it's cold and it's dark – and with equipment to fix.
Hello, says the doorman. Oh I see it's you.
If only I'd known, I could have slept through.
Come in since you're here – and put down your case
No – not there – that's just clean – there must be a place.
But please don't sit there – you'll be in the way
'Cos that's where the cleaner puts down her tray
You look very fit and you look very brown
- You have a great time on location.

In lifeboats, in factories, in churches and mines
On farms and on islands of various kinds,
With statesmen and gypsies, with sportsmen and kings,
With vicars and whores and all sorts of things.
Like footballers, actors and dogs who can speak
We must get a programme from out of this week.
When hungry and tired and feeling forlorn
- We have a great time on location.

If the early retirement of Jock Mearns gave me an opportunity to dip my toes into the water of television production, I was to benefit from another fortunate break within a year of my joining the television service when producer Pat Chalmers was appointed Head of Television for BBC Scotland.

He asked if I would be prepared to assume the role of producer of *Landward* on a six-month trial basis. He didn't have to ask me a second time. I jumped at the chance. I chose as my assistant producer a farmer's son from Yorkshire, Chris Middleton, then working in radio as a graduate trainee. With his help, I hoped to prove myself over the next six-months. I felt that if I could cut the mustard and earn my producer's spurs I would then enjoy the freedom to shape the programme and continue the broad-based approach to the content that had already begun. On the contrary, if I was found wanting, the management of BBC might want to shift me sideways or down – or out.

I was on tenterhooks by the end of the six months as I awaited the internal advertisement for the producer's post for which I would naturally apply. In the event, there was to be no advertisement and no subsequent board. Instead, I received a letter from BBC Scotland's senior personnel officer saying that the management had approved of my work over the six months I had been acting producer and had decided to appoint me to the full-time position with immediate effect. With my promotion came a decent increase in salary. I felt I had won a lottery jackpot.

The extra income was welcome not least because on August 9th 1979 our fourth child was born – a little girl called Ailsa. That made four youngsters around Andrea's feet. Something was causing all this. Whatever it was, it had to stop. Well, up to a point...

TV Diversity – Landward Style

And so began the latest stage in my life as a television producer. Over the next 24 years that role was to take me to every corner of Scotland, many parts of the wider UK and 27 countries around the world.

Filming stories in Scotland about Scottish farming and rural topics for the Scottish audience was our bread and butter business but I felt that where the story was justified and the budget allowed it was also important to occasionally see what was happening outside Scotland. My attitude was that we could not look into a mirror image all the time. We were part of a rural and political scene that was changing socially, economically and agriculturally, and that this should be reflected when possible.

In each series we broadcast 26 fortnightly programmes over the year and I tried to produce certainly one or hopefully two from overseas within each series. Because I had one of the smallest television budgets in the BBC I was often asked how I could possibly afford to make even *one* programme outside Scotland.

I reckoned that it was a simple case of careful accounting. In today's administratively top-heavy BBC most departments have a Business Manager whose salary very often eats up licence payers' money that would be better spent on programmes – but that's just my cynical view. When I began producing television there were no Business Managers. Inside the office the producer was the editor and the accountant. On location he or she was also the BBC representative, diplomat and director. I remember a long-serving senior financial manager telling me: *Before the advent of all these business managers, I knew where every single penny of money was being spent. Now I haven't a clue.*

In addition to myself as producer of *Landward*, there were in the beginning two full-time production staff – an assistant producer who would shoulder the research burden and also direct on location where and when necessary. The other central figure of this tiny team was the production assistant, a role that was largely secretarial but also carried a greater responsibility both on location and in the office.

On location in the days of film the production assistant had a vital role in logging the number and detail of every shot. Back in the office there came the laborious business of transcribing most of the longer interviews so that the producer and film editor could together establish over which section of speech various complementary pictures, or overlay as we called it, would be seen in the final broadcast. With the advent of videotape a few years later and the consequent ability to transfer location tapes to domestic VHS with a burned-in time-code, identification of content and structure could be done much more easily by the producer back at base and thus dispense with the need for a production assistant on location. It was a contentious issue at the beginning but I believed it was resolved amicably - eventually.

Working closely with the producer, the other central role for a good production assistant was sitting on top of the budget. Inevitably some programmes cost more than others but it was always important to know week by week what the overall picture was and how adrift we might be on the overall cash at our disposal.

And small though the amount was, I was usually able to squirrel away in the books enough to pay for one or maybe two more geographically ambitious trips in each series. Jokingly, my colleagues used to look forward to what they termed the *Landward* outing.

Even on a tight budget, filming overseas didn't need to be any more expensive than filming at home in Scotland. Give or take an exchange rate or two, bed and board is more or less the same anywhere in the world; the staff and freelance costs are the same; car hire is the same. The one extra factor is the cost of getting there – the airfares. However, if you take the cost of four international airfares – economy class naturally (but cross your fingers for an upgrade) – for producer, reporter, cameraman and sound recordist and spread the cost of those four fares over the budget of 26 programmes in the series then the price becomes a very small part of the total programme budget.

In reality for the *Landward* programme there were few financial brick walls that we hit over the years. Most of the farming families we filmed with throughout Scotland welcomed us with warmth – plus much hospitality if we ever had the time to sit and share it with them.

However, broadcasting is full of paperwork and it was invariably necessary for the BBC in Glasgow to issue a contract to someone if they had been interviewed. This contract gave the BBC freedom to broadcast the interview where and when they wanted to and in order to get people to sign the contract, it was normal practice to offer a tiny sweetener – say £50 which came out of my budget. I never grudged it. When you hear the crazy fees demanded and often given in other areas of broadcasting today I reckon I was lucky to get away with £50.

Once, however, our offer of a £20 contract (it was a long time ago) came back and smacked us in the face. We were filming the opening of the grouse-shooting season on the Glorious 12th of August in 1989 in the Lammermuir Hills south of Edinburgh. It was an idyllic occasion. The sun shone and we were there with the full and friendly co-operation of the local landowner who had invited a small but select party of shooters for this first day of the season – some of them well-heeled Americans, one of whom went by the name of Jean-Jacques Rousseau. He was a banker rather than a reincarnated 18th Century French philosopher.

The cameraman was Colin Maclure and he filled his creative boots as the birds flew, the guns roared and the spaniels and labradors raced through the heather to retrieve the game.

At the end of the shoot, the landowner capped the day by giving his BBC visitors a brace of grouse each. It was a generous gesture by any standards. If anyone was worth a £20 facility fee it was the landowner and on my return to the office I organised the paperwork for the BBC contracts office in Glasgow.

I was surprised, therefore, a few days later to be sent from Glasgow a letter from the landowner. He was furious, he said, to be charged £20 by the BBC when he had gone out of his way to offer us any facilities we had wanted on this special day of the year. More than that, he went on, he had given each of the

Landward team a brace of grouse. Did we have any idea what the grouse were worth on the Glorious 12th. And yet we had the audacity to ask *him* for £20.

Had he read the contract a little more carefully and a little more slowly he would have found that we not asking for money. We were *offering* him £20.

Sheila Stewart in BBC Contracts department in Glasgow wrote to the landowner gently suggesting that he have another look at the contract. To his credit he replied to her thus:

Oh, Sheila shame on me it be
When on the contract could not see
That payment was indeed a fee
So twenty pounds I get with glee
And you – a deep apologee!

Proving that creativity also exists in the BBC administrative staff, Sheila wrote back:

Graceful sorrow takes no small skill
And doubly so when from a quill
My faith in others you helped to mend
Thank you kind sir for the words you penned
No grouse hereafter will be heard of me
For reading payment instead of fee
And of the latter this letter rounds
Off - with enclosure of twenty pounds!

It might be appropriate here to explain the acceptance of the two grouse from the landowner. From time to time over the years, various individuals or organisations would offer a small gift. Inevitably this was by way of a kindly gesture rather than any crude inducement for greater publicity. Whether producers should accept these gifts comes down to common sense.

Once we had been filming on a large commercial salmon production enterprise in the north of Scotland and at the end of our filming each member of my small team was presented with a freshly caught 10lb salmon. I felt it was acceptable for my colleagues to take the gift in good spirit but that I should not lest anyone perceive that the slightest hint of subsequent favourable coverage on television could be linked to the fine salmon in my family freezer. I diplomatically explained this to the company representative and he accepted my reasoning.

On the other hand, I recall filming on a bitterly cold winter afternoon on an agricultural college dairy farm near Edinburgh. As we were leaving to head further south through the thickening snow flurries, the farm manager tapped on my window and passed a bottle of whisky to Ross Muir, the programme presenter, and me. It was, he said, just a little something to warm our bones when we reached our destination. It would have been churlish to refuse. We accepted it gladly.

In years gone by, gifts from commercial companies - and occasionally from individuals - to journalists were much more common than they are today. Harking back to my days on *The Scotsman* I recall that each Christmas my boss Bob Urquhart received a brace of pheasants from Lord Lovat, chief of the Clan Fraser and Second World War hero. He also used to receive festive gifts of whisky. One afternoon Bob received a parcel that he opened to reveal a fine bottle of malt courtesy of an animal feed company.

Bob looked at it with longing then turned to me and said: *Look at this. Do they think they can bribe me with a bottle?* He paused for a second. *They should know by now it takes at least a case.*

I wouldn't swear to it but I'm sure I saw him wink.

While television is clearly a picture-led medium and the leader of the technical team on location was undoubtedly the cameraman, it would be remiss of me not to pay tribute to the work of sound recordists. Men like Peter Brill, Ken Mutch and Roy Argyle who helped turn my early film programme ideas into technical reality.

Sometimes this help extended far above and beyond the call of duty. That was certainly true of Roy Argyle who was the sound recordist on duty when the *Landward* team spent two weeks in France and Spain in 1981. The film we made in France was the story of Billy Hogg who farmed in the Scottish Borders but as a committed Francophile Billy also had a farm in South East France near Limoux that he stocked with Blackface sheep and Galloway cattle. A little corner of Écosse in La Belle France – what better a subject for a BBC Scotland farming programme.

We had flown to Carcassonne, the walled city that has been occupied by man since the 6th century BC and then picked up hire cars and drove to Limoux in the Languedoc-Roussillon region. We checked into our 18th century hotel which went by the charming name of Moderne et Pigeon with a delightful cobbled courtyard dappled with late afternoon sun. All seemed well with the world – until the allocation of rooms. The camera team seemed to be first in the queue and were quickly allocated accommodation that seemed to please them. Then it came the turn of Ross Muir and myself. Sorry – only one room left, we were told. We would have to share. Merde.

Not only that but the one remaining room had but one bed. Whatever you might hear or think about the proclivities of some members of the BBC – that was a step too far for we rustic Scots.

Mais attendez! – the hotel owner had a solution. He disappeared into a small storage room and emerged a couple of minutes later with a small fold-up camp bed with a wafer-thin mattress. It was the best he could do. He looked at us pleadingly. Ross and I viewed this stopgap solution with dislike and disdain. Still, we were in Limoux for three days and had to sleep somewhere. But who should enjoy the comfort of the full-size bed – the producer or the freelance presenter - and who should slum it in the make-shift alternative? We decided to toss a coin. I lost. Ross got the good bed. Encore du Merde.

Of course, I should have known that I was never in the van-guard of grabbing the best sleeping quarters. Some time before, Ross and I had been filming on Fetlar in the Shetland Islands. For some reason – I guess stupidity on my part – a coin was tossed for the only available beds in the only decent bed and breakfast around. The crew won and Ross and I had to settle on sharing a tiny caravan on a nearby croft. The owner kept a large variety of poultry which we discovered when the only access to our caravan was by picking our way slowly and carefully round the many highly aromatic deposits from the flock of bantams, ducks, turkeys and geese. In the dark, it wasn't easy.

Meanwhile back in Limoux, sitting in the hotel's small courtyard having a drink before dinner lessened my disappointment at yet again coming off second best in the sleeping arrangements. At the owner's suggestion we tried the local wine – Blanquette de Limoux, the region's answer to Champagne. According to legend, Blanquette de Limoux was the world's first sparkling wine dating back to 1531. At the time the monks of the Benedictine abbey of Saint-Hilaire, near Limoux, were producing white wine in an unusual style – instead of using oak vats the wine was fermented in a glass flask with a cork top that gave it a natural sparkle. Apparently, Dom Perignon passed through the valley on his way north from Spain, chanced on the abbey, took careful note of the technique and carried it off to the nobles of Champagne.

Who knows if the story is true – the fact is that Blanquette de Limoux, made exclusively from Mauzac and Chardonnay grapes, produces a dry creamy-textured wine with fruity aromas. Needless to say, after a few glasses I wasn't much caring what my bed was like.

Despite the wine, the uncomfortable bed and an un-seasonal thick fog that blanketed the area for the first day, our filming with Monsieur Billy Hogg went well. Eventually the sun broke through the fog and we filmed Billy in the hills of the south of France with his Galloway cattle and Blackface sheep. We even managed a brief filming visit to one of his neighbours to whom he had sold a Border collie. They say if you want to learn a language, start young. Certainly, it worked for the dog because he put on a faultless display for our camera when he was summoned to fetch the sheep by his French master.

We ended our final day's shooting in France in baking heat and were invited into the farmer's modest home for lunch. Cautiously side-stepping a Golden Eagle on a perch at the farmhouse door that scrutinized each visitor with a cold gimlet eye, we entered the cool of the house for home-baked bread, wild boar paté and locally produced red wine. It was a marvellous and memorable meal.

For all Roy Argyle's diligence and abilities as a sound recordist during that first week, his real contribution was still to come as
we began our second film on the implications of Spanish entry to
the EU, or the EEC as it was then called.

Entry to Spain meant a long hot drive from Limoux to
Perpignan then south on the motorway to the customs entry point
at La Jonquera about a hundred miles north of Barcelona.

As usual our Customs Carnet – the official document enabling
goods to be taken through international frontiers – had been
painstakingly prepared by the BBC Shipping department in
London. Accordingly we were duly stamped through the customs
as we left French soil and after one hundred yards of no man's
land, we reached Spanish customs and offered our documents for
inspection.

The speed of this process depends on the nature of the bureau-
cracy endemic to the country you are entering. In Eastern Europe
and Russia it was wise to set aside a couple of hours while each
piece of the camera crew's equipment was minutely inspected and
cross-referenced with the serial numbers of the Carnet documentation. In Western Europe the process could take less than five
minutes.

But not so that hot afternoon in Spain. There was a problem.
It appeared that we were missing a vital piece of paper inviting us
into the country. Remember this was just before Spain became a
member of what we now call the EU and the customs officer
sitting sweating in the cramped office seemed determined to wring
the last bureaucratic detail out of the situation before him.

He was resolute and immovable. No piece of paper, no entry.
My problem was that we were in a kind of no man's land. We
were out of France – with no documentation to get back in – but
not yet into Spain. The worst-case scenario was that all the BBC
camera gear could be impounded plus the rolls of film we had shot
in France. It was too early to be suicidal but I knew the germ of
the idea would soon emerge from where it had been slumbering
since our out of synch nightmare with the Royal Smithfield Show
programme.

My salvation came in two forms – Jeni Warburton and Roy Argyle. Jeni was my PA at the time and before taking up her BBC post had lived for some months in Mexico. For me, her master card that day at La Jonquera was that she spoke a little Spanish. She helped decipher some of the nuances of what the customs officer required. If we couldn't produce the piece of paper he said he would need a phone call from someone in BBC authority to sanction our onward journey into Spain. But this was Saturday afternoon. Even if I knew someone who might fit the bill the chances of raising anyone on a summer weekend was highly unlikely.

Enter Roy Argyle, our intrepid sound recordist. By happy accident, Roy knew a contact in the newsroom in BBC Broadcasting House in London. He rang him and explained the position. In turn, Roy's London contact passed on the telephone number of an occasional BBC freelancer in Madrid. Roy rang him too and once again our luck was in – he answered the phone. The phone was passed to the customs officer who eventually seemed placated. He had also seemed placated a little earlier when I had discreetly passed him a large denomination note. Our carnet was duly stamped and we drove on into Spain. After all that tension and rising blood pressure, I could have done with a couple of glasses of Blanquette de Limoux. But I was in the wrong country for that. I needn't have worried. A certain wine maker called Miguel Torres was about to take care of any of our vinicultural needs.

While the name Torres is now well known to every consumer who visits the wine section of any British supermarket or off-licence the situation was very different almost thirty years ago when Miguel Torres welcomed us to his home near the town of Vilafranca del Penedès.

Miguel was the fourth generation of his family in the wine business. Branches of the family were also busy producing wine in Chile and California but back at home base, Miguel was keen to take any opportunity to raise his profile in the wider European market that was awaiting Spain's entry into the EU.

Clearly there was no real link between wine production in Spain and the kind of commodities that interested our core audience of farmers back in Scotland. Nonetheless, Spain was one of the world's biggest wine producers and we felt that we could not produce a film on Spanish production without touching on the significance of wine.

We arrived in the morning and hoped to begin filming immediately. Not quite. Miguel's father insisted that my whole team descend a stone stairway into the family wine cellars. There we saw a long oak table immaculately laid out with places for our hosts and BBC Scotland's six-strong team.

Beside each place were six or eight glasses. It looked ominous. Mr Torres senior insisted that before we started filming it was important that we had a good understanding of the range and quality of the wines that the family had been producing for generations.

One by one we were given a small amount to taste. Glass followed glass as one variety led to another. Our hosts were tasting their own product in a wholly professional way – rolling the varieties round their mouth then spitting it out. But Scottish drinkers, even at that time in the morning, don't do spitting out. It was 10am and I felt that if this continued, and it looked very much as if it might, we would have to be carried back to our hotel with no filming accomplished

I gestured to John McNeil the cameraman that he and I should at least begin some work and with a brief explanation to our hosts he and I slipped back up the stairs leaving our colleagues to continue the tasting – and the diplomacy.

John grabbed his camera and the two of us attempted to walk purposefully towards the nearest vineyard where we hoped to get some establishing shots in the can of the area, the mansion house and any activity that happened to be passing.

Alas, too late. The fierce sun beating down upon us added to the wine we had already consumed combined to weaken our early resolve. I was carrying John's camera tripod that seemed unusually heavy. He agreed that his camera too seemed unduly weighty that morning. So we did the only thing we could do under the circumstances. We sank to our knees between the vines and John took various close up shots of a single grape, a small group of grapes and a bunch of grapes – and yet another shot of a single grape for good measure. Not our most productive start to a day's shooting but it ensured our survival to get through the rest of the day. For the record, John's shots of the grapes, like all his work, turned out to be splendid.

In the event, the rest of my team eventually emerged from the bowels of the mansion house blinking in the harsh daylight and our work continued well enough, ending with a Hollywood-style interview with Miguel Torres beside his swimming pool and a bottle of chilled white wine in the ice bucket at his elbow. Once the interview was over, Miguel's beautiful German artist wife Waltraud offered us all another glass. It would have been impolite to refuse.

Today the Torres family are one of the world's biggest wine producers producing more than thirty million bottles of wine and ten million bottles of brandy each year.

The Spanish Ministry of Agriculture could not have been more helpful and even laid on a translator at their own expense. Our main guide and mentor was one of the Ministry's agricultural advisers called Senor B. I have truncated his surname for reasons of courtesy as you will discover.

At any rate, Senor B. was energetic, enthusiastic and knowledgeable and nothing troubled him. For the most part he was a pleasure to work with and have him as a temporary member of our small team. It therefore seemed reasonable that near the end of our trip we should give him a little gift on behalf of BBC Scotland and the *Landward* programme.

For just such eventualities I always kept a couple of bottles of malt in my luggage. Senor B. was delighted with his gift and insisted on opening it after dinner on our last night and sampling the best that Scotland could offer.

Either he wasn't in the habit of drinking at all or unused to first-class malts because very soon he had to excuse himself and went out to be sick. Undaunted, he returned and tried another dram – and then another. And then he went out to be sick again. And returned again. He had stamina, I'll give him that. By the time we went to bed Senor B. was feeling no pain but his night – or ours - wasn't over yet. By an unhappy coincidence he was in a room beside the two rooms allocated to Ross Muir and myself. The walls were thin and for the rest of that night we could hear that poor man trying to rid himself of what he must have assumed was some deadly Celtic poison which I suppose, in sufficient quantities, it is.

But Senor B. was to get his revenge. Next morning at breakfast he appeared ashen-faced and shaking. We had plenty of time before our flight, he agreed, so might there be any last thing he could help us with?

Yes there was. We had one more item to film – two pieces to camera by Ross Muir that would serve to open and close our film. Olive oil production was one of the main commodities produced by Spanish farmers and I asked Senor B. if he could take us to an olive grove, a little away from the main road so our sound recordist Roy would not have any interference from the noise of passing traffic.

Senor B. thought this should be possible and went off to make a phone call. Within a few minutes he had returned. No problem. He knew the perfect spot. *Let's go*, he said.

We drove for about an hour until suddenly he directed our small convoy off the main road and down a track into an olive grove. He stopped. I told him we were still a little too close to the main road for our sound recordist's peace of mind so could we continue a little way and stop in front of a fine example of an olive tree?

Senor B. absorbed this latest request. *We go again*, he said.

On and on and on we went. For almost an hour we drove past hundreds of thousands of well-formed olive trees any one of which would have served our purpose as a background for Ross's pieces to camera.

Eventually after an eternity of driving through what seemed the world's largest olive grove, Senor B's car stopped with a squeal of brakes. Once we were able to locate him in the fine cloud of red dust we could see he was gesticulating proudly at an olive tree.

This one, he said. *This is the one.*

We looked at his special tree. It looked exactly the same as the thousands of others we had already driven past.

We brushed the fine dust off our clothes and began filming. Once finished, the gear was loaded back into our cars and, a trifle disgruntled, we began the long drive back to the main road while we quietly speculated that no olive grove could be so large and perhaps we might have been driving in a giant circle. Ah well, with a bit of luck we would still make our flight in time.

What made life on the road producing a regular television programme throughout the year constantly challenging was the variety of subjects that were thrown up in the normal round. Over the years many colleagues in other departments would raise an eyebrow and question either my sanity or my ability to keep filling the programme by hitching my wagon to farming and rural affairs to the virtual exclusion of all else.

In reality, it was never boring and far from repetitive. The rhythm of the changing seasons brought its own harvest of stories be they political, economic, technical or offbeat and off-diary. Serious issues dominated our schedule and covering the main farming and rural news of the week meant we came into contact with all the movers and shakers on the scene in Scotland and, occasionally, outside the UK. I always reckoned, however, that whether a story was pro-active or reactive the point at issue was always more sharply defined for a mass audience if we looked at it through the eyes of an ordinary working individual who would benefit or suffer as a result. Interviews on contentious issues with the chairman of this organisation or the president of the other were naturally included in our reports but where possible we would try and also embrace the views of the small tenant farmer or meat processor or haulage contractor who might be personally affected by a particular story

From time to time, we also tried to put a smile on the face of the tiger. In the hard-nosed business of food and farming that wasn't always easy so we grabbed the chance when it arose.

One such chance came when I noticed well in advance that April 1st was due to fall on a Sunday that we were due to broadcast. It was about two years after the Falklands War and I came up with the idea of a story on how the bombing during the conflict had rendered sterile some of the penguins on the islands and that the British government were trying to breed virility back into the birds.

Half-baked, naturally, but I managed to persuade Keith Chalmers Watson who farmed south of Edinburgh to go along with the idea. Keith's late father Rupert had been the leading turkey producer in Scotland for many years and part of our fabricated story was that the family had been given a contract by the government to develop disused turkey rearing sheds for new breeding work with penguins. Keith was an articulate and engaging communicator and he was happy to take part in our innocent subterfuge.

Central to making the idea work was being able to persuade Edinburgh Zoo to allow us to film in the penguin enclosure so we could pretend that their resident birds might form the nucleus of new virile strains to be sent to the Falklands.

To my delight, Edinburgh Zoo agreed so we were able to film Keith Chalmers Watson and Ross Muir walking through the penguin enclosure identifying what birds looked like offering top quality breeding potential. We had our story. Not only that but when inter-cut with library footage from the Falklands and presented with a straight face it looked like the genuine article.

The reaction to the broadcast was overwhelmingly favourable and unlike my radio spoof about the four-legged turkey some years earlier this time there was no phone call from teachers wanting more information. To be fair, of the feedback we received, one or two took it at face value but most realised the report for what it was – pure moonshine.

At other times, lighter moments can come unscripted and unbidden. In my early days working on film, the clapperboard was central to our work on location. This identified the name of the programme, the cameraman and number of the shot. At the start of every shot the camera was switched on and the sound recordist also started his tape recorder which in the days of film was quite separate from the camera. After a few seconds when the camera was up to speed the instruction "Mark it" would be given and a striped bar, usually metal, was closed sharply from an angle of 45 degrees   The picture and the sound would then subsequently be matched in the film cutting room thus ensuring that the ensuing contents of the shot would be in synch.

The job of using the clapperboard could fall to the assistant cameraman, the production assistant or the director.   I rather enjoyed doing it in the early days – visions of Hollywood movies and all that.

One day I wished I had never heard of a clapperboard.   We were on a farm in central Scotland filming a story about the opening of one of the country's largest egg production units. What made it unusual was that it was a deep litter system rather than the normal battery cages.   The hens were free to roam around rather than being confined to rows of wire cages and I have no doubt the deep litter system would have found favour with the animal welfare lobby.   The farmer proudly opened the door of his deep litter house and there before us in a shed approaching the scale of an aircraft hangar were tens of thousands of hens.

We were advised not to make any sudden movements and film what we wanted - slowly and quietly.   It made sense to me. Coming from a farming background, I was aware of how flighty poultry can be and so reinforced the need for a calm approach to my team.

Once the camera was ready I prepared the clapperboard. "Mark it", said the cameraman. I marked it. Within a split second of the sharp noise of the clapperboard closing, thirty thousand birds rose two feet off the ground in a cacophony of noise accompanied by what might have been the biggest cloud of dust and feathers ever seen in the poultry industry.

The farmer was far from happy. I didn't blame him. I learned later that egg production dropped sharply for a couple of days until the birds had overcome their unscheduled introduction to our filming techniques.

For me it was also a learning experience – what we should have done in those circumstances was to record what was termed an "end board" where the shot is filmed first and the clapperboard, turned upside down so the film editor can spot it easily, identifies the shot at the end. In the cutting room the film editor then synchs up his material from the end of the shot to the beginning thus still maintaining synch. The hens would still have been frightened out of their wits by the noise of the "end board" but at least by then we would have the shot safely in the can.

I would know the next time.

As the hens would testify, the arrival of a BBC crew can see carefully laid plans go askew for reasons that might never have been remotely contemplated in the production office when the story was being set up.

Ross Muir and I were shooting a story on one of the ongoing problems in the Scottish dairy industry and our work had taken us to Ayrshire to film around one of the bigger creameries in the area where the future of butter production was under threat.

All of our filming in the creamery went perfectly but at the end I asked the creamery manager if I could take my camera crew into a nearby field where we could get good establishing shots of his plant with an agricultural setting in the foreground.

He suggested that as the field was owned by a local farmer I should ask him for permission but he knew he happened to be picking potatoes that day and if I went to the field I was sure to find him.

We found the field. I asked the camera crew to hang on while Ross and I walked into the field where potato harvesting was in full swing to try and find the farmer and seek his approval for five minutes of filming of the distant creamery.

What followed was surreal. In the field around 30 pickers were following a mechanical harvester. As the harvester turned the potatoes from the soil, the pickers descended upon them like busy ants, bent over filling their plastic baskets with flying hands and fingers. Piecework brings out the grafter in all of us.

Ross and I walked up the field towards this scene of activity. Because of the earlier filming with the chairman and the chief executive, we were reasonably well turned out with clean shirt and tie – certainly more office worker than potato picker.

As we walked towards the pickers we heard a shout and saw old men and young men, women and youngsters stop dead in their tracks and look at the two BBC men walk towards them.

There was a second shout and in an instant everyone started running in every direction – in every direction apart from towards us. Within moments the field was empty apart from the tractor that had been pulling the potato harvester.

We approached the tractor that now stood silent and stationary. The field that had been a scene of frenetic rural activity minutes earlier had taken on the semblance of a rural Marie Celeste.

Suddenly we spotted a slight movement behind the large rear wheel of the tractor. Quietly, Ross went one way and I went the other in a pincer movement to find the farmer trying to make himself invisible.

He looked up, immediately recognised Ross from his television appearances, and slowly got to his feet.

Oh thank God it's you. We saw you come up the field and we thought it was the DHSS Inspectors!

It emerged that all his casual potato pickers that day were locals who were on social security payments and they had thought we were local Department of Health and Social Security officials out to check on them.

We looked at the farmer. But why we asked, did *he* have to hide?

Sheepishly, he explained that he too had been receiving social security payments for a bad back and didn't want to be seen working.

We sympathised – and, more than that, we apologised for disrupting the important work in hand. How, we wondered, would he find more pickers?

Don't worry about that son, said the farmer. *They'll soon be back. You see, they haven't been paid yet.*

He put two fingers in his mouth and whistled. Within moments, dozens of potato pickers began to emerge from the trees, ditches and hedgerows of Ayrshire. It seemed the tatties would be picked after all.

Expecting the unexpected is a good rule of thumb in location filming. Certainly it always worked for us on *Landward*. But sometimes the unexpected can hurt like hell as I found out to my cost when we filmed with the British Lions rugby team.

It was 1989 and the British Lions rugby squad were about to depart for Australia. Fittingly there was a strong Scottish contingent in the team and within their number were a good few players with strong links to Scottish farming.

That seemed a good peg on which to hang a story and presenter Dan Buglass and I decided that it was enough reason to build a television feature on the strong links over the years between Scottish farming and top-flight rugby.

Dan was a recent addition to the team and had quickly proved himself a knowledgeable contributor about farming matters. That wasn't surprising as he was a farmer himself from the Borders and, like all good Borderers, he also had a deep knowledge of rugby.

So we filmed various items for our feature including a farm visit to John Jeffrey, the so-called Great White Shark, and his Charolais cattle on his farm near Kelso; we interviewed Bill McLaren the doyen of rugby union commentators; and we filmed with team captain Finlay Calder and his team in training. But we needed one more section of the story – another brief pen portrait of a star player.

We decided on Gary Armstrong, the team scrum half, a brilliant player who was then working on a farm near Jedburgh. When the *Landward* team arrived, there was no sign of Gary. We parked our cars and I told my team to hang on while I scouted around the farm steading.

In the distance I heard a noise of metal on metal. I followed it to its source and eventually found Gary Armstrong fixing the ploughshare on a large reversible plough.

We had a brief chat and I told him that if he didn't mind we would like to film him doing exactly what he was doing and I would be back in moments with cameraman and sound recordist and the rest of my team.

All of this brief conversation took place as I looked at Gary and walked backwards at the same time. The plough he was working with was attached to a large tractor and when I reckoned I saw the end of the tractor in my mind's eye I turned to walk back to my waiting team.

What I hadn't bargained for was that at the front of the tractor was attached a front-end loader which had been raised off the ground to a level approaching the height of my head. I bid temporary farewell to Gary, then turned and in that same instant felt raw metal bite into my face followed immediately by something warm and wet running down my cheek. Blood.

By all accounts by the time I made it back to my team all of a hundred yards away I looked as if I had been on the receiving end of the entire British Lions front row. My day with the British Lions was over. Dan Buglass our intrepid presenter took over for the rest of the afternoon. As for me, Sandy Fraser, our lighting electrician, whisked me off to Jedburgh Cottage Hospital where a couple of sterestrips above my cheekbone soon turned me from casualty to walking wounded.

There are three postscripts to that story. First, when we came to package the programme on tape, we secured the approval of the Scottish Rugby Union to have Ross Muir introduce it from Murrayfield stadium in Edinburgh, the home of Scottish rugby. Given the location and the subject matter it seemed reasonable that Ross should be holding a rugby ball while he welcomed our regular viewers to the programme. We asked the SRU if they could supply a ball. Remarkably, they had plenty – but every one was deflated. We finally found a pump to blow up a ball and Ross duly recorded the programme links. As the camera gear was being packed up Ross and I thought it might be the one chance in our lives when we could race up the pitch and touch down for Scotland. We did – but without the cheers of tens of thousands of supporters our supreme sporting moment fell a little flat like the ball.

The second postscript to my British Lions story is that, many years on and in a certain light, I can still see a small scar on my cheekbone from my unscheduled encounter with Gary Armstrong's tractor. I look forward to the day when, with grandchild on my knee, he or she should point to my scar and ask:

Where did you get that Grandad?

I will reply simply but truthfully:

I got that with the British Lions.....

And leave it like that. After all - what's a little white lie within the family?

The third postscript concerns our reporter Dan Buglass. I had known Dan for some years when he was a farmer in the Borders and he had cut some of his broadcasting and journalistic teeth with me on the programme before private circumstances dictated his move out of farming and into full-time journalism. He was a pleasure to work with because of his engaging enthusiasm and his knowledge of commercial and technical agriculture and I was delighted years later to watch his progress to the job he had always coveted when he took over the challenge of Agricultural Editor of *The Scotsman* following the retirement of our mutual friend Fordyce Maxwell.

Dan's family background on his father's side was much the same as mine – we had our roots in shepherding families in the Cheviots. But it was to be many years after my retirement from the BBC that I was to discover that we were distantly related.

According to Dan's sister Gay, who had been researching the family tree, Dan's great great grandfather was Andrew Buglass, a shepherd, who had married a Margaret Anderson at Alwinton in Northumberland on January 5th 1849. Her father was George Anderson, my great great grandfather.

Margaret and Andrew had two children – Elizabeth born in 1851 and Ralph in 1853. Sadly, it appears that Margaret died giving birth to Ralph and her widower Andrew Buglass subsequently married her sister Elizabeth Anderson and they went on to have seven children.

Small world. Following the discovery of our family links Dan and I promised we would drink to our mutual health the next time we met. Sadly, we never had that drink. Dan took ill in November 2009 and was dead within a few weeks. He was only 63 and his passing was a big loss to agricultural journalism in Scotland.

If 1989 brought me into contact with some of Scotland's rugby heroes, I had cause to reflect on how three years earlier I had had another rugby hero as my boss, albeit briefly. In 1986 I had been seconded from Aberdeen to Edinburgh to work as one of the liaison officers during the Commonwealth Games. My duties were at the velodrome at Edinburgh's Meadowbank where I had the pleasant duty of being the link between the host broadcaster, the BBC, and visiting broadcasters from various Commonwealth nations. There was a team of around 15 of us covering all sporting venues and drawn from all areas of the BBC. Our boss was the legendary former Welsh rugby internationalist Cliff Morgan who had won 29 caps for his country between 1951 and 1958 and was a member of the successful British Lions tour to South Africa in 1955. After his playing days were over, Cliff had found a new career in broadcasting and with a natural gift for communicating rose to become Head of Sport and Outside Broadcasts for BBC Television. I was to discover another gift he had – remembering people. After a brief introductory meeting with him one evening before the Commonwealth Games began Cliff Morgan jumped on the bus containing all his team of liaison officers the next morning and remembered all our names despite having briefly met us only once before. Impressive.

What was less impressive about the 1986 Commonwealth Games in Edinburgh was how political issues and financial mismanagement threatened to spoil the international sporting festival. The political matter was a boycott by many African, Asian and Caribbean nations over Britain's continuing sporting links with South Africa – at that time still in the grip of apartheid. The brouhaha surrounding the Games only intensified when the newspaper tycoon Robert Maxwell assumed the chairmanship of the event and claimed to have "rescued" the games from its £4 million deficit – a claim later to prove something of a bombastic smoke-screen from the now late and disgraced Cap'n Bob.

Apart from being a close colleague, Ross Muir over the years proved to be one of BBC Scotland's most dependable and professional presenters. At one point he was the front man for BBC Radio Scotland's daily afternoon current affairs show and his commitment to that occasionally made it difficult for me to get hold of him for *Landward* filming. However, with careful planning and scheduling he and I usually managed to keep everyone happy.

Ross was well known throughout the rural community and his abilities as a broadcaster were highly respected. As far as I was concerned he was as solid as a rock - wholly professional and, on location, always diplomatic.

Well, apart from one occasion.

We had been filming on a large private farming estate at Gatehouse-of-Fleet in Galloway. Known as Ardwall, the estate owners were the McCulloch family and the subject of our film was the family's devotion and commitment to rare breeds of cattle and sheep. Our film was to be called *The White Galloways of Ardwall*.

We had arrived separately and I noticed on reaching the farm that Ross had got there before me in his brand new black Ford Granada. Parked in front of the large mansion house on a hot summer morning, it looked like an advertisement from a glossy colour supplement. Looking at my own beat-up old Ford I was deeply envious.

Filming began. The estate owner proved clever, able, articulate – but slightly eccentric. He had taken us on a small boat from his main farming estate to a small island about two hundred yards off the coast so that we could film some of his sheep flock summering on fine organic pasture. During the short journey he began painstakingly rolling up his smart trousers until they were but a couple of inches below his knees. Then, within a few yards from the island, he leapt out into two feet of water and began pushing the boat into the surf – still wearing a pair of high quality black brogues. I doubt whether the shoes would ever have recovered from their immersion in salt water - but at least his trousers were dry.

At the end of our filming our hosts generously asked my team to join them for tea and sandwiches on the lawn. We did. It was idyllic. The afternoon sun beat down strongly as we eagerly dug into the delicately cut cucumber sandwiches and others refreshments.

In the midst of this bucolic scene, the gentle chink of cup on saucer and polite conversation was suddenly interrupted by the sound of a fast rat-a-tat-tat......rat-a-tat-tat...rat-a-tat-tat.

Your resident woodpecker seems busy this afternoon, we suggested.

No woodpeckers round here, said our host.

So what was responsible for the insistent banging which by now had taken on a distinct metallic tone.

Good lord, look at that, said someone.

About twenty yards away one of our host's proudly strutting peacocks had chanced on seeing its own reflection on Ross's new car and, no doubt imagining its mirror image to be an adversary, had begun to peck seven bells out of the door of Ross's immaculate vehicle.

Ross dropped his cup and was on his feet within a split second. No time for diplomacy now. He raced from the lawn towards the peacock.

You.....bastard......leave my ......car alone or I'll wring your...... bloody neck! For any readers of a tender disposition, many expletives have been deleted.

Obviously recognising that discretion was the better part of valour, the chastened peacock quickly retired behind the nearest rhododendron bush.

We thanked our hosts and left shortly afterwards. I think it took the rest of us about an hour to stop laughing.

Having an eye for the birds seemed to be par for the course over the years – if you know what I mean. We've heard about the four-legged turkey, the penguin spoof and the thousands of hens leaping in terror when they heard the clapperboard. But maybe the most memorable of all the birds was a dead goose. No, not the one I shoved feet first into the waste bin at an Edinburgh bus stop many years before. This was a different dead goose........

Now it is axiomatic that the worker deserves a decent break. Well, at least once a day. No doubt taking a lead from my days in local radio, over the years I tried to sidestep old BBC traditions of morning tea breaks, one-hour lunches and afternoon coffee. My stance tended to be that if we could restrict lunch to half an hour all to the good. This made the working day more productive and to a greater or lesser extent my colleagues on location went along with me knowing that at the end of the day, wherever we were, I would do my best to ensure a good evening meal. And if that included the programme budget putting a couple of bottles of house wine on the table so be it.

However, it is also axiomatic that a good dinner can lead to a late night. So it proved on one occasion when the *Landward* team were staying in Perthshire in the only hotel for miles around. The fact that it was an upmarket country house hotel was all to the good. We had dined well and felt we should end the meal with a fine liqueur – this time not paid from programme funds but out of our own pocket.

We were enjoying our drink when one of the team returning from exploring some of the many rooms on the ground floor reported that the hotel had a snooker room with a full-size table.

What could we do but take advantage of these wonderful facilities and organise a sporting tournament. But to get the event off to a decent start it seemed reasonable to have a second liqueur to fire us up for the sporting challenge that lay ahead.

We sporting heroes set to with a will and the tournament began. As the competitive tension reached fever pitch (well, kind of) we felt it could only help our game to have another small liqueur.

Then things got out of hand slightly. As the night porter arrived with one tray of drinks he was immediately despatched to prepare the next. Tray followed tray and it seemed to us that our snooker abilities were improving in direct proportion.

That is, until someone decided to open the chest freezer in the corner of the snooker room. There we discovered a cornucopia of frozen game – hare, rabbit, grouse, snipe and venison, all no doubt part of an overflow store for future a la carte delights from the hotel chef.

In the midst of all this culinary treasure trove was a goose. For reasons we never discovered, the goose had never been plucked. It lay there, frozen hard, immobile and fully feathered. More than that, for another odd reason its legs were stretched out to their full rigid extent. And, for a final bizarre touch, someone had cut a small section off its beak. Instead of the end of the beak being gently rounded, it had been sliced straight across.

It seemed to represent a snooker cue with a difference. And so it proved. For the next half hour or so four of us took it in turns to play our shots using the frozen goose as a cue. It took a little while to learn to adjust our play accordingly, but eventually it worked well enough and the straight edge of the beak seemed to offer an encouraging contact with the balls on the table. Sadly, they were not always the balls we had been aiming at. In the end we had to put the goose back in the freezer when the warmth of the room and our constant handling caused its neck to lose a little of its rigidity. There was also the small matter of one or two of us being put off our game by the puzzled look the goose seemed to be giving us. All in all, it seemed time for bed.

Although there was a strong social thread running through our working lives in those days – quite different I suspect from the politically correct disciplines of the present day - I never experienced the excesses that were alleged to have been commonplace among newspapermen of yesterday's Fleet Street.

One alcohol-related anecdote concerned the late Hannen Swaffer, a giant of newspaper folklore who was a former editor of the Daily Mail. Famous for taking long liquid lunches in Fleet Street hostelries, one afternoon - unable to support himself vertically - he was crawling up the marble staircase towards his office when he became conscious of a pair of highly polished shoes directly in his path. Looking up he saw the stern image of the paper's proprietor Lord Northcliffe glowering down.

"Swaffer – there's too much damned drunkenness in this office," he shouted.

"Yes, sir," said Swaffer, "and if I can get to the top of these stairs I'll fire the bloody lot of them."

The *Landward* team with a few special friends at the Royal Highland Show. They were farmers from Poland getting their first taste of family farming in western Europe.

From *Landward* to seaward. About to set sail with the crew on the fishing trawler Jenmar. With me in the front row are, in the centre, sound recordist Terry Black and, on the right, cameraman Janusz Ostrowski. Within hours of posing for this picture at Mallaig, I was so seasick I had little contribution to make. Despite days of stormy seas the film crew battled on without me to bring home the bacon...er, fish.

A little light relaxation after another hard day. This time in Jutland, Denmark in 1999. With me from the left are Lindsay Cannon the presenter, Colin Maclure then a sound recordist but soon to become a respected cameraman in his own right and Ken Gow the cameraman whose skill and commitment proved such a strength in the *Landward* team for so many years.

Janusz Ostrowski the cameraman and me in western Norway. As a regular freelance over many years, "Jan" proved another safe pair of hands on many productions both in Scotland and overseas. His knowledge of the Polish language and culture was an indispensable asset in Poland.

The *Landward* production and presenting team. From the left: Euan McIlwraith, Lindsay Cannon, Eric Robson, me, Ross Muir, production assistant Noreen Harding and Ken Rundle.

All work and no play? A few frenetic years of sporting excess. This was the first - and the fastest - of my six marathons when I finished the Aberdeen event in 3 hours 24 minutes - but not quite good enough for Olympic selection!

But all that running gave me the stamina to play squash – and the strength to replace lost sweat in the bar afterwards.

You can't have too much of a good thing. Relaxing with friends on the Swiss-Italian border.

From the left:

Matt and Kay Dick, John Milne, Andrea, Margaret Milne, and me.

My friend Fordyce Maxwell joined me for the last leg of the 213-mile Southern Upland Way walk when more than 100 supporters from Scotland's farming and rural communities celebrated the centenary of the RSABI charity in 1997.

Fordyce and I also shared another memorable day when we both received journalism awards, presented at the Royal Show in Warwickshire in 1992.

My sister Monica and her husband John McTurk with their beloved black Labradors. John died tragically early of an heart attack in October 2014 at the age of 60.

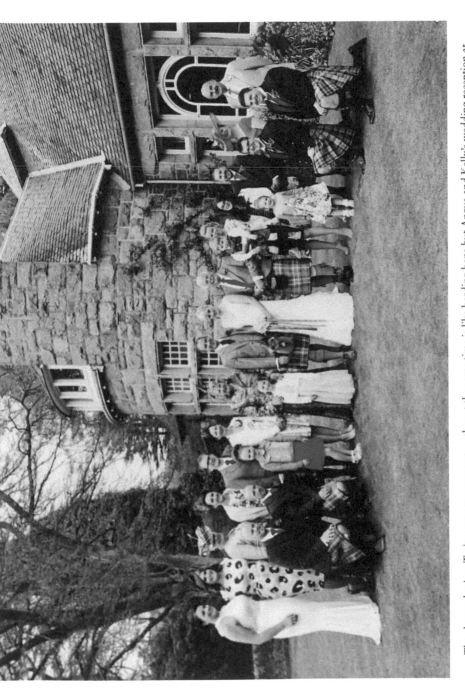

The clan gathering. Trying to get everyone together at the same time is like herding hens but Angus and Kelly's wedding reception at Glen Tanar in 2015 gave us the rare opportunity for the entire family to be in one place at one time. On the left are McTurks and Chorleys, centre stage are the Adams, Andersons and Richardsons and on the right are the MacKenzie family from Qatar.

Journey's end – but hopefully not quite yet. Andrea, still my leading lady after nearly half a century, at a Glasgow reception ending almost 30 years with the BBC.

Gallimaufray

I've often been asked what makes a good programme. My answer has always been the same – people. Not only the larger than life characters that you stumble on by chance as interviewees but the special talents that you are sometimes lucky enough to have as part of your team. That might be the cameraman or it might be the presenter.

Presenters, naturally, have a central role to play in any long-running series. They are the individuals that the viewers can identify with and come to accept as bringing a constancy of style or polish to the programme in question.

Over the years I was lucky with my presenters – John Harle and Dan Buglass with their deep specialist knowledge of the agricultural industry; Lindsay Cannon with her ability to bring a lightness of touch to her own family farming background; Euan McIlwraith with his willingness to tackle any subject; Claire Powell who had an encyclopaedic knowledge of livestock matters; Ken Rundle with his deep political insights into EU farm policy and his contacts in the corridors of power; Eric Robson and his never-ending ability to enhance the final shape of any subject he tackled; and the ubiquitous Ross Muir, the programme's sheet-anchor for so many years. How many times when, after a shoot had ended, seeing I was despondent that somehow the story had not seemed to live up to my expectations Ross would say: *Don't worry son – my commentary will lift it!* He wasn't always wrong.

Over the years, however, the programme embraced other great stalwarts like Ben Coutts, the Perthshire farmer who for decades was one of the most kenspeckle figures in Scottish farming circles. A son of the manse, he was one of five brothers most of whom went on to become high profile figures in public life. They included Sir Walter Coutts, the last Governor General of Uganda and Brigadier Frank Coutts, career soldier, international rugby player and later president of the Scottish Rugby Union.

Ben's early life was stranger than fiction and read like an adventure story penned by an over-fertile mind. He had trained as a vet but failed his exams yet still pursued his love of the countryside and became a pony boy in Sussex until the outbreak of war. Then, as a 23-year-old, he sailed to North Africa with the Surrey and Sussex Yeomanry. After service in Sudan and Abyssinia he was sent in 1941 to join the besieged British garrison at Tobruk. Within days, German shrapnel removed most of his nose.

The hospital ship taking Ben to Alexandria was bombed by the Luftwaffe and he spent the next year in hospital before it was decided he should be repatriated back to the UK. En route home aboard the Cunard liner Laconia carrying more than 2700 prisoners, crew and military personnel, the liner was torpedoed by a German U-boat U-156 off the west African coast between Liberia and Ascension Island. Around 2000 passengers and crew perished as a result of the sinking.

The sinking of the Laconia, on September 12th, 1942, was the second worst Allied maritime disaster of the war. It was also the last occasion in the history of the sea when a submarine tried to help its own victims. Although 2000 thousand died, nearly a thousand people were saved by the humanitarian efforts of the German submarine commander Gustav Julius Werner Hartenstein who called on international shipping in the area to come to the aid of the survivors. This later led to the Laconia Order from the Nazi government forbidding the rescue of surviviors of sunken ships.

Somehow, Ben survived and spent five days on a raft as others died around him. On the fifth day after the sinking, Ben and a handful of other survivors were rescued by a Vichy French cruiser that had been summoned by the commander of the German U boat who had apparently been appalled to discover the large numbers that the Laconia had been carrying.

Eventually he reached the UK and over the next few years underwent a series of 15 operations to rebuild his face under the skilled hands of Sir Archibald McIndoe the pre-eminent plastic surgeon of his day. Most of Sir Archibald's patients, known as his guinea pigs, were from the RAF yet Ben, an army man, managed to become one of the famous surgeon's patients at the Queen Victoria Hospital at East Grinstead.

Ben was a born raconteur and had the happy knack of being able to produce as many good stories on camera as he could off camera. Someone once said, a little unkindly I thought, that if Ben couldn't talk he would starve to death. Yet there were times when he could be silent. Long before we worked together on television I recorded a personal profile of his life for radio. At one point I asked him if, having returned from the war still a young man but with a face severely disfigured, he had felt cheated by fate. Unusually for him, he did not respond immediately. I looked across the studio table to see him quietly weeping. After a few seconds he recovered his composure and emphasised his deep belief in God and His ability to see him through an experience that for any young solider must have been Hell on earth.

As for the U-boat captain Gustav Julius Werner Hartenstein, he and his entire crew of U-156 were killed in action by depth charges dropped by a US Catalina aircraft east of Barbados on March 8th, 1943.

There were other more senior citizens too that I had great pleasure in working with over the years – men like Tom Barry, who turned away from a family business in Edinburgh to pursue his love of farming and the land. He had an infectious enthusiasm for history too and was at his best when in 1981 we spent a memorable week on the west coast island of Rum filming a deer stalker's course which included five nights accommodation in Kinloch Castle, a gothic red sandstone mansion built in the latter half of the 19th century by the millionaire English mill-owner industrialist Sir George Bullough.

Truth to tell, our visit to this island in the Inner Hebrides was one of those occasions when we were almost more interested in the sideshow than the main event. Kinloch Castle cost an estimated £250,000 to build – equivalent to £15 million today. The sandstone was shipped to Rum from the island of Arran and it took 300 craftsmen three years to complete.

It was the first private residence in Scotland to have electricity with a dam built across a local stream to provide the hydro-power.

Kinloch Castle also boasted one of only a handful of the world's Orchestrions which was an organ driven by an electric motor that played perforated card rolls – for all the world like a giant cassette player. When we filmed on Rum the Orchestrion was in full working order but over the years I have heard that woodworm was becoming a problem.

Most of the bedrooms at Kinloch Castle boasted a private bathroom – with a difference. Each apparently conventional bath had a second bath upturned at right angles that enveloped the bather like a large protective enamel shelter.

On the upturned bath were a series of taps which, when turned on, would direct jets or sprays of brown peaty water upwards, downwards and sideways.

I guess it was my first experience of a spa – only nobody connected that word with Highland accommodation in 1981.

In its heyday, Kinloch Castle also had heated pools in the garden with alligators and turtles, an outdoor squash court, a conservatory with hummingbirds and a billiard room with air conditioning. Not surprisingly this little island became a mecca for expensive parties thrown by the Bulloughs for the aristocracy and the nouveau riche of the time.

Spending time in Kinloch Castle was like taking a step back into the Edwardian age. Dining was a surreal experience. With the minstrel gallery above and a stuffed Monkey-Eating Eagle on the wall – a gift from the Emperor of Japan no less - the dining table was a magnificent surviving piece of furniture rescued from the Rhouma, Sir George Bullough's yacht that saw service as a hospital ship in the Crimean War and for which magnanimous gesture George Bullough secured his Knighthood.

But our historic surroundings didn't please everyone. We were working that week with a freelance sound recordist from Newcastle who had just finished a long and arduous stint for BBC News and current affairs on the streets of Liverpool covering the Toxteth riots when over nine days pitched battles between police and youth throwing missiles including petrol bombs saw 450 policemen injured and 500 rioters arrested.

I guess our intrepid freelance had looked forward to his week on a Scottish island, a world away from the dangerous streets of

Toxteth. At least, that might have been the case until he visited the island's only shop, a small store near the jetty where the ferry from the mainland called but twice a week.

A heavy smoker who was also fond of his beer, he went into the store on our second morning on Rum to replenish his supplies of both.

No cigarettes, he was told, *until the next ferry in three days time.*

In an effort to seek solace elsewhere, he asked for a dozen cans of beer.

No beer - it'll be on the next ferry too.

He came out of the small store with the look of a condemned man. No fags and no beer and no prospect of either for three more days.

For Christ's sake, said the ashen-faced freelance, *I'd rather be back in bloody Toxteth!*

Sir George Bullough died playing golf in France in 1939. His widow, Lady Bullough – a society beauty in her time with the exotic name of Monique Lily de la Pasture – died at Newmarket in 1957 at the age of 98 but not before selling Rum and Kinloch Castle to the then Countryside Commission for Scotland for £1 an acre. Both the Bulloughs are buried in a family Greek-style mausoleum at Harris on the west side of the island overlooking the Atlantic. As for our film on the island's deer-stalking course, that went well too - thanks to the course organiser Robin Fleming of Flemings Bank, a mainland laird who owned the Blackmount Estate in Argyll and a cousin of the author Ian Fleming who created the legend of James Bond. Competent though our short film turned out to be, it was our week in Kinloch Castle that was to live longer in the memory.

Eddie Straiton was another stalwart who was to contribute memorably to many *Landward* programmes. Born in Clydebank, Eddie was one of Britain's highest profile vets and was a lifelong friend of James Wight, better known in later years as James Herriott. Both men had been students at the Glasgow Veterinary College long before the enormous success of Herriott's *All Creatures Great and Small* books and television series. Once he qualified as a vet, Eddie Straiton was soon carving out a significant reputation for himself as an author and broadcaster and became known as the first TV vet from his many appearances on the BBC *Farming* programme produced in the Birmingham studios.

After setting up in practice in Stafford, he also built the first veterinary hospital in Britain which specialised in the treatment of large farm animals and had a regular veterinary advice spot on the *Jimmy Young Show* on Radio 2.

Like Ben Coutts, Eddie Straiton was a born broadcaster and could have made a full-time career on the airwaves if he had not sought another path through his professional life. As it was, he enriched any programme he was involved with and one of the most memorable was when I invited Ben and Eddie – both then in their 80s – to sit together in Ben's cottage in Perthshire and reminisce about farming and rural life in the days of their youth. Throwing budgetary considerations to the winds, we shot it on two cameras to create greater spontaneity and subsequent ease of editing and the resulting programme, steeped in nostalgia, created more positive feedback from our regular audience than any of our normal editions on matters of the moment.

Fyfe Robertson was a revered figure in broadcasting that I had the pleasure and privilege of working with. A former journalist on *Picture Post* magazine he went on to blaze a trail in BBC television as one of the pioneering team on *Tonight* throughout the 1960s with Cliff Michelmore, Derek Hart and Alan Whicker. Although no longer a young man when I met him in 1981 he turned out to be an exceptional and engaging presenter on a special documentary that I managed to have commissioned – unimaginatively entitled *The Bog People* that looked at the potential for harnessing the fuel in the vast peat-lands of Scotland and Ireland. He was known by one and all as Robbie and we had an enjoyable two weeks shooting that included celebrating his 80th birthday in the Irish Republic.

However, there were one or two little difficulties along the way. Robbie was a heavy smoker and over the years his fondness for tobacco had not done him any favours and the resultant hardening of the arteries in his legs meant that I had to be careful not to suggest anything too physical. Any suggestion of leaping over moorland ditches was definitely ruled out.

This was especially true during one morning's filming at Braehour in Caithness, where, during the 1950s attempts were made to run Britain's first peat-fired power station using peat from the nearby Altnabreac Moor. Technical problems meant the scheme was abandoned in 1960 but rusting machinery still evident among the bog myrtle of this bleak northern moor made it central to our story. Getting Robbie from the nearest vehicle access point to where we wanted for our piece to camera was a challenge we had not envisaged. The rough terrain made it impossible for him to make the short walk on his own. In the end two of us had to gently lift him into position.

Robbie also liked a dram or two of an evening – and he had the disconcerting habit at the end of his dinner of falling sound asleep in the hotel lounge. The worry for me was that he slept so soundly and without noise or movement I feared on one or two occasions my presenter may have expired. However, I was to find that the gentle offer of a nightcap whispered in his ear had remarkable restorative powers – especially on the night of his 80th birthday during our filming in Southern Ireland.

After our film had been edited I had gone to Glasgow airport to meet Robbie who had flown up from Gatwick from his home in Eastbourne prior to a weekend of commentary writing and recording the final words to the edited picture. But as I watched the passengers emerge from the Gatwick flight, there was no sign of my important presenter.

The came an announcement on the PA – would I go to the first aid station at the airport. There I was to find Robbie white and shaken. He had fallen on the steps of the aircraft when boarding at Gatwick and had gashed both legs – a nasty injury which would have caused most men half his age to have called off his flight north.

But Robbie was made of sterner stuff than that. I took him to the local hospital where his legs were bandaged and then we borrowed a wheelchair for the weekend. The next day in our Glasgow hotel he was clearly still in pain yet he was able to make steady progress with his commentary writing as I kept up an equally steady progress ferrying drams of whisky and plates of cheese sandwiches to his room.

The following day I took him into the film dubbing theatre in Glasgow - still in the wheelchair. I asked him if he wanted a glass of water:

Only if you put a wee dram in it, he said.

At 80 years old and after what he had gone through who could have denied him that small libation. Certainly not me.

Later that day at Glasgow airport, waiting for his flight to Gatwick, he thanked me for asking him to be presenter for the story but wondered if I would mind a little advice. I said I would welcome it.

Well, he said in that rich gravelly Scottish tone that was so singularly his trademark:

It's a good film we've made about an important subject. But there's one thing wrong with it son - there's no belly laughs. Always try and work a belly laugh into a programme if you can...

I said I would try. We shook hands and he disappeared into the departure lounge. It was the last time I saw him. He had presented his last documentary and he died in 1987.

In 1982 I was to venture further than ever before in *Landward*'s programme-making interests when I travelled round the world to New Zealand and came back with a programme that had cost less than £2000 - a bargain by any standards.

There were a couple of principal reasons for the bargain basement price. That year New Zealand was playing host to the annual congress of the International Federation of Agricultural Journalists. Air New Zealand was one of the congress sponsors and was offering a special return fare for less than £500.

Additionally, Television New Zealand provided a cameraman and a sound recordist on a rota basis to be shared between our TVNZ hosts, BBC Scotland and BBC Northern Ireland whose experienced and genial producer John Johnston had also made the trip to the other side of the world. The deal was that the three producers would sit down and study the schedule that had been organised for the delegation of around 100 international journalists. We would then cherry-pick the visits to farms and agricultural research stations that we felt would be of most interest to our own domestic audiences and try and earmark the resident New Zealand cameraman and recordist for those specific days. Given the comprehensive schedule that had been set up for us there were few clashes of interest and both BBC Northern Ireland and BBC Scotland returned to Belfast and Aberdeen respectively with half-hour television programmes made at no more cost than had we stayed on our own home patch.

It had proved a splendid example of international co-operation thanks to my farming producer counterpart on TVNZ, Colin Follas. An engaging man with a wonderful knack of telling amusing stories, he and his wife Doreen were to become great friends in the years ahead.

Returning from New Zealand all those years ago carried an extra responsibility. Not only did I have all those precious rolls of film safely wrapped in the luggage rack above my head in the aircraft about which I could not relax until I had passed them safely to the film processor in Aberdeen. Apart from that I knew that the moment I returned to Scotland I had an important task awaiting me on the domestic front – I had to look at a house.

Our semi-detached end-terrace property in Stonehaven that we had moved into nine years after leaving Carlisle was all right up to a point but with four growing youngsters it was becoming a little cramped for space. By that time the continued growth of the North Sea oil industry had seen an upward spiral of house prices and we reckoned that we stood a fair chance of making enough profit on our home to fund the purchase of a larger detached property. As chance would have it, Andrea found one while I was in New Zealand. The closing date was twenty-four hours after my arrival back in Scotland. The house in question was a cottage in the village of Auchenblae ten miles south of Stonehaven.

In essence it was no larger than our Stonehaven home but this former mill manager's dwelling offered significant opportunities for improvement and expansion.

I made it back to Scotland in time to see the property and with just hours before the closing date Andrea and I agreed to make an offer. It was accepted and thus began a 35-year commitment of investment and enlargement.

But that, as they say, is another story for another day apart from the fact that we felt our first winter in Auchenblae would be our last. Heavy snow had virtually cut off the village for five days. Huge mounds of snows were piled high on each side of the road. There was no electricity. The only semblance of comfort during this miserable period was when local farming friends John and Margaret Milne made the daily trek to our home with their generator so that we could fire our central heating system. It was a generous and neighbourly gesture and with the warmth flooding back into our system we knew we might just survive the Auchenblae winter.

There was one humorous incident in those dark snow-bound days of our first winter in the village. I was shovelling snow from our front path when around the corner came the rare sight of a car slowly snaking its way towards me.

It drew abreast of me and stopped. I could see it was full of Chinese men. The driver rolled down his window and asked:

Where is house of joy?

I stopped shovelling. Was I inadvertently being given some new information about the village that had not been disclosed in the estate agent's prospectus?

I could think of no reasonable answer for this anxious Chinese gentlemen who I presumed might be looking for an evening's activity a little more relaxing than shovelling snow.

Fortunately, Andrea came out at that moment and discovered the Chinese were looking for the home of a local lady called Joy whose husband had business links with the Far East.

Ah well. It seemed Auchenblae was not about to offer any bacchanalian surprises after all. I returned to shovelling snow.

Meanwhile *Landward* continued its public service broadcasting remit but there was a constant self-induced pressure to try and create other strands of programming that would continue to justify the small Aberdeen operation as part of BBC Scotland's television operation.

Years before, my colleague Mike Marshall – the original producer of the *Beechgrove Garden* television programme – had produced two highly successful series called *Breathing Space* and later *The Food Programme*. But by now Mike had left the BBC to set up his own commercial video production company which left the television arm of Aberdeen hanging onto only gardening and farming television programmes.

So I put up an idea for a new countryside series called *Up Country*. Either my pitch was good or Jim Hunter my then Head of Television in Glasgow was in benevolent mood because the idea for a short run was accepted.

Our first programme was broadcast in 1985 and was a half-hour feature on the life and work of John Ridgway, the former Parachute Regiment officer who in 1966 with Chay Blyth spent 92 days in a 20-foot dory rowing boat and became the first to row across the vast expanse of the Atlantic Ocean.

By 1985 he and his wife Marie Christine and young daughter Rebecca were based at Ardmore in a remote part of North-West Sutherland. It was a magnificent setting at the edge of a sea loch and anchored just offshore was the English Rose VI, John Ridgway's yacht that the year before he had sailed non-stop round the world in a record-breaking time. Accompanied on that occasion by Andy Briggs it was the fastest-ever circumnavigation of the globe taking 203 days from Ardmore via South Africa, Australia, New Zealand and South America before finally returning to their Scottish base.

Now settled at Ardmore, John and Marie Christine had set up an adventure centre designed to foster greater skills of self reliance on individuals or groups, many of which were sent on the course by their employers in the hope that they would return to their work better equipped for both leadership and teamwork.

I felt that if we were to tell this part of John Ridgway's story to best effect, our presenter would benefit from being one of a group being put through John's demanding paces with the story unfolding through the eyes of a participant. I put the idea to Claire Powell, an enthusiastic and energetic freelance journalist who had recently turned to broadcasting to add an extra string in her bow. Accordingly, she agreed to become a temporary member of a team of middle managers from a biscuit manufacturimg company from the south of England.

The other members of my team were Gordon Penfold, the cameraman, Jim Patchett, sound recordist, and Sandy Fraser, the lighting electrician. They too entered into the spirit of this unusual assignment and we all looked forward eagerly to what our week in Ardmore might bring.

We were not to be disappointed. The first part of the course for this group from the south turned out to be the most daunting. After reaching Ardmore via a two-mile trek through the heather – there was no public road to the adventure centre – personal gear was safely stowed after all participants heeded John Ridgway's instruction to put on swimming kit below their normal clothes. The group then boarded a trawler that headed for the open sea. John Ridgway asked everyone to don a lifejacket, remove their outer clothing and secure their kit in a plastic bag tied tightly at the neck. They meekly complied – including Claire Powell. That was just as well – as a former officer in the Parachute Regiment John Ridgway was not the kind of man who would take kindly to dissent in the ranks.

He pointed at a small island several hundred yards behind in the wake of the trawler that was now picking up speed.

See that island? he said. The group nodded as one.

That's where you're going to spend the night.

How are we going to get there? a brave soul ventured.

You're going to swim, said John Ridgway. *Now jump!*

The group were bright enough to realise that the quicker they leapt from the trawler the less distance they would have to swim to the island. Consequently, one by one, clutching their wrapped clothing they made cold contact with the waiting sea and struck out for the island.

John Ridgway looked at me with an inquiring glance. I nodded and whispered to Gordon Penfold the cameraman to keep recording what was happening in front of his lens.

You too Claire, said John.

What? she queried.

This was no time for debate. Two of John's instructors on the course quickly walked up to Claire at the rear of the trawler and with one swift motion heaved her into the briny. I'm sure I heard the words *You bastard Anderson* as she hit the water.

We had agreed in advance that the best film would be made if our presenter became totally immersed in the subject – although Claire never imagined immersion in the literal sense.

Truth to tell, the decision to throw Claire into the water to join the others on the survival course was a spontaneous one taken by me at John Ridgway's suggestion just before we boarded the trawler. With her lifejacket on neither she – nor the others – were ever in any real danger. Nonetheless, I would be chary about having any presenter thrown into the ocean today without their prior agreement. In any event, by the time I had ticked all the boxes that would be required in one of the BBC's modern-day hazard assessment forms I expect I would have lost the will to live.

In the event, Claire survived to swim to the island and join the rest of the guinea pigs in building a shelter for the night, catching a fish then helping construct a raft to return to the mainland the next day. All of this we filmed and all of it made for a good programme.

On our last day filming we also got a chance to sail on the record-breaking English Rose VI when John Ridgway allowed the course members to take alternate turns at the helm of what was his ocean-going pride and joy.

Well, at least that was the intention. Shortly after we left Ardmore en route for Handa Island, a storm blew up and it was felt that the control of the English Rose VI remained in the safe hands of the owner himself. The half-day voyage would have added an strong extra dimension to our film but in the event we filmed very little – the storm was so severe and Gordon our cameraman so seasick that the camera stayed in its box for most of the time.

Jim Patchett, the sound recordist but also in those days a second string cameraman, eagerly embraced the challenge of keeping his feet as the yacht rose and fell in the mounting waves. A mountaineer of some note, Jim was taking all this in his stride and suggested that if he could use the camera he could climb the main mast and get some superb shots of the raging open sea and the group of huddled humanity far below on the deck.

I told him firmly the camera was staying in its box and he was staying on deck. I don't think Jim ever forgave me. In retrospect I have no doubt Jim would have delivered the goods if I had given the go-ahead. After all, wasn't he the hardy soul one afternoon when filming was over for the day on the island of Fetlar in the Shetlands who had stripped off to his underwear and gone for a "refreshing" swim in the cold grey waters of the North Sea.

And so we left Ardmore with our film that turned out to be a successful portrait of the work of one of the country's most charismatic adventurers. Since those days many thousands have attended John Ridgway's survival and leadership courses at Ardmore. I gather that while John is now semi retired, his daughter Rebecca continues her father's pioneering work. Somehow that doesn't surprise me. Within a few short years of our filming at Ardmore, Rebecca followed in John's trail-blazing footsteps when she became the first woman to kayak around Cape Horn. She was 16 years old.

Another programme in our *Up Country* trial series consisted of a day salmon fishing on the River Dee near Balmoral Castle. This time we had no presenter – maybe Claire Powell thought we would throw her into the river as well. Instead we let two enthusiastic anglers do the talking – mainly to each other. One of the fishermen was the playwright, author and broadcaster Roderick Wilkinson and the other was a rapidly rising star called Billy Connolly.

The two men had never met before but given their mutual love of fishing they bonded immediately and the interaction between them on camera helped underwrite a memorable short piece of television.

Yet perhaps the most memorable part of our time with Billy Connolly that day did not take place on camera. Over lunchtime sandwiches in the nearby hotel he regaled my team with stories of his days in the Territorial Army when he was training to parachute. As he explained, the first few times he took off in an aircraft he never landed. Told in his inimitable style with expletives not necessarily deleted we could hardly eat for laughter. Mind you, you had to be there......

Yet if working with Billy Connolly on the River Dee brought memories of laughter another occasion on the River Tay near Perth could have had tragic consequences for our cameraman Alistair Black and sound recordist Larry Pirie.

We had gone to film white water canoeing near the village of Stanley. At first sight it seems a straightforward exercise. The BBC's two-man team would be in one canoe securely roped to a second canoe in the capable hands of two experienced canoeists. The idea was that this home-made mini catamaran would then run parallel with the sporting canoes as they tackled the white water challenges on this most famous of rivers.

What no-one had considered was that the handling characteristics of a lashed-up double canoe are unpredictable. Despite the best efforts of all concerned our four-man filming vessel was pulled closer and closer into the raging vortex until it capsized throwing everyone into the river.

All of this was happening out of my sight. I had helped the team push off from the bank and then by arrangement left in my car to meet them at an agreed spot about a mile downstream.

Although only a mile or so as the crow flies, by road the distance was about three miles and by the time I reached the rendezvous I found the team waiting for me sitting forlorn and drenched on the riverbank.

Because Alistair Black and Larry Pirie had been wearing life jackets, they were fine. Sadly the camera was not – lost somewhere under the foaming deep black water of the Tay.

It was a salutary experience for all concerned – and embarrassing. Having to telephone Jim Hunter, my boss in Glasgow, and tell him I was instrumental in having lost an expensive camera was bad enough. What was worse was that a local freelance reporter had got hold of the story and it hit the headlines in the tabloid press.

Because the astronomical cost of insuring all the BBC equipment would have meant there was little cash left over to make programmes, much of the organisation's technical apparatus is not insured. We therefore had to assume the camera was lost and gone forever. However, the single over-arching comfort was that while the camera may have been lost, human lives were not.

Many weeks later when the waters of the Tay had receded, a local found our shattered camera lying entangled among branches on the riverbank. Eventually returned to the BBC studios in Aberdeen, it was widely assumed it would be scrapped. However, John Cowie, a brilliant television engineer began to take it apart and painstakingly put it back together. It took months but it survived to become a working spare in our small television studio.

Sad to relate but shortly after the River Tay incident, our sound recordist Larry Pirie died following complications as the result of a simple knee operation. I happened to be checking details on his passport when I received news of his untimely death. He had been due to go filming for *Landward* in Canada the following week. At short notice, Brian Webb, a long-serving and respected BBC radio studio manager took his place.

Equally sadly, John Cowie, the television engineer, is also no longer with us – a brain tumour having taken him well before his time.

Our short series of *Up Country* was duly completed and broadcast but sadly was not re-commissioned. Still, nothing ventured nothing gained.

New challenges, however, come out of the blue – although not always in the way you might expect. Some time after the River Tay incident, I found myself in BBC Scotland headquarters in Queen Margaret Drive in Glasgow. Walking along the carpeted corridor of the third floor, the sanctum sanctorum of senior management, I happened to pass my boss Jim Hunter's door when it suddenly opened and Jim saw me:

Oh Arthur – good – come in.

I entered his office to find sitting opposite his desk was Jimmy Shand the ageing grandfather of Scottish dance music. Could it be, I instantly speculated, that I had been chosen to produce the definitive documentary on one of Scotland's most popular musicians?

Jim introduced me briefly to Jimmy Shand and then came my challenge:

Arthur – would you mind showing Jimmy to the toilet!

It was good to know what my boss thought of my talents as a director – even if on that occasion it was only to direct an old man to a toilet.

The rolling commitment to *Landward* continued to demand my attention and my energy. At this time my assistant producer Chris Middleton had decided that a future in television was not for him and he returned to farm with his father in Yorkshire although he was to continue as researcher and writer for many years with a commercial video production company specialising in agricultural topics.

To the surprise of many of my colleagues, I chose as his successor as assistant producer a young chap called Sandy Milne, an engineer at the BBC in Aberdeen. He had no particular knowledge or experience of the farming industry but at the BBC board I was struck by his enthusiasm and open-minded attitude to trying something new. He proved a great success – so much so that he soon moved on to what he felt were pastures more challenging in BBC production and in a few years had become a senior manager with the BBC in the south of England.

The next to occupy the demanding hot seat as Assistant Producer-Director was Dick Colthurst. Dick was then a reporter on the Aberdeen Press & Journal and had impressed us all at his BBC board as a young man with an infectious enthusiasm and driving commitment to move from print journalism to television. We hired him.

Dick quickly made his mark, not least when I set him to direct a film with Jack Webster, one of the leading figures in Scottish journalism. Although a journalist all his working days, Jack was a son of the soil having been brought up on a farm called Honeyneuk in Aberdeenshire.

A few years after Jack's father died he realised that his future lay in journalism and he decided to sell the family farm. He approached me to see if I would be interested in filming the farm roup – the North-East Scotland name for a closing down sale of cattle and equipment.

And one more thing, he asked, could he write the commentary?

Jack was a fine writer with a special gift for touching the emotions. I quickly gave it the green light and set Jack and Dick to work together to record the unfolding story of one man's life set around the Honeyneuk roup of June 8th, 1986.

The end result – *Webster's Roup* – became the most popular and fondly remembered film of all the hundreds of editions of *Landward* I produced over nearly 25 years. The cameraman was Dennis Callan with Colin Maclure on sound and Jack Webster's writing took the viewer on an emotional roller-coaster journey from his boyhood as war broke out to the public auction of the cattle and the boxes of nuts and bolts from the farm's dusty workshop and to his mother and father's final resting place in the local churchyard. Dick Colthurst pulled all the component parts together to make a fine and lasting film that would, as they say, bring a tear to a glass eye.

Our film of Webster's Roup went on to compete for the award as the best specialist programme of 1986. It didn't win, beaten into second place by a programme made by commercial television, part of a series that reputedly had cost the best part of a million pounds. Our hard cash costs had been little more than £1000.

The irony is that Webster's Roup had so stirred the emotions of tens of thousands that many years later it is still fondly recalled by many in Scotland's rural communities and for some time copies of the film were sold to raise funds for RSABI, Scotland's only national charity helping those who have depended on the land for a living.

Dick went on to make many good films as part of the *Landward* team. They included a memorable story with Patrick Gordon-Duff-Pennington, the charismatic laird who ran the Ardverikie Estate beside Loch Laggan and which in later years was used as the backdrop for the long-running BBC television series *Monarch in the Glen*.

Queen Victoria and Prince Albert had considered Ardverikie as a potential Highland home but they were so appalled by the multitude of midges that the Royal pair went further east and settled on Balmoral instead.

They were right about the midges – when Dick and I filmed at Patrick's stately pile, we recorded one interview in the garden overlooking Loch Laggan. The fact that I was doing the interview rather than one of our small team of freelance presenters possibly indicated that it was a question of budget rather than ego. Patrick, wearing his kilt, sat on a garden seat beside the supposed burial spot of King Fergus, an ancient king. It was late on a warm summer afternoon and the midges were out in even greater force than usual. During the interview, Patrick, on camera, had to endure extreme discomfort from his airborne attackers. I, being off camera, could at least scratch. Poor Patrick. Never mind the agony – it was a lovely scenic setting.

Patrick was liked and admired throughout Scotland's farming and landowning community not least for his commitment to putting people above policy or politics. He was also a poet – a gift that no doubt sprang from his deep insight into the human condition and many of his poems are contained in his own autobiography *These Blue Remembered Hills*.

Issues of land use then, as now, were never far from the headlines. When pursuing stories on land use it was very easy to step on toes. Unrelated to the Ardverikie film but about the same time I was reporting and directing on one land use topic about how the then Highlands and Islands Development Board sought Parliamentary powers to compulsory acquire land that they thought was not being properly managed – getting rid of the absentee landlords and all that.

My resulting film was, I hoped, balanced and objective. However, I was quickly to learn that balance – like beauty – is in the eye of the beholder. The day after our Sunday broadcast there was a complaint from the Labour Party that my reporting had shown too much right wing bias.

I was naturally anxious - but I needn't have worried. The following day a second letter arrived, this time from the Conservative Party suggesting that my commentary had been too slanted in favour of the left. Presented with both letters, my bosses in Glasgow reckoned that I must have got it about right.

While our work continued on *Landward* with the bread and butter issues of the day, there were lighter moments that linger in the memory – sometimes for the wrong reasons.

We had gone to Paris for three days to cover the Paris Show, one of Europe's biggest food and farming events with plenty of Scottish involvement to justify our presence.

On the first day shooting we would occasionally find ourselves competing for tripod space with another farming team from Norwich where Anglia Television also produced a farming programme. We knew the principals involved – the producer Bill Smith had cut his broadcasting teeth in radio with the BBC in Aberdeen years before while the presenter was David Richardson the Norfolk farmer who in a previous broadcasting existence a few years earlier had worked for the BBC in Birmingham and who memorably had to conduct an extended interview with the Minister of Agriculture when we screwed up our end of the programme in Aberdeen.

Why don't we join up for an evening meal, suggested Bill Smith. *Anglia TV will pay.*

We readily agreed and that night had a memorable meal in Le Coupole the famous brasserie in Boulevard du Montparnasse. At the end of the meal I thanked our ITV hosts and said:

Tomorrow night's dinner is on Landward. Where shall we go?

A well-known restaurant was suggested and Bill Smith who knew his way round Paris a lot better than I did duly booked a table for the following evening.

When we arrived for our meal the next night I knew something was amiss. Unlike La Coupole there was no excited tumult of diners from within. Entering from the street, our feet fell into a deep luxury carpet and throughout the small restaurant an air of sepulchral calm prevailed in the almost deserted basement dining room with the silence occasionally broken by the sound of silver cutlery on bone china tableware. The restaurant turned out to be La Marée, a famous fish restaurant near the Champs Elysées. Six of us were seated at a round table and my sense of what I might have let myself in for was heightened when a waiter leapt from the darkness to place a perfectly fitting jacket over the shoulders of Dick Colthurst who had arrived in his shirtsleeves. They don't do that in a cheap diner.

The menu arrived and everyone eagerly looked at the Michelin-starred delights that awaited us. I didn't. I could only see the prices and my mouth went dry.

While the others looked forward to the gastronomic delights that awaited them, all I could think of was the common thread that linked my predicament with that of the man in the short story by Saki who met by chance a woman friend and took her for lunch at an expensive restaurant only to find it was the first day of the asparagus season with all the demands that that implied for his wallet.

What did we eat that evening in Paris? I can't remember. What did it cost? Don't ask. Somehow I got through the meal and even more miraculously I paid the bill – but it made a dent in the *Landward* budget and I was content to visit a MacDonalds on my last night in Paris in a poor attempt to redress the balance.

Mind you, expensive restaurants and dangerous bidets apart, Paris can offer other traps for the innocent Scot abroad. In the early days of the European Union and on the occasion of the Paris Show the British Embassy hosted a glittering reception for the movers and shakers of Europe's agricultural industry. Among them was a leading light in the Scottish farming scene, an upright and sober Presbyterian of unsullied reputation.

Doing his best to speak French in this international company, one attractive lady asked him what nationality he was.

He meant to reply:

Je suis Écossais.

A slip of the tongue, however, saw him respond instead:

Je suis Corse.

Our upright Presbyterian was pleasantly surprised how he very soon came to be surrounded by admiring young women.

Diplomatically extricating himself from this posse of young female admirers, he asked a colleague why he seemed to have become the centre of attraction.

It was delicately explained to him that his French might have left a little to be desired. Instead of saying he was Scottish he had identified himself as Corsican. It was further revealed to him that Corsicans have a reputation for their sexual prowess. History relates that he had a stiff drink and spoke English for the rest of the evening.

In due course I realised I couldn't hang on to Dick Colthurst and that his talents deserved a larger stage and soon he found a new berth as a producer working with John Craven on the newly-launched *Countryfile* television programme made in the BBC's Pebble Mill studios in Birmingham. In later years he was to continue his onward progress with an executive role in BBC Bristol before securing a senior management position post with Tigress, one of the UK's leading independent production companies.

With Dick gone, I needed another assistant producer and I was pleasantly surprised to receive a late night international call from Colin Follas in New Zealand who had done so much to make my first filming visit to New Zealand some years earlier a success.

He informed me that TVNZ was ending its farming programme. He had plans to go independent but wanted to spend some time in Europe first. Did he have any chance if he threw his hat into the ring for the post of assistant producer on *Landward*. I told him to go ahead.

The board for the post was some three weeks hence and he flew to Scotland for the interview. Despite strong domestic opposition, I selected Colin for the job on a six-month contract. Maybe one or two of the other candidates might have felt the appointment smacked of favouritism but there was no question of that. Of course I knew him and liked him but I also knew the high standard of production values he had brought over many years to his own farming programme on New Zealand television. He got the job with *Landward* strictly on merit.

So Colin and his wife Doreen packed their bags and headed for Scotland to fulfil his six-month contract. While he was with us he did a splendid job both professionally and personally. Colin was the life and soul of any party and could tell stories with a laid-back style that soon had his audience helpless with laughter.

The story he dined out on most was of the annual duck shoot that a local farmer near Auckland used to host for his neighbours and friends of whom Colin was one.

Around the farm was a network of small rivers and streams that invariably boasted wild ducks in abundance. Sadly, on this occasion there were no ducks to be found. Hours went past and the two or three groups of shooters quartered the patch to no avail. Ducks were not to be in their sights that day.

Walking slowly back to the farm one of Colin's group heard the sound of a duck in the reeds. They crouched down behind some cover and waited. A few seconds later, a small brown duck swam courageously into view. Colin's gun blasted and the small brown duck was no more. Colin reached into the water and fished out the unfortunate bird.

That's funny, he said. *This duck has only got one leg.*

The group continued back to the farmhouse where they joined the farmer and his wife for lunch during which the farmer commiserated that there had been such a poor morning's sport.

I reckon that means the only duck around today will be Archie the family pet, said the farmer. *For God's sake don't shoot him. He's been part of the family for years.*

What's Archie look like, said Colin.

He's a small brown chap, said the farmer. *Very friendly. Easy to recognise. He's only got one leg.*

Colin went silent and left shortly afterwards.

His other story concerned the same shooting party a year or two later. Walking well away from the farmhouse and homestead after a long and indulgent lunch, one of the shooters collapsed clutching his chest. His pals did their best to make him comfortable while another ran back to the farm to get help.

The farmer's wife phoned the ambulance service while the farmer set off with his tractor and trailer over rough ground to bring the casualty back to the farm.

Still clutching his chest, the shooter was gently loaded onto the flatbed trailer. Knowing speed was of the essence with suspected heart attacks, the farmer set off for the farm as fast as he could with his precious human cargo bouncing awkwardly on the bed of the trailer as it raced across the rough ground.

They reached the farmhouse just as the ambulance was arriving and the casualty was gently transferred from one transport to the other. In the event he was in hospital for several days – not for the feared heart attack that turned out to be no more than chronic indigestion as a result of the convivial lunch he had consumed earlier - but for the broken leg caused by his host's humanitarian dash across the fields in a bouncing farm trailer.

In 1988 Australia celebrated its bicentenary – a perfect reason it seemed to me to make two films on how Scots had helped shape the farming industry of that great nation. Accompanied by presenter Ross Muir, cameraman Alistair Black and sound recordist Colin Maclure we spent a memorable and productive two weeks working in New South Wales, South Australia and Victoria.

Our first film was a report on the history of the Australian wool industry that centred on the life of Peter and Sue Dowling, a delightful couple who ran the Keri Keri Sheep Station near Moulamein in the Riverina region of New South Wales. It was one of the smaller properties – Peter could fly round his acres and his tens of thousands of Merinos in his own plane within the hour.

In different circumstances our story might not have had a successful ending. I had picked up our hire car at the local airport to drive to Keri Keri and about one mile short of our destination the engine died. It was a fairly new vehicle and there was no apparent reason for the sudden loss of power. And then I realised the problem – there was no fuel in the tank. I had failed to check the petrol gauge when I signed for the car. Had I not had another team car behind me; had I not been within spitting distance of our hosts; had I been on my own hundreds of miles into the outback. Not for the first time in my career was I to face a not so gentle ribbing from my colleagues. Significantly perhaps I was to discover that in the native Aborigine tongue Keri Keri literally translated as *Place of the Bones*.

Our second film profiled two Scots who had left their native land to build a new life on the other side of the world. One of them was Jimmy Young from Castle Douglas in Galloway. I knew his father and brother who still farmed in Scotland and it was an eye-opening experience to see the difference between the small fields he had left behind and the huge expanse of the 5000 acres he and his wife Christine now farmed near Penola in South Australia.

The other Scot we profiled was Archie Stevenson whose family was well known for the high quality of Ayrshire cattle produced on the family farm near Stranraer. It was to prove that old habits die hard – on his 400 acres of land in Victoria he was still surrounded by his brown and white Ayrshire cows. However, there were two small differences from his Scottish home.

The first was when we walked through the pasture to film the cows we sought a higher vantage point on a pile of stones.

Don't do that, Archie suggested. *Those stones will be full of snakes*. We came down fast.

The second obvious difference came when we were having a coffee in the farmhouse kitchen with Archie and his wife Susan. I happened to remark that I had recently read that most Australians had never seen a Koala unless on television or in a zoo.

We've got our own here, said Susan.

Where? I asked.

Right there, Susan said pointing.

195

We looked and there in a eucalyptus tree beside the house were two Koalas.

Grabbing our camera took precedence over a second cup of coffee.

For our last night in Australia, Ross Muir and I had booked into the Sebel Town House, an upmarket Sydney hotel favoured by show business luminaries.

We signed in and went to our rooms agreeing to meet in the bar in an hour. I came down early and noticed a display board in the foyer indicating that high profile guests that week included rock musicians Mick Jagger and Bryan Ferry and the actor James Fox.

I approached the young man at the reception desk and indicated the display board. I asked if they knew that Ross Muir of the BBC was also in the building.

Who is Ross Muir? I was asked politely.

I feigned astonishment at such ignorance and suggested that Ross was one of the best-known broadcasters in the business.

I went further and suggested it might be no bad idea from a public relations point of view if Ross's name was added to the star-spangled list on public display.

Certainly sir, we'll see to it right away.

I was sipping my drink when Ross walked into the bar.

Well, I said, *I see you've made it.*

What do you mean?

Go into the foyer and look at the display board of visitors.

He did and returned with a huge grin.

Courteous to a fault, Ross bought the next round. I had a double.

Vanity of vanities, all is vanity – as we are reminded in Ecclesiastes. Mind you, a little bit of innocent vanity is no great sin.

Many years ago there was a well-known television presenter admired and adored throughout the land. He believed himself perfect in every respect apart from one – he was sensitive about his rapidly approaching baldness. He was so sensitive that he grew the last remaining strand of his hair to such a length that he was

196

able to coil it round the top of his head that briefly created the illusion that he had some hair after all.

One winter evening he was at a dinner party. Behind him a roaring log fire was blazing. Towards the end of the convivial meal when sensible conversation became dulled with wine, his hostess began extolling the friendly nature of the family budgerigar and, to prove it, proceeded to release the bird from its cage. For a few moments the liberated bird flew from side to side in the dining room before perching on the head of our erstwhile television presenter. The port flowed and another chunk of Stilton was cut. By now the bird was curious at what it had landed on and began enthusiastically to tug at the coil of human hair with its beak. Mortified that the bird might unravel the entire coil and expose the fact that he was less hirsute than might at first appear, the presenter waited until he thought no one was looking then took a mighty swipe across the top of his head to persuade the bird to move elsewhere. Sadly, his quick movement took the bird by surprise and the blow hit it amidships hurtling it across the room behind the presenter – straight into the fire where the hot updraft carried it up the chimney. It was never seen again. Vanity of vanities, all is vanity.

After we completed our stint in Australia our cameraman and sound recordist returned to the UK with the recorded tapes while Ross Muir and I flew to New Zealand to record a third programme – thanks to the co-operative spirit of Colin Follas, now running his own independent production company and who was able to supply us with a local crew at a knockdown price.

We managed to make our third film of our visit within less than three days and with some time to kill. Colin asked us if we would like to see a boat he was working on for a client.

The boat turned out to be another ocean-going yacht – the Fisher and Paykel - owned by Gary Paykel the New Zealand white goods tycoon who had commissioned Colin's company to video the preparation of his yacht for the forthcoming Whitbread round the world race.

And so it was that Ross and I spent an hour on the Fisher and Paykel during her sea trials off the coast of Auckland. It was a memorable experience – and I can report that the Antipodean ocean was a lot calmer than when John Ridgway took me around Handa Island on the English Rose VI three years earlier.

One year later, in 1989, came the opportunity to pursue one of the most challenging shoots we had ever done on *Landward*. We went to Papua New Guinea to film with two young people who, in different ways and in different parts of that vast country, were spending part of their young lives helping Papua New Guinea nationals overcome the recurring problem of food shortages.

Papua New Guinea occupies the eastern part of the world's second largest island and is prey to volcanic activity, earthquakes and tidal waves. Linguistically, it is the world's most diverse country with more than 700 native tongues and some 80 per cent of the nation's population live in rural areas with few or no facilities of modern life. Many tribes in the isolated mountainous interior have little contact with one another, let alone with the outside world and live within an economy dependent on subsistence agriculture.

One of the young people we filmed with was Theresa Redding who had qualified as a fish biologist at the Institute of Aquaculture at Stirling University. Now she was putting her skills to use in the far north of Papua New Guinea working with the communities living along the banks of the mighty Sepik River where the river's bounty was so little that tinned fish had to be imported from Australia. Theresa was working on a project funded by the Food and Agriculture Organisation of the United Nations which involved netting fish in different areas to assess populations. One species introduced in the 1950s was the tilapia a fish widely known in Africa and which over the years has found increasing popularity in many other parts of the developing world. With over one million tonnes farmed each year, the tilapia is second only to carp as the most popular freshwater fish in the world.

The Sepik River project was ambitious and so were our plans for the *Landward* programme. In many respects this was possibly the most logistically complex shoot that our small department had ever tackled and the various threads of the schedule were superbly pulled together by my production assistant at the time, Sarah Johnson.

Despite Sarah's best efforts we were to suffer a few hitches before Ken Gow the cameraman and Jim Patchett our sound recordist and second operator were able to unpack their gear. The first setback came when we changed aircraft at Singapore for our flight to Port Moresby.

The air conditioning on the aircraft was not working properly but we were invited to remain in our seats while it was fixed. To suggest that it was hot and humid would be an understatement. After an hour the airline took pity on us and handed round beer and soft drinks that merely encouraged the passengers to visit the toilets. A second hour went by and then a third. More beer and soft drinks were dispersed and more visits to the toilets made by the hundred or so passengers.

After four hours captive in the aircraft, our clothes sodden with the humid conditions, the air conditioning was fixed and our aircraft was on its way at last. But by then the odour from the over-used toilets had permeated the whole plane so the flight to Port Moresby became one of the least enjoyable travel experiences we had ever shared as a team.

And then just when you think things cannot get worse – they do. Having reached Port Moresby, the down at heel capital of Papua New Guinea we checked in for our flights north to Wewak the small town on the northern coast overlooking the Bismarck Sea. The usual assortment of suitcases and camera boxes were checked in and we checked in – or at least some of us did. Despite Sarah's splendid organisational skills we had not bargained on the arbitrary seating arrangement of some third world airlines.

That was why Ross Muir and I flew north to Wewak with all the BBC gear leaving our cameraman Ken Gow, sound recordist Jim Patchett and Sarah Johnson to sample a night of the dubious delights of Port Moresby.

Our flight to Wewak was uneventful. We disembarked and collected all our gear from the ramshackle luggage area, loaded it carefully onto the only two trolleys we could find and looked for a taxi.

That's when the lights went out. We had been on the last plane into Wewak that night, we had collected our baggage, so the airport authorities clearly assumed there was no further need to keep the lights on.

Standing there in the pitch darkness with gear that was separated from their operators by several hundred miles I could feel a rising tension within me. Friendly locals approached us from the darkness, arms outstretched offering to help.

We refused. Let one camera case disappear into the Wewak night and there was a good chance we might never see it again. And who knows what vital piece of filming gear might be in any box that might go astray. For the want of a nail the battle was lost...and all that.

Taxi? We asked.

No taxi came a response in pidgin English from out of the darkness.

But we were in luck. Out of the night came a pick-up truck. It had been sent from the nearby Paradise Hotel where we were staying. It was salvation - at least of a sort.

Darkness comes quickly in the tropics and as it was still reasonably early evening I decided to put a call through to Theresa Redding to discuss our filming over the next two or three days.

We fixed up the filming from Aberdeen via phone and fax but Theresa and I had never met and like everything done by the seat of your pants it always helps to cross your fingers and hope for the best.

But crossing my fingers on this occasion didn't seem to work. Theresa was friendly but a bit reserved and said she wasn't sure if she really wanted to go through with the filming after all. She wasn't being unhelpful, merely suggesting that she wasn't sure if her work was of sufficient moment to justify 30 minutes of television.

This turn of events struck me like a hammer blow – here I was, having spent a considerable sum, by our standards, flying a team of five from distant Aberdeen to Papua new Guinea and not only were most of my colleagues missing but one of the subjects of our filming was having second thoughts.

Once again suicide seems a realistic prospect but Ross persuaded me that a couple of cold beers might prove a better option. I chose the beers.

But a new day brings fresh hope. Ken, Jim and Sarah managed to get a flight to Wewak, we met Theresa and after a convivial chat we had the green light to go ahead. I could feel my blood pressure drop.

Our schedule was tight and we had already lost a valuable day yet I was soon to discover the art of the possible when all conditions fall in your favour.

That day we left for Angoram, about sixty miles inland from Wewak where we would do most of our filming. We were advised to get there before darkness fell as there had been some trouble recently with "rascals." In our parlance a rascal may be a mischievous youngster but in Papua New Guinea it means something quite different where a rascal can be a member of a local tribe who can constantly be warring with members of other tribes of which there are hundreds spread throughout this vast country. These sporadic tribal conflicts have gone on for generations and each year there are many murders. We had no wish to be added to the statistics.

We were advised that the one local small hotel was considered too dangerous to stay in but thanks to Theresa's contacts we found accommodation for the night in a fisherman's hut. The hut was raised about ten or twelve feet above ground level and access to our accommodation was via a wooden ladder. We all slept on the floor in sleeping bags and there was much mirth from my colleagues when, despite our rudimentary surroundings I felt it incumbent to wear my Marks & Spencer yellow pyjamas. After all, a producer must have standards.

I looked down from a hole in the wall of the hut and saw the security that had been arranged on our behalf – two armed guards patrolling the trees below, each armed with a bow and arrow. My mind now at peace I surrendered to the night and fell quickly asleep.

We rose shortly after 4am and within an hour, as dawn was breaking over the jungle, we began filming. We saw the villagers come through the trees to set up their stalls at the open-air market laying out their little piles of catfish and smoked gudgeon, shrimps and snakeheads. We saw the sun's early heat burn off the mist from the river and then headed with Theresa to an ox-bow lake to film her and her aides laying out the nets and assessing fish-stock populations. We even managed to film on the local crocodile farm where local fishermen could earn a little extra by offering the farm any small crocodiles they might catch by chance on the river.

I recall the appalling stench and the primeval quality of hundreds of small crocodiles, poised as petrified, as we filmed over the fence of their enclosure. When mature, the reptiles were killed and their skins salted for a week before being exported to Japan and France to be turned into shoes, handbags and wallets.

We interviewed the owner of the crocodile farm, Ludwig Schulze, a local entrepreneur. Ross Muir asked if there wasn't something of an apparent contradiction that many of the local people were malnourished and short of protein yet his crocodiles were consuming around a quarter of a tonne of fish every week.

He looked at Ross and smiled:

It's business, he said softly. *Just business.*

Ken Gow and Jim Patchett worked like Trojans that day – I guess we all did, but Ken and Jim had the added burden of heavy equipment to carry around in the baking tropical heat. But it proved worth it. When the time came to leave Angoram we had a complete programme in the can. One day – one programme. Bliss, perfect bliss.

We celebrated by buying at least twenty small cans of chilled orange from the small local store, owned – naturally enough - by local entrepreneur Ludwig Schulze, and packed our gear into the 4 x 4 for our drive back to Wewak. All was quiet as I hung grimly to the steering wheel trying to avoid the potholes on the yellow dirt-track road through the jungle. After a little while I made a general comment about our day's work. There was no reply. I chanced a quick glance around at my colleagues. Everyone was sound asleep. They'd earned it. Two days earlier I thought we were going to be stuck up the creek without a paddle but we got there in the end. Mind you, we usually did.

Our first film was maybe safely in the can but my day wasn't finished. In far-flung destinations around the world where I couldn't be sure of the acceptance of credit cards for payment I always carried a large amount of notes in the national currency in a body belt under my shirt. Today, the £ sterling is equal to around four PNG kina. I can't recall what the exchange rate was all those years ago but I do remember that I had about £1500 equivalent in low denomination kina notes. When I got back to our hotel, I took off my money belt and realised that sweating for twelve hours in the blazing tropical sun had turned my thick wad of notes into something approaching a limp and sodden brick. It took me the best part of an hour to dry them sufficiently with a fan to allow me to gently peel one note then another off the top of the sweat-drenched mass. Life is a learning curve. On future trips to sticky climes, I wrapped the notes in a plastic sandwich bag before putting them in the money belt.

The subject for our second film was Phil McCabe, a former farm worker from Ayrshire who was working near Goroka in the Eastern Highlands of PNG trying to introduce rudimentary systems of sheep management. He had left school at 15 with the aim of becoming a jockey but rising height and weight soon put paid to that ambition.

Looking for a challenge in life he had left his native Scotland to join the staff of a horse-breeding stud in Kentucky where he was one of a team in charge of $200 million dollars worth of bloodstock. Yet he felt there had been something missing in his life and as he had always had a yearning to teach he had found an opportunity to do just that by coming to PNG as part of a Voluntary Service Overseas project.

If the lack of protein for the local populations along the Sepik River was a perennial difficulty, the situation was worse in the Eastern Highlands where there was a distinct shortage of nutritional food for six months every year. The locals called it *Taim Bilong Hangri* – three words in pidgin that translated into one in English - *Famine*.

Phil McCabe believed he could help to do something about that if he could persuade a greater involvement in sheep production that in turn would increase protein and reduce the endemic problem of malnourishment.

There was no real tradition of sheep production in the area. Pigs were the livestock of choice. But in PNG pigs were seen as more than a means to a commercial end. The pig has a revered place in PNG society and Phil advised us that if we happened to accidentally kill one on the road on no account should we stop and try and placate angry villagers. Some time before our arrival, a passing doctor had done just that. He got out of his car to offer his sympathy – and a little money – to the family whose pig he had killed.

He was hacked to death.

With 700 tribal languages spoken in PNG it is little wonder that there is much tribal rivalry that can trace its roots back many generations and it will be many generations yet before the traditional clan violence is extinguished.

While filming with Phil McCabe we chanced across one group of tribesman – a war party of some twenty men, faced daubed with paint and carrying bows and arrows.

They were a frightening sight – more akin to something out of a movie- maker's imagination than an everyday vision of country folk. Phil assured us that they never attacked outsiders like us – they kept their murderous tendencies for their tribal rivals. We spoke to them with Phil translating the pidgin English. They had just come from a raid on a rival clan but apparently it had been a relatively quiet affair. Only one person had been killed that day.

Phil turned out to be a natural subject for television combining as he did a relaxed style with a sharp mind and articulate turn of phrase. Even in the short time we spent filming with him in the hilltop villages of the Eastern Highlands it was clear he had struck up a rapport with the villagers.

Whether it was advice on disease prevention, sheep nutrition or shearing – each one of his training courses guaranteed an attentive audience of locals all anxious to absorb some of the skills being imparted by this young man from the west of Scotland.

By the end of several days filming in the Eastern Highlands, the villagers developed a wish to establish a stronger bond with this strange team of camera-bearing people from Scotland. Maybe it was their fascination for the hairy white legs of Ken Gow, the cameraman, or the unknown gifts in what my colleagues called Arthur's beanbag that I took to the villages bearing small gifts like BBC pens or pencils for the youngsters. On the other hand, their fascination with us may have been that they saw a potential for the sale of soft drugs. On several occasions we were quietly approached for our addresses and asked if we would be interested in receiving regular small parcels from a far off land containing mind-altering substances. We declined politely. A few glasses of claret had all the power to relax that I could ever wish for – not that there was any sign of that in the hinterland of Papua New Guinea.

Meeting committed young people like Theresa Redding and Phil McCabe was an enriching experience. They may have been from different backgrounds but they were united in common cause of doing something positive to help the people of a developing nation.

Although very different in content than anything the *Landward* team had ever produced, both our Papua New Guineas films were well received both by our audience and the television industry in general, so much so that we were delighted when *Taim Bilong Hangri*, the film about Phil McCabe, won the 1990 One World Broadcasting Trust Premier Award for Regional Television.

Not only did we enjoy the kudos of winning a national award for our work but I also took a quiet satisfaction in knowing that a television team of five had travelled from Scotland to the jungles of Papua New Guinea, made two 30-minute films and still had a handful of change from £8000.

Often over the years, I was asked for updates on stories we had filmed years before. Very often I had no answer for them – the remorseless hunger of the television schedules always demanding that the production caravan move on to pastures new with what had happened before disappearing into the dark recesses of the memory or to gather dust on the shelves of the film and video library.

But with our two subjects in Papua New Guineas there was a follow-up. Phil finished his stint in PNG and returned to Scotland with his wife, Lasia, who he had met in the Eastern Highlands. Over the coming years the marriage produced three daughters, Susan, Carolyn and Charmaine. In due course, the *Landward* camera team were invited to share a family Christening ceremony at the little church in Girvan, Ayrshire, where Phil had returned to his roots to work for the local authority.

As for Theresa Redding, she became Network Manager for CoastNet, a national charity whose focus is the coast and sea, raising awareness about climate change.

There was a final postscript to our award-winning Papua New Guinea programme. About a year after the two programmes were first broadcast, I was asked to compile a one-hour version embracing the best of both to fill a gap in the schedules. This I was delighted to do and the 60-minute "special" was carefully compiled and completed and sent to Glasgow for subsequent broadcast. In the event, someone somewhere in BBC Scotland's transmission headquarters proved a little less conscientious than normal and the programme was broadcast without the commentary soundtrack faded up. This meant that the Scottish viewers enjoyed the vivid colours of our exotic visit to the Far East and the words of our interviewees but of Ross Muir's dulcet tones there was none. For the second time in my broadcasting career I felt ready to inflict bodily harm to whatever hapless colleague had been responsible. For all that, it proved not to be the transmission disaster or embarrassment I feared. Our Papua New Guinea "special" drew a healthy audience but we received not one single complaint about the missing commentary soundtrack. Perhaps our audience thought it was a deliberate production effect. To his credit, Ross Muir saw the comic irony of it all although it took me a little longer.

Much of the success of our long trek to Papua New Guinea was due to the diligent research and logistical detail tackled by Sarah Johnson, my PA. I felt that she showed an enthusiasm and ability that would equip her for becoming a producer in her own right.

Although it was a risk for Sarah, she took the plunge and was eventually to resign from her *Landward* post and take up a place on the BBC's highly competitive graduate trainee scheme.

However, before she began to stretch her wings in other areas of the BBC, there was another short film that I asked her to pull together with the help of a new assistant producer in the team – Nick Ibbotson.

Nick was, and is, a remarkably talented man. He had begun his working life as a doctor in Cambridge but when he took off his white coat and stethoscope he also possessed great musical talents. In fact he was to eschew the medical profession to pursue a career in show business after becoming a founder member and tenor with Cantabile, the close harmony group he helped form as a barbershop quartet at Cambridge University in 1977.

Some ten years later Nick then took another significant turn in his life when he became a director with BBC's *Tomorrow's World* team in London but after a few years he wanted a taste of rural life so left London and became my assistant producer in BBC Aberdeen.

Nick, Sarah and I worked well together – never more so than when Pat Chalmers, by now Controller of BBC Scotland, rang me to say that he had met in Edinburgh the last Onion Johnnie in Scotland and it seemed to him a good idea that we should make a short film on the last of a line for *Landward*. *Did I agree?* Pat wondered. Didn't I just!

And so it was that in 1990 Nick, Sarah and I spent three days in Britanny filming with Yves Rolland, the last of the Onion Johnnies. We filmed him harvesting his small crop, packing it in his van then taking the ferry to the UK before cycling round the streets of Edinburgh selling his strings of onions door to door in the time-honoured fashion. I recall a memorable short film with, off-camera, much garlic, wine and laughter.

In due course Sarah headed south to a successful career as an award-winning documentary maker in the BBC's Bristol studios but after some years drew that chapter in her life to a close and took on a fresh challenge to study medicine. She gained entry to Bristol Medical School and qualified in 2010. She will prove a fine doctor. Nick, too, has returned to his Hippocratic roots and is working as a family doctor in Yorkshire. With old age and infirmity slowly creeping up on me, it's something of a comfort to know that there's not just one friendly doctor in my contacts book - but two.

The pace of life for the *Landward* team never slackened; we worked hard but enjoyed life and there was the added bonus of receiving a constant feedback from our audience – the farming families of Scotland – that they enjoyed the programme. They felt that what we were producing week after week was for them and about them. That pleased me. I had always felt – and still do – that family farming was the sheet anchor of the rural economy of Scotland and that a public service broadcaster like the BBC should reflect that strongly in its schedules, even if for only 30 minutes a week. Fortunately I had the support of senior management in the BBC in Glasgow and that commitment from them to me and to the rural viewers was to continue until I retired.

There is, of course, impermanence to all things. My mother Frances died suddenly in January 1992. She had never sought the limelight, choosing instead to pursue a hard working life as a tenant farmer. Not only did she shoulder all the work and the worries that go hand in hand with trying to make a living from the May Farm; in addition she and my father had the extra challenge of providing nursing care and support for both my grandmothers who spent the last years of their lives at the May Farm.

My mother was the most unselfish person I have ever known. She never had much by way of material luxuries of her own and any time she had a little extra of anything she sought to give it away to someone she felt had greater claim to it than herself. In quiet moments of introspection she sometimes wondered what she might have done if her life had taken a different course. Academically bright and musically gifted as a youngster, she had been a pupil at Esdaile School in Edinburgh but after two or three years the demands of the family farm meant she had to forsake her studies and return to Airyolland to milk cows.

The hearse bearing my mother's coffin from the May Farm to Mochrum Church began its short journey down the farm road at walking pace. As my mother travelled down the farm road for the last time I walked behind the hearse and looked up and beyond to the Galloway hills that had filled her horizon for all her days. Now she would lift her eyes to the hills no more.

It has been one of the abiding regrets in my life that I was never able to find the means to offer her – and earlier, my father too – some of the material things that neither of them had ever enjoyed in their lifetime. Not that they had ever sought them but having sacrificed so much for myself and my sister Monica it would have been satisfying to lift from their shoulders their constant worries about money. Never did a couple more personify the old farming joke that they had started with nothing and at the end still had most of it left.

As for the future of the May Farm, the position after my mother's death was very different to that when my father had died nearly twenty years before. Then I had flirted briefly with the idea of leaving the BBC and going back to the farm until my mother persuaded me otherwise. I had considered the prospect again soon after moving from radio to television when I felt I was not pulling my weight.

Now I had no such thoughts. In the intervening years my sister Monica had married John McTurk, a well-known name in Galloway farming circles, a fine man and a born stockman. In turn Monica had forged ahead with a successful career and become the senior speech and language therapist with the National Health Service based in Dumfries.

Together, John and Monica had continued the tenancy despite the pressures and challenges of this type of marginal farming. In the intervening years John and Monica had raised two fine daughters in Katie and Hilary. My mother may have gone but in my sister and brother-in-law the May Farm was still in safe and caring hands.

Meanwhile I was now working for a new boss. Colin Cameron had taken over as Head of Television for BBC Scotland and with a strong track record across a broad range of programmes on the network he was keen to see his producers stretch themselves and encouraged any new initiative if he felt it had a place on the schedules.

209

Around the same time a former freelance cameraman called Mike Herd made contact with me in Aberdeen. Mike had been one of the first cameraman I had worked with and had proved a tower of strength to me in the early days after leaving radio when I was gingerly feeling my way with this new medium of television.

Mike's first love as a cameraman was natural history and very soon after I first met him he had found his talents increasingly in demand from the BBC Natural History Department in Bristol. For many years thereafter he became a valued cameraman working throughout the world on award-winning programmes.

But now he wanted to travel less and spend more time around his home base in the Highlands. He suggested an idea for a series of four programmes looking at the wildlife on and around a Highland loch over four seasons of the year. Colin Cameron and I discussed it and it seemed the kind of project that with Mike Herd's steady hand on the tiller could work well for BBC Scotland and the small Aberdeen production unit. Mike could do the work, I could do the worrying – and still produce the *Landward* programme. And so *The Loch* began to take shape with Mike shooting and directing his own programme and our committed and talented picture editor Rob Shortland cutting the material together in Aberdeen.

Apart from keeping an eye on the budget and the progress towards transmission, I had little hands-on involvement with the programme – with two notable exceptions.

Mike wanted a fox to be filmed in a short winter sequence prowling around a small island in the middle of our chosen loch. As the producer, could I find one for him? It wasn't the kind of challenge I was used to but I did find a fox at Camperdown Park in Dundee and those in charge at the park could not have been more supportive and helpful. When they realised why it was required they volunteered to take the fox north in a cage and let it loose on the island while Mike filmed it doing whatever it is foxes do when prowling around a small island.

The fox duly obliged us and everyone seemed happy with the afternoon's work. However, at the moment it came time to recapture the fox for its return journey to Dundee, it clearly decided that it had been presented with a once and for all opportunity to return to the wild. It looked round at its human pursuers, dived into the water, swam swiftly the fifty yards to the mainland and took to the hills – never to be seen again.

As producer with an infinite capacity to worry, I wasn't sure if litigation would follow given that I had been instrumental in causing Camperdown Park to lose one of its local attractions. However, once again those in charge of the park were pragmatic. *Dinnae worry son*, I was assured, *we'll easy get another fox*.

The other sequence I was briefly involved with on *The Loch* was helping Mike construct an underwater net enclosure, fill it with trout, rig up a camera just below the water then lie in wait with a remote control until a passing osprey decided to fly past and partake of one of the said trout.

Actually, the set was not built quite as quickly or as apparently easily as I have just described it. Getting the trout was easy – we bought them from a local fish farm – but setting up the net and the camera took a lot longer. The main work in setting up the net and camera was done by Matt Leiper who had been a lighting electrician with BBC in Aberdeen before spreading his wings and becoming a sound man and later a cameraman in BBC News in London. He was also a qualified scuba diver and on a weekend visit to Aberdeen he volunteered his services. Mike and I eagerly accepted. Matt worked eagerly all day and by the end had achieved the set-up that Mike required. But it was exhausting work and as I drove Matt back to Aberdeen late that evening with a fish supper as his only reward, he remarked that he had had easier days at the sharp end of BBC News. Matt's efforts were not in vain. Mike Herd got his shot of the osprey.

There was one significant difference between *The Loch* and the normal run of natural history programmes. We would have no commentary. Instead, Mike's camerawork for the four programmes covering the spring, summer, autumn and winter seasons were accompanied by specially commissioned music written by four leading contemporary Scottish composers – Sally Beamish, Eddie Maguire, Alasdair Nicolson and Bill Sweeney. Add the talents of BBC music producer Martin Dalby and music performed by the Chamber Group of Scotland and we felt certain that we had produced a short series that would stand comparison anywhere in the television industry.

All of us were quietly pleased that *The Loch* was nominated for outstanding achievement as the Best Special Interest Programme in the BAFTA Scotland Awards for 1995. It didn't win. Damn.

Still, it was a start and Colin Cameron and I were sufficiently buoyed up by the success of our first tentative steps into natural history that we felt we should try and build on what had been achieved with *The Loch*.

As a result, Sally-Ann Wilson was appointed to produce a new series of natural history programmes under the umbrella title of Operation Survival. Sally had a passion for nature. Born in rural East Sussex, she got a degree in ecology and a Masters in anthropology from the University of East Anglia and had worked in many parts of the world for the BBC Natural History Unit.

The series was a success and embraced three compelling stories – Local Heroes on the life of the Bottlenose Dolphins of the Moray Firth; the Call of Coll on the fight to increase the shrinking population of corncrakes on the west coast island; and Back to a Future on the successful work over many years to reintroduce the magnificent White-Tailed Sea Eagle to Scotland.

There were some magnificent shots of the sea eagle catching fish but on this occasion we didn't call on Matt Leiper and his scuba gear. He would probably have wanted a greater reward than a fish supper the second time around. In any event he was probably otherwise occupied filming in Baghdad.

Eastern Approaches

Eastern Europe had always held a fascination for me – a fascination that had grown from the seed corn of cloak and dagger films of my boyhood and no doubt reinforced by my brief visit to Czechoslovakia in 1968 shortly after the Russian invasion.

After all, these were the countries behind the Iron Curtain that for a generation had represented the stultifying hand of communism – of individualism suppressed and freedoms denied.

Eastern Europe represented too an echo for my generation of the hapless reference made a generation earlier by Neville Chamberlain when he talked of *faraway countries of which we know little.*

Certainly I knew little about Eastern Europe but was keen to learn more and if the opportunity ever came to visit any eastern bloc nations with a BBC team I was ready to grasp the chance.

In 1987 I got my wish. Thanks to a contact in an international animal medicine company who dealt in Eastern Europe I was able to go to Hungary and was granted permission to film on some the giant state farms that had grown up since the Second World War, the product of the Russian philosophy of collectivisation.

Part of my reason for wishing to go was to try and look ahead to what it might mean for we in the west if the dead hand of state control was removed from the east and a resulting free market economy could unlock the vast untapped potential of the great productive land masses that lay behind the Iron Curtain in nations like Hungary, Poland and East Germany.

Like other countries in the eastern bloc, a large proportion of Hungary's workforce were on farms – nearly 20 per cent – split between 1300 co-operative units and 120 state farms each occupying several thousand hectares. There were also one and a half million small farms.

In our film *Land of the Magyars* we looked at the prospect of increased trade links between Hungary and what was then the Common Market. We captured on film the vast herds of beef and dairy cattle, goose production, fish farms and meat processing. One of the abiding memories the *Landward* team shared was that while we had never witnessed such vast herds of beef cattle during our working day, in the evenings we never tasted beef. Beef was never on the menu. Instead we dined well on pork every night but during the working day we never saw a pig.

Hungarians love their horses and Hungary is one of the most respected horse-breeding nations in the world. Part of our filming was in and around the vast Babolna State Farm that had been the headquarters since 1922 of the Royal Hungarian Babolna Stud. Communism may well have seen the royal connections officially abandoned but Babolna was still the nation's top stud with dozens of Arab stallions filling the historic old stables and remained the nation's centre for breeding full and half-blooded Arabian horses and Lipizzaners.

It therefore seemed fitting that on our last day's filming, Ross Muir the programme presenter should introduce the film from a stagecoach pulled by six magnificent white Arab horses beside the majestic dancing fountains in front of the 15th century Manor House of Babolna.

It seemed less than fitting later than night, however, when we attended an impromptu disco in a restaurant beside the Babolna stud. For a weary producer with another programme in the can it seemed perfectly natural to sit with a relaxing glass of sweet Tokaji wine and admire the energy of the dancers in front of me. It seemed less than natural to turn the other way and be eyeball to eyeball with an Arab stallion. The disco was part of the stables.

We also filmed in the Hortobágy National Park, part of the great Hungarian plain, or Puszta, where the nation's equestrian traditions are best preserved. This is a vast flat land with echoes of the American west. If you have a hunger for the empty places of the world, go to the puszta. Here you will see the traditional Hungarian grey cattle, ancient racka sheep with strange spiral horns and flocks of cranes beside the river Tisza.

It's on the puzta too that you will find the csikós, the Hungarian cowboys who have an unrivalled prowess on the back of a horse.

The horsemen ride with a girthless saddle, called a patrac, which is a felt or leather pad with rings to hold the stirrup leathers. The csikós gallop at full speed, cutting in and out among the herd. They can also mount from the ground by holding the pommel, putting the left foot in the stirrup and swing up. Impressive stuff – and it made for wonderful television.

I had no doubt about the supreme horsemanship of the csikós and before we left the Hortobagy I asked them if they would do one more thing for BBC Scotland.

They felt sure they could.

All right, I ventured, if our cameraman Ken Gow, sound man Jim Patchett and I crouched down in one fixed spot to get a low level shot, could the csikós drive as many horses as possible straight towards us – and hopefully the herd would see us and part left and right leaving us without the imprint of a hundred hooves on the camera - or us.

Ken seemed happy with the idea. He loved horses. Jim seemed happy. He loved a challenge.

No problem the csikós said. *Get ready.*

What followed was like a scene from a Hollywood Western – only our budget was a little smaller. The csikós gathered together forty or fifty horses and then galloped them directly towards us from a distance of one hundred yards. I crouched beside Ken who was busy capturing the moment. I hoped it wouldn't be his last moment – or mine. It was a stirring and alarming sight – the thunder of a herd of horses coming straight for us at full gallop with no place to run to.

I needn't have worried. At the last moment the herd broke into two and swept past us to left and right leaving with us only the swirling dust in our hair and nostrils.

Another memorable television sequence was in the can but in the same way that I would now hesitate before having a presenter thrown into the open sea as in our John Ridgway film, I would not ask a cameraman or sound recordist to tackle such a sequence like we recorded on the Hungarian puzta. In today's sensitive environment the mere idea would make a health and safety officer's hair turn white overnight.

It is appropriate here to make special mention of my high regard for the work of Jim Patchett – ever the enthusiast wanting to scale the mast of John Ridgway's yacht all those years before or help record the galloping horses on the Hungarian puzta or work tirelessly in the baking heat of Papua New Guinea. In due course he was to become a cameraman in his own right and ended his career as a dedicated and respected news cameraman. Having taken early retirement because of a shoulder injury he developed pancreatic cancer and died at the age of 60 just two years after laying down his BBC camera. Jim was one of those remarkable people that you occasionally meet on this short walk through life – never complaining, always enthusiastic and someone who always gave more than 100 per cent in the interests of the programme and the BBC. Those of us who were privileged to work with him were enriched by the experience.

Travelling around Hungary was in itself a memorable experience – for all the wrong reasons. Our guide, interpreter and fixer was a decent chap but like tens of thousands of Eastern Europeans he didn't boast the latest in motor cars. He drove a "Trabbie". This was the affectionate name given to the Trabant, a noisy and smelly car with a two cylinder two-stroke engine that had only five moving parts – it was often reckoned to have more in common with a lawnmower than a motor car. There were no disc brakes, no radiator, no oil filter or oil pump and no fuel guage. The petrol flow was powered by gravity so there was no need for a fuel pump. Wheezing, sputtering and belching clouds of oily blue smoke, it could accelerate from zero to 62 mph in 21 seconds. The engine was small and light and could be lifted from the car by one person. Developed by engineer Werner Lang, production of the Trabant began in 1957 in the Saxony factory that had once built Audis before the post-war separation of East and West Germany. Because of the shortage of steel the car's body was made from a plastic material similar to fibreglass that in reality was a type of plastic containing resin strengthened by wool or cotton.

Inside the "Trabbie" the noise of the two-stroke engine meant it was virtually impossible to carry on a normal conversation. Despite its shortcoming, the Trabant became much sought after in Eastern Europe and buying one involved joining a waiting list that could last up to 18 years. Production of the Trabant ended with German reunification in 1991. Because of the challenge of this mode of transport we managed to lock two jokes about the "Trabbie" into our consciousness.

Why do all Trabbie drivers go to heaven?
Because they've already experienced hell on earth.

And:

What do you need to measure the acceleration of a Trabbie?
A calendar.

The two films we made in Hungary had gone well but I was destined to leave Budapest with a further entry in my diary.

On our first night in the Hungarian capital we had stayed in a smart city centre hotel that boasted a swimming pool and gymnasium area. Returning my towel to the swimming pool attendant on that first night she asked if I wanted to book a massage during my stay at the hotel. I have to point out at this stage that the receptionist was a strikingly beautiful girl with long legs and whose heavily accented dusky English accent offered a further *je ne sais quoi*. I explained that we were leaving in the morning but would be back in five days and most certainly, a massage might be the very thing I needed after a week's hard work filming in the Hungarian countryside. I'm sure she didn't understand a word I said – but she booked me in.

On our last night in Budapest I turned up at the appointed time for my massage and the beautiful receptionist was on duty – as I had hoped she would be. She smiled and pointed to one of the massage cubicles where I was told to strip to my swimming trunks and wait. I keenly did as I was asked.

I was lying face down on the cubicle bed imagining the soft hands and long fingers that would soon be kneading my shoulders and driving out the tension of the working week when the door burst open and a harsh voice addressed me in Hungarian.

I whirled round. Instead of my expected long-legged lovely, there stood the reincarnation of Tamara Press, the Ukrainian field athlete who won many gold medals in the 1960s as a result, it was alleged, of having taken male hormones – there were even some suggestions that she might even have *been* male.

To suggest that this colossus looked more like a refugee from the sharp end of an eastern European steel-making plant would not have done justice to the creation before me. She was less than five foot tall – and possibly more than five foot wide. I tried to engage her in conversation and suggest there had been a great mistake but she would have none of that. With one mighty tree trunk of an arm she forced my shoulders down onto the bed and proceeded to subject me to an agonising fifteen minutes of mindless brutality.

As she worked on my shoulders I looked down and saw her white footwear. Was that the point of a dagger protruding from one of her shoes? I had always wondered what happened to Rosa Klebb after her appearance in *From Russia With Love*.

When I met the rest of the *Landward* team in the hotel bar later they were keen to know what my massage had been like. I didn't answer – I just sipped my gin and tonic and looked out over the River Danube. After all, I was still a man in great pain.

In 1990 we continued the eastern European theme – with a difference. We brought Poland to Scotland. Mikhail Gorbachev, the Soviet President, had been awarded the Nobel Peace Prize for his work in defusing East-West tensions and his policy for economic and social reform proved a heady cocktail for the millions who had lived under Soviet control since the end of the Second World War.

Glasnost (openness) and perestroika (restructuring) were in the air and I made arrangements to bring four Polish farmers to the Royal Highland Show at Edinburgh to film them at our main national farming event as well as on local farms so that they could sample at first hand something of the western agricultural economy. The quid pro quo was that later that summer the *Landward* team would go to Poland and film them on their own farms and thus compare and contrast the two economic philosophies.

It worked well. Our new-found Polish farming friends made for compulsive viewing as we filmed them seeing part of our western world for the first time and we parted looking forward to our next meeting three months later in Poland.

I knew that our filming with our Polish farming friends would be of interest to our regular viewers but I had another motive in wishing to film in Poland. During my research and setting up the Polish visit to Scotland I had stumbled on a little bit of history I never knew existed – the fact that thousands of Scots had emi-grated to Poland between the fifteenth and seventeenth centuries to be followed by hundreds more in the nineteenth who helped build and maintain some of the great farming estates.

One of the Polish landowners who "imported" many Scots rural artisans was Count Ludwik Pac who had inherited the Dowspuda Estate near the north-east Polish town of Suvalki near the border with Lithuania and Belorussia. Count Pac had been a general in Napoleon's army and later made a visit to Scotland in 1814. At that time Britain was in the forefront of farming development and there was much to be seen and admired for the ambitious Count Pac to embrace and adopt for his own estate.

I felt if we could find some evidence of the Scottish heritage it would make for a memorable programme. So after a few days filming with our Polish farmers that had earlier visited Scotland we set off on the long drive north to Suvalki to see if we could uncover any trace of the Scots who set up home in the area one hundred and fifty years before.

I was confident that we might. I had a good team – the ever-green Ross Muir was the presenter-reporter and my Production Assistant was Maggie Mutch who had recently joined the *Landward* department. Ross and I had known Maggie for years – she had first worked with the BBC in Aberdeen shortly after leaving school but left after a few years to run the pub in her local village. Now married to Ken Mutch a former freelance sound recordist and later a BBC radio music producer, she had decided that in the long term a career in the BBC was a better bet than pulling pints for a living. She was to prove a splendid choice as PA for this and many programmes to come – hard-working, loyal and full of energy and enthusiasm.

The sound recordist was Wiesiek Znyk, a Warsaw-based freelance and the cameraman was Janusz Ostrowski. I had worked with Janusz, or Jan as he preferred to be called, only a couple of times before when I discovered he was a freelance based in Northumberland but was of Polish extraction and could speak a little Polish. The fact that he was a first-class hard-working cameraman also helped.

We found Suvalki and the Dowspuda Estate, now something of a shrine in the area. We also found two small rooms along a narrow street that contained the Suvalki archives. The door was unlocked and a large bound ledger produced. The archivist gently laid the large tome on a small table and invited us to inspect the contents. There, in fine copperplate, written by John Lowman, the Count's Scottish Secretary and dating from July 1817 were the names, ages and contract details of all the rural craftsmen that Count Pac had brought from Scotland to his Dowspuda Estate. The contracts included guaranteed benefits for work well done, like wagonloads of wood, but also stipulated that none of the Scots could set up a brewery or distillery on the estate.

A few miles away we also found the tiny village of Szkocja – Scotland in Polish – where several of the families had lived. We had been told that poverty and disease had wiped out most of the Scottish families over the years, a fact reinforced by a small monument outside the village that read: *Protect us from hunger, epidemics and war. Provide us with quiet times.* The Scots lie under a canopy of Scots pines in a nearby Protestant cemetery.

But there was one Scot left – his ancestors had the surname of Burns and they called their small farm Berwick. Over the years the family name had been transformed from Burns to Boerma.

Through an interpreter he told us of how things were better now than before. He was now in his 70s and had been a boy during the Second World War. He had no love for the Germans when they occupied Poland, he said, but they were not as bad as the Soviets who would demand food and livestock and pay very little for it.

When our filming on his small patch of land was finished, Mr Boerma invited us into his home. Like everywhere in the world, it is the poorest people who are the most hospitable and the Boermas were no exception. They invited us to sit around their tiny kitchen table while a meal was prepared. Vodka too was produced.

I was sitting beside a broken window. Within a short time I had become aware of a pungent odour coming through the window from outside. It didn't take me long to work out what it was – the family cesspit was placed just below the broken window and it was overflowing.

We were all aware of the stench but Maggie Mutch was the first to react. She leaned towards me and whispered that she had to leave to go outside for a cigarette.

Within seconds of Maggie leaving the kitchen to seek clean air wherever she might find it, Mrs Boerma entered with our meal - pork knuckle swimming in a vast pool of rapidly congealing fat. Somewhere in there I suppose there must have been meat but all I was conscious of was my gorge rising. The smell of the pork did not mix with the stench from the cesspit on the other side of the broken window. Excusing myself, I rose and left the kitchen before I made a public spectacle of myself. I found Maggie in the car, smoking. Without ceremony I grabbed her packet of cigarettes and lit one, inhaling deeply. It was my first cigarette for twenty years.

On my return to the kitchen, Wiesiek Znyk the sound recordist looked at me then looked at his watch. He did not speak much English.

Artoor? More work?

No, we have finished for today.

OK Artoor – ees time for you?

He pushed the Boermas' carafe of home made vodka across the table towards me. As I could still smell the cesspit mingling with the pork knuckle, I thought it advisable to pour myself a large one - for medicinal purposes only of course.

Two years later we went further east – to Russia. The year before we had made a programme in Scotland following a group of young Russian farmers who were spending some weeks on Scottish farms. That was August 1991 when President Gorbachev was briefly overthrown in a coup led by hardliners fearing the break-up of the Soviet Union. Thanks partly to the rallying call of Boris Yeltsin climbing defiantly on a tank as the Red Army surrounded the White House, the headquarters of the Supreme Soviet, the coup collapsed after several days enabling Gorbachev to return from brief exile in the Crimea.

We filmed the young Russians in Scotland, inter-cutting their work on farms with them watching the unfolding BBC News as they anxiously awaited political developments in their homeland. It made for riveting television.

Would it make equally good television, I wondered, if we were to travel to Russia the following year and film the young Russian farmers trying to put into practice something of what they had learned from their Scottish hosts. As the huge Russian collective farms were being broken up in the drive towards a more market-driven economy would the Scottish experience stand them in good stead and help them build a more certain future. We resolved to find out.

And so it was in April 1992 I found myself in Moscow on a recce. People with a military background will always tell you that time spent on reconnaissance is never wasted. That is also true for television production. Most decently financed television programmes will always build in time for a recce. Sadly, we normally never had the time – producing twenty-six programmes a year with a team of three meant we had to do most of our setting up and research on the hoof. Usually the closest we came to a "recce" was a long telephone call.

Be that as it may, I was able to get a cheap flight to Moscow because I had found it impossible to talk to the people I needed to talk to by telephone. The old communist regime might be crumbling but I wasn't prepared to go to Russia with my team without having a clear idea in advance of how we would travel and where we could film.

Once in Moscow I met my Russian fixer – a middle-aged, friendly factotum from the Foreign Office who dealt with visiting television producers. We sat down for a couple of hours and I outlined my hopes and ambitions as he nodded and took copious notes. No problem, he said. All this can be fixed. All I needed to do was to pay him - in cash – when I returned with the *Landward* team. One more thing, he said – the money had to be in US dollars - $4000 to be precise. He assured me the money would cover all my team's food, accommodation and transport while we filmed in Russia. It seemed reasonable. We shook hands.

As usual when overseas, as a courtesy I let my presence be known in the local BBC office, if there was one. In 1992 the two principal BBC correspondents in Moscow were Ben Brown and Angus Roxburgh. They were friendly and supportive when I revealed my programme-making ambitions but underlined the vast geographical compass that made up the Russian Federation and advised me that I couldn't expect to reproduce in one day in Russia what I might expect to at home. How right that was to prove when I returned to Russia with my team some weeks later.

Some snapshots of life stay locked in the mind forever. Before leaving Moscow after my brief two-day visit, I bought a ticket for a violin recital on March 5th at the Small Hall of the Moscow Conservatory. From memory the ticket cost the equivalent of 20p.

The recital, by an Israeli violinist, was due to begin around 5.30pm. I took my seat in plenty of time and watched as the auditorium gradually filled to capacity with one significant difference from any concert in the UK. A large proportion of the ticket holders were manual labourers – men and women – who were taking in a little classical music en route between work and home. Some were dressed in boiler suits, others in sweat shirts and old trousers. Most wore working boots.

The recital lasted a little more than one hour. The violinist gave a virtuoso performance and the Russian workers cheered him to the echo. As he took his final bows, a little girl about four years old sitting in front of me with her mother and father took a large bouquet of flowers up to the stage to present to the violinist. But the stage was taller than she was and the violinist could not see her. He walked to the right and took another bow and she walked to the right but still she could not attract her attention. There was same fruitless result when he took a bow to the left. The girl, now in tears, returned to her seat with the flowers.

But all was not lost. An adult rose from the front and approached the violinist, whispered in his ear and pointed to where the little girl was sitting. The violinist beckoned her to come forward. This time he came to the front of the stage and bent down and she was able to deliver her flowers into his welcoming hands. The thunderous applause the girl received will live long in the memory. This time she returned to her seat with a broad smile.

Within a few weeks I was back in Moscow, this time with presenter Ross Muir, cameraman Ken Gow, sound recordist Colin Maclure and production assistant Maggie Mutch. Getting into Moscow as a BBC crew, however, was to prove very different than arriving alone.

Despite the Russian Embassy in London having received all the proper paperwork well in advance for the issue of visas, the appropriate documentation arrived only one day before our flight – and wrongly dated. We flew anyway only to find our onward passage into Moscow barred by officialdom at Sheremetyevo Airport. All our BBC equipment was confiscated while our visas were revised. Within two hours – and at a cost of around £30 each – we received our updated visas. Could I have a receipt, I asked. Sorry - no receipt possible. Ah well, I had to hope the BBC accountants would trust my expenses claim.

But of the BBC equipment there was no sign. That was still impounded. Only day one and my blood pressure count was steadily rising. We went into Moscow, checked into our hotel and had a meal while the fixer and a colleague made various phone calls. Eventually, around 5am, Ken Gow and the fixer went to the airport by taxi and were able to collect the gear. I had earlier given the fixer a few hundred dollars to help oil the wheels should it prove necessary so to do. That was the last I saw of it. Truly this was a nation that believed corruption was a rite of passage to capitalism.

I had earlier given the agreed $4000 dollars to our fixer and was assured that all the facilities we wanted for our filming over the next ten days had been laid on. After the debacle at the airport, I sincerely hoped so.

In truth, our filming began well enough – a news story on the signing of a trade deal between Russian and Scottish grain merchants. We then decamped to the main railway station for a 36-hour journey to Nalchik, the capital of the Kabardino-Balkarian Republic in the foothills of the Caucasus between the Black Sea and the Caspian Sea.

There's a strange notion in the west that travelling on a long-distance Russian train is somehow glamorous. Don't believe a word of it. It's purgatory in motion. Slow motion.

Naively, I had expected that we would fly to Nalchik from Moscow. The train journey was tedious and while it's said that no experience in life is ever wasted I considered that our time on the train from Moscow to Nalchik was indeed wasted time.

The main purpose of being in Nalchik was to visit a young man called Anzor Dikinov, a local young farmer who had earlier spent some time working on a farm in Aberdeenshire. He could speak English, was personable and had a clear commitment to follow in the footsteps of his grandfather – his father had become a university professor – as a farmer. Only for Anzor it would be different. He did not want to be part of the traditional collective farm. He wanted to make his own mark as a private farmer and had been given a credit of five million roubles – then about £10,000 – to set up a beef, sheep and cashmere goat production enterprise outside Nalchik. It was to be the first of its kind in Russia.

On our first day in Nalchik we filmed with Anzor and captured on tape the house he was building as he proudly walked around the construction site with Ross Muir. We then filmed on pastureland that he had carved out from the collective and on which he was building his hopes and dreams for a farming future.

The bonus for us with Anzor was that until he purchased cattle and sheep and cashmere goats, his daily commitment was on hold even though his dreams were very much alive. Because of that we made him an offer he couldn't refuse – he agreed to accompany us for the rest of our filming trip to act as guide, adviser and interpreter.

We were all delighted. He was a fine young man and a good companion and he could offer a guiding light for the rest of our filming schedule. I began to relax a little – well, at least for a few hours.

The following day Anzor arranged that we visit the home in the centre of Nalchik of the local Communist Party boss to talk about the move from collectivisation to privatisation.

On schedule we arrived at a large house within a compound in the outskirts of the city. As we were led through the compound to the Communist Party boss's home we passed a group of men using a blowtorch to burn off the skin on the face of a large dead ram lying on the dusty ground.

I made some quiet comment to the *Landward* team that I hoped the ram's head wasn't destined to be offered to us as some kind of local delicacy. I had eaten some strange things over the years but had never had a sheep's eye and didn't want to start now.

We were ushered into the home of the party boss to see a great spread of food and drink laid before us – it was to be the first of many over the next ten days. After the many expected speeches and vodka toasts even at that very early hour we then left to start filming agricultural activity on the collective farm outside Nalchik. I quite forgot about the ram's head.

At the end of our filming that day we were invited to join our hosts for a small barbecue in a birch wood near the collective farm. It had been a long and tiring day and we accepted gratefully. Darkness was falling and although we could scarcely see what we were eating it tasted reasonable and anyway, what were the bottles of beer for if not to wash down food morsels of doubtful origin.

Towards the end of our meal in the birch woods we saw headlights approaching and soon three cars drew to a halt within a few yards of where we sat. A group of about ten men got out of the vehicles, opened the boot of one of the cars and walked towards us bearing a large salver covered with a white cloth. The salver was placed in front of me and with a flourish the white cloth was pulled off. Despite the fading light there was no mistaking what was there in front of me – the ram's head that I had earlier seen being prepared that morning. Not only that, but both eyes were looking right at me.

Before I could say anything, our mysterious nocturnal visitors leapt upon the ram's head and began cutting and slicing and generally tearing it apart and dividing the spoils into portions that they then offered to the company. I was terrified I would be offered the eyes. Instead, I was offered what was reckoned to be the most important part of the sheep – the nose. Suddenly I wasn't hungry any more. I pretended to nibble the nose but with the barbecue area now almost in complete darkness I reckoned I could get away by shoving the nose round the plate and leaving it untouched and untasted.

The meal ended. We said goodbye and drove into the night back to Nalchik. We were staying in rooms at the Communist Party headquarters that were basic but reasonable. It was 1am and the *Landward* team was enjoying a beer in my room when we became aware of the sound of car horns and headlights sweeping into the accommodation block compound. Car doors were slammed and the sound of feet came thundering up the stairs towards us. We looked at each other anxiously.

The door of my room burst open and a small group of Russians entered.

Their spokesman stood in the centre of the room holding a plate. On the plate was the sheep's nose.

Artoor – you forgot your nose!

I promised I would eat it and laid it gently on the small bedside cabinet as the group proceeded to consume the few cans of beer we had left. However, they had another purpose of coming to find us in Nalchik. As they drank our beer they opened a bag and produced two beautiful drinking vessels made from silver and horn which they presented to Ross Muir and me as a gesture for showing a little bit of their lives on the BBC. Naturally, that was an excuse for many speeches and toasts. After all, what else was there to do at that time of the morning in Nalchik.

I awoke the next morning in Nalchik, minus a few hours sleep and a few more brain cells as a result of the late night beers.

Slowly I began to focus on the world and the object on the bedside cabinet. It was the sheep's nose. For the record, I did not eat it for breakfast. That day we left Nalchik and the sheep's nose stayed. However, that silver drinking vessel has had pride of place in my home for many years and I treasure it.

We then embarked on the second stage of our trek across Russia. Once again I had hoped we would fly to save time and increase the opportunities for productive filming. Once again my hopes were dashed when our fixer arranged seats on a train from Nalchik to Ufa, a city on the edge of the Ural Mountains.

We were on our way to Bashkortostan, an oil-rich republic to see a young farmer who had recently also spent time in Scotland. Only this was to be no 36-hour train journey like our first leg from Moscow to Nalchik. This time we were due to be incarcerated for 54 hours.

Robert Louis Stevenson said to travel hopefully is a better thing than to arrive. Don't believe a word of it. He would never have written those words if he had ever been on a Russian train.

So began the longest two days of my life. It was to seem like a week. There were five of us in the BBC team but the sleeping quarters could only hold four.

By some strange logistical juggling – and I didn't take it too personally – Ken Gow, Colin Maclure, Ross Muir and Maggie Mutch were granted one sleeping compartment while I was in another. I didn't particularly mind being separated from my colleagues – in any event we didn't normally sleep together. What I did mind was sharing my sleeping quarters with three babushkas, the diminutive term for grandmothers or old women.

There were three of them, a formidable bunch who spent all day talking with, I suspected, occasional strange references to the strange Scotsman in the top berth. At night – all night - they snored like a perfectly rehearsed choir from hell itself.

The three babushkas had one saving grace. They fed me. There are two facts to take on board here. One, Russian trains do not travel quickly and they stop at frequent intervals at stations in small towns and villages. Two, dining cars on Russian trains should be avoided at all costs. Traditionally therefore, passengers on Russian trains eschew the dining car in favour of buying fresh produce from the vendors who set up stalls on stations along the route.

My three travelling babushka companions were street wise – or rail wise. They would quickly get off at most stops and purchase fruit or vegetables. Then, having divided most of the spoils between themselves they would chatter among themselves then hand me on the top berth slices of apple, carrot or tomato. It wasn't the Ritz but I guessed I would survive.

As to filming on the train, forget it. First, our resident fixer said it would not be allowed. Second, we quickly realised if it had been permitted we would not have had much to sink our teeth into. Any thoughts I might have entertained about asking Ken Gow to stick the camera out of the train window and capture great vistas of the Russian hinterland with life along the route were quickly dashed. To prevent snowdrifts sweeping over the track during the winter, the Russians had planted dense avenues of birch trees on either side of the track for hundreds of miles. We may have been travelling across Russia but we saw precious little of it.

We were able to pick up one or two short sequences like pieces to camera by Ross on bustling platforms as the passengers scrambled to replenish their supplies of fruit and vegetables. Ken Gow, a splendid cameraman, could always get the best out of any given situation and he did a masterful job in capturing the atmosphere during these brief halts. Only once did I think he had been a little too enthusiastic – he was still filming from the platform as the train began moving. The last thing I wanted was to leave our cameraman behind. I leaned out of the carriage to tell him to jump aboard only to discover that Ken was filming in my direction. The edited film includes a brief glimpse of a balding producer anxiously seeking a lost cameraman. After all, if Alfred Hitchcock managed a walk-on part in his movies, why couldn't I?

Inside the train we could do precious little other than record one sequence with Ross taking advantage of the great stand-by of Russian train travel – the samovar.

But a short sequence of our presenter making a cup of tea wasn't going to amount to more than a few seconds of our finished film and the enforced idleness as the train slowly trundled towards the north-east didn't help my mood. Had we flown instead, I reasoned, we would have managed two or three days more of productive filming. I made a mental note – maybe next time. Immediately I made a second mental note – don't let there be a next time.

The monotony was broken by two alarming episodes. First, Ross and Ken discovered that some of their valuables had been stolen from their compartment while they had been elsewhere in the train. The valuables included the horn and silver drinking vessel that Ross had been presented with in Nalchik.

Ross and Ken reasoned that the theft had taken place since the train's last stop. Therefore their property must still be on the train. We found what we took to be the train's senior guard and raised merry hell - and our voices. He promised he would look into the matter.

Within the hour the property was restored to Ross and Ken. They had been "found" under the floor of the train near a small room used by one of the attendants responsible for our carriage. We had come to know her well. She was an ageing woman with a ready laugh that revealed a mouthful of gold fillings in her teeth when she spoke to us even though we hadn't a clue what she was saying. After the theft, however, we ensured that someone was always in the compartment. The attendant knew that and her demeanour changed. She didn't laugh any more so we never caught another glimpse of those gold fillings.

The second episode happened shortly after the recovery of the stolen property. To lose some of your belongings was bad enough. To lose your Production Assistant was far worse. I lost Maggie Mutch.

Maggie was as bored as the rest of us by the tedium of the seemingly never-ending rail journey. But, being of lively mind and friendly disposition, she passed the time by making friends with anyone who crossed her path and she could usually be found trying to converse with some of her Russian travelling companions.

Somewhere south of Volgograd when the train had stopped at a station I needed to talk to her about work but she wasn't in her compartment. Russians trains are long and the carriages are many. I walked through them all one way and back again. There was no sign of Maggie.

I jumped from the train onto the platform. There was still no sign of her. The guard's whistle sounded. The train was about to move. I felt a mounting sense of panic. In moments like these dark thoughts can run through a man's mind. They certainly ran through mine. Not only was I going to have to explain to the BBC that I had lost an important member of the team, I was also going to have to explain to my old colleague Ken Mutch that I had lost his wife somewhere in eastern Europe. Neither prospect was appealing.

Standing on the platform feeling helpless I noticed the public toilets some yards away – a grey concrete structure through which there was a constant flow of people, men and women. I walked to the entrance and peered into the dark and uninviting interior. I called Maggie's name.

Answer came there none. The only response was some dark looks and untranslatable insults from the users of the toilet.

The guard's whistle sounded again. The train began to move. I jumped aboard and once more began the long trek up and down through the carriages as the train picked up pace. I was close to desperation.

Then I found her, engrossed in conversation with a Russian woman who had befriended her. The Russian woman spoke a little English and was well dressed and friendly. She also had a bottle of vodka in her handbag. When I found them, Maggie and her pal were drinking the latest of what had clearly been many toasts to international sisterhood.

How I had missed her on my first trawl through the train I don't know – maybe she had been in the toilet when I passed. That didn't matter. She was aboard the train and safe.

Maggie introduced me to her new friend, a citizen of Volgograd, where the train would be stopping shortly. As the train would be at the platform for about an hour, the Russian woman offered to take Maggie on a brief tour of the city then return her to the station before the train left for the next leg of its journey.

Maggie thought it was a fine idea. I didn't. I told her it simply wasn't an option and I would get the rest of the team to tie her to her seat if she so much as thought of disappearing into Volgograd. Reluctantly, she promised to stay aboard.

The first sight of Volgograd stays forever in the mind. Dominating the city is the Motherland Statue. More than 250 feet tall, the giant sword-wielding memorial is twice the height of New York's Statue of Liberty. Looking out over the River Volga, the Motherland Statue commemorates the longest battle in military history when over six months of the winter of 1942-43, three quarters of a million Russians and Germans perished in the fight to control the city before the Russians finally prevailed and turned the tide of the Second World War in Europe.

Seeing it, it's hard not to feel the weight of history and I had no wish for any additional historical footnotes with the disappearance of a BBC production assistant. Maggie stayed on the train.

Somewhere towards midnight the train drew to a halt at a lonely station and we alighted. Our rail marathon was at an end. After 54 hours on the train we were exhausted and all we sought was a long sleep. It was not to come. Any relief we felt at having ended the misery of travel tedium, poor food and filthy toilets was soon shoved to the back of our minds when we met our Russian farming hosts. They were stoned out of their mind – all apart from one of their number, a bright and personable woman professor who was to spend a couple of days with us doubling up as interpreter with Anzor Dikinov.

We loaded our gear into a minibus and headed into the night. Every moment I hoped our hotel would appear. It didn't. The least drunk of our male hosts drove for an hour through the pitch-black countryside until eventually we came to a Scandinavian type chalet.

Inside a large table had been laid out with enough food to satisfy an army. There were also glasses and bottles of vodka. We had need of neither. It was well after midnight and all we wanted was to collapse into bed.

Our hosts didn't give us the chance. They insisted we begin with a sauna and then join them at the table. From time to time there's a temptation to ignore tact and diplomacy and ride rough-shod over what seems courteous. We wanted to but we were too tired even for that. We had a sauna and ate our meal.

Sometime around 3am we managed to extricate ourselves from the table. Our Russian hosts were now even more drunk and had even stopped trying to talk to us through the interpreters. Instead they talked and drank among themselves. Bed and sleep was the only option.

I don't suppose I had been asleep for more than an hour or so when I sat bolt upright. I thought I had heard a scream in the night. I listened. Then it came again, a loud high-pitched scream followed by a woman cursing in Russian and the sound of a door banging followed by heavy footsteps disappearing down a corridor.

I rose to investigate. While the male members of our team had been allocated a room each, Maggie Mutch was sharing a room with the woman professor. It seems that one of the drunk Russians had entered the girls' room and woken the professor who angrily had sent him packing.

Who knows what might have transpired had the two women been sleeping separately. In the event, all was well but it had been a frightening experience. I went back to bed and slept only fitfully. Once again my imagination began to work overtime. Maybe Maggie would have been safer in Volgograd after all.

The next day, still exhausted by travel and tension, we met the second subject who would be part of our film. He was Ravil Khamedulin, a fine young man who had spent time on a Scottish farm near Inverness. When he had completed his stint on the farm in Scotland, his generous host had bought him a second-hand Lada as a gift and Ravil had spent ten days driving from Scotland to his Russian home. Now his plan was to start a dairy herd and join the 300 other private farmers in the area who had each been given a section of land on what had previously been a huge collective farm.

With no more setbacks, within a couple of days we had fin-ished our filming and were due to fly to Moscow from the city of

Ufa, a distance of around a thousand miles. My Moscow fixer had delegated a local political colleague to ensure we caught our flight. I was grateful for that. I felt I could handle anything but another Russian train journey.

We were taken out onto the tarmac with all our BBC gear where our Aeroflot jet was waiting. There was a hurried discussion between our local fixer and the cabin crew. It seemed the aircraft was already full but if we didn't mind waiting for a few minutes the problem would be solved. We waited. Within five minutes half a dozen passengers disembarked, glowering at us. I don't know who our local fixer was but clearly he had some clout.

We took our seats near the front of the plane and settled down for the flight but not before baggage handlers carried our suitcases and BBC boxes onto the aircraft and stowed them beside us – totally blocking one of the emergency exit doors. Still, as long as the plane didn't crash, who cared where the gear was stacked. And who cared that there were three passengers standing at the back of the still overbooked plane. This was Russia after all – and we were going home.

If filming in Russia had a dampening effect on my enthusiasm, it was further compounded the day before we left Ufa for Moscow. Our translator showed us a local newspaper that a few days before had sent a reporter and photographer to record our visit to a local farm. The report was detailed and accurate and mentioned all my hard-working team until it fell a little short on objectivity – in my opinion – when it mentioned that the team had been led by an *ageing but sprightly Arthur Anderson*. I knew I was ageing but by then I didn't even feel sprightly!

It was to be another six years before I found myself filming once more in Eastern Europe – this time in Poland and Romania in the company of presenter Eric Robson.

By this time Eric, one of the country's most experienced all-round broadcasters, had become one of the mainstays of the *Landward* programme. Chairman of BBC Radio 4's *Gardeners' Question Time* – one of the longest running programmes in the world - he had also, for more than 35 years, been one of the recognisable voices of British broadcasting as commentator on the great events of State like Remembrance Sunday and Trooping the Colour. I had first come across Eric in my early days in BBC local radio in Carlisle. As I was leaping around North Cumbria with quarter inch recording tape hanging round my neck, he was across the road in the comparatively more glamorous role as a reporter with Border Television.

Over the coming years he had presented a raft of programmes for both BBC and ITV and by the time I caught up with him again he was presenting *Farming Outlook* on Tyne Tees Television. Sadly for the rural communities of the north of England, *Farming Outlook* came to an end. When I heard of the programme's imminent demise, I rang Eric. Would he consider working for *Landward*? He would – and did.

While Eric did many fine reports for the rolling *Landward* series, some of the highest profile output came in the form of special documentaries that my small team put together over a period of years. Colin Cameron was still Head of Television and he continued to encourage new thinking and better programmes across the whole range of BBC Scotland's output.

As a result of the support of senior management we came to produce what we called the *Landward Specials* presented and strongly authored by Eric Robson. Each year the "specials" consisted of a series of three programmes looking at a single issue. They included *Whose Land Is It Anyway* which dealt with land ownership in Scotland and the increasing moves towards community possession; *One Man's Meat* on the way ahead for our food and farming industry in the wake of various crises relating to BSE, E-Coli, Salmonella and Listeria; and *Troubled Waters* on the future of our fishing communities which took the team to Spain and Canada as well as our home waters off the Scottish coast.

They were memorable documentaries not least for some of the lasting images they brought in their wake – like filming one of Eric's pieces to camera off the hamlet of Bay Bulls in Newfoundland as whales and icebergs came into view in the grey and fog-laden Atlantic waters behind him. Or spending three days out at sea in a Scottish fishing boat with cameraman Jan Ostrowski and sound recordist Terry Black.

That fishing trip began badly for me – for the first day I was so seasick I could not rise from my bunk and could only lie in abject misery as the redoubtable Jan and Terry got on with the job. I also recall vividly the toilet arrangements on the boat – in truth there were none. You peed over the side and if you wanted to tackle a bodily function of greater ambition you had to carefully weave your way through the roaring engine compartment before carefully – very carefully – crossing the rotating propeller shaft which spun alarmingly fast about four inches below your crotch then open the door of a small cupboard where a tiny loo awaited. Somehow I found that the tension and physical challenge of getting to the damn loo transcended the physical need for wanting to go there in the first place. Next time maybe I would try and hang on till I was back on dry land.

Perhaps the most important of the special documentaries the *Landward* team produced with Eric Robson was *Eastern Approaches* which in 1998 was to take us to many parts of Europe

As Scotland prepared for the challenge of devolution it was inevitable that such an important political development would be seen as a step on the road to independence. There were those who believed that nothing less than complete self-determination and a full expression of national identity would do. But others feared that the liberation of such nationalist sentiments would lead inevitably to the division and xenophobia that stalked many parts of an expanding Europe. Our ambitious aim in making the programmes was to examine the quest for national identity that sprang from the land in Scotland, the Czech Republic, Romania, Germany and Poland.

It was a memorable series to be involved in and filming with pioneering Scots like Aberdeenshire farmer Jack Lind who had taken the lease of a thousand hectares of a former state farm in Poland to grow cereals and seed potatoes and Doug Niven from Berwickshire with his ambitious plans for developing his agricultural enterprise in the Czech Republic a few miles south of Prague.

But as so often it was the stories and images encountered along the way that are likely to stay longest in the memory.

We began our filming in Northern Poland, at Gdansk, at the memorial at Westerplatte at the entrance to the city's port. It was here that the Second World War began when the German cruiser Schleswig-Holstein opened fire on the Polish garrison on September 1st, 1939.

The following day Eric, Jan Ostrowski, Terry Black and I managed to gain access to the town of Borne Sulinowo hidden deep in the pinewoods near the German border. At that time the town was not marked on any map. It once housed 25,000 people but in 1992 it had been deserted overnight when the Russian Red Army left. This was a chilling reminder of the cold war because Borne Sulinowo had been the Russian front line with its nuclear arsenals pointing out over the Baltic to the capital cities of the West. When we filmed, the buildings and the tenement blocks lay empty and exposed – a ghost town serving only to remind us of the deep political divisions that once destroyed the lives of millions.

Although originally part of Poland, the area around Borne Solinowo became German territory in the 18th century and in 1933 the German authorities began the construction of a large military base. Most of the local inhabitants were resettled and their homes levelled to the ground. The new facilities were opened by Adolf Hitler on August 18th, 1938. Soon afterwards the Artillery School of the Wehrmacht moved to Borne Solinowo and during the later stages of World War II an artificial desert was built there for training units of Erwin Rommel's Afrika Korps.

Nazi anti-Semitism was evident from the point that the Germans began construction. Gravestones from local cemeteries were used as paving flags on the site and those with Jewish inscriptions or symbols were laid face up, an expression of contempt by walking on the memory of the Jewish dead.

After the war, Borne Solinowo was taken over by the Red Army where the Soviet military established a huge military camp. The town was excluded from Polish jurisdiction and erased from all maps. In official documents the surrounding land was called forest area and remained a secret for 50 years. Under Russian control, a 20-kilometre exclusion zone was imposed around the town. Anyone trying to leave without permission was shot.

There was emotion too when we filmed with Count Wilhelm von Schwerin in what had been part of East Germany before reunification in 1990. I had known Count Wilhelm slightly for several years because of his long years as head of PR with the John Deere organisation in Europe and his support for the International Federation of Agricultural Journalists where in our more egalitarian age he was known simply as Bill Schwerin.

For more than half a century, the Count's family had been dispossessed when the Nazis commandeered the Schwerin estates of Göhren in Mecklenburg-Strelitz and Sartowitz in then Polish West Prussia. Later, after the war, the land was once again confiscated – this time by the East German Communist Party.

The reason the estates were appropriated by the Nazis was because the Count's father, Ulrich-Wilhelm Graf von Schwerin von Schwanenfeld, had allegedly been part of the plot to assassinate Hitler on July 20th 1944.

Called up as a reserve officer on the outbreak of war he worked on the staff of Field Marshall and Commander in Chief Erwin von Witzleben from 1939, the same year he was to hear of mass shootings of Polish Christians and Jews in a gravel pit on his Polish estate of Sartowitz.

Having earlier witnessed the Hitler putsch in Munich in 1923, Von Schwerin found Nazism loathsome to his Christian social convictions and these convictions must have been recognised at the highest level because in 1942 he was transferred from Paris to Utrecht as "politically unreliable". After a transfer to Berlin in 1943 he became involved in the preparations for the coup against Adolf Hitler as a member of the group led by Colonel Claus von Stauffenberg.

When von Stauffenberg's briefcase bomb failed to kill Hitler on July 20th, 1944, the alleged conspirators, including von Schwerin, were arrested the following day within the Bendler Block, the headquarters of the Army High Command. In a public trial at the Volksgerichtshof, the Nazi Peoples' Court, von Schwerin was sentenced to death on August 21st and later hung with piano wire at the Plötzensee Prison in Berlin on September 8th, 1944.

In a further chilling reminder of the event, I later discovered dramatic archive film of the show trial in Berlin and was able to include it in our BBC programme.

His son, Count Wilhelm von Schwerin, could recall with absolute clarity the day of his father's arrest. He was seven years old and had been out on the family estate shooting. He returned about 7.30 in the evening with two rabbits and his small shotgun over his arm to find a car outside the family mansion. He knew it was unusual because in those days nobody other than the police or the Gestapo had cars. It was the Gestapo. He was told to pack a small case with some clothes. Also arrested were his mother and his two brothers the youngest of whom was only six weeks old. The family nurse told the Gestapo that if the baby was arrested then she would go to prison also. So the Gestapo took her too.

There was a strange twist to the arrest of the von Schwerin family. There was no room in the car for the two eldest brothers so the Gestapo told the boys to buy a rail ticket to a nearby town where they would be met by Gestapo officers and then imprisoned with their mother and baby brother. Wilhelm von Schwerin admitted to us on camera that when he tried to explain over the coming years that he and his brother had bought their own tickets to jail, nobody believed him.

When we filmed with the Count in 1998, it was clear that his bond with the family land was as strong as ever. As he stood with Eric Robson and surveyed the abandoned and ruined buildings that had once been part of a great estate, Count Wilhelm von Schwerin pointed to a family of storks nesting on top of a nearby tall brick chimney. He said that when he was a boy the storks had always nested there but since the family lands had been forfeited the storks had abandoned the chimney for half a century. But now the von Schwerins were home and the storks were too. I hope Bill Schwerin eventually found the peace that had been denied him years earlier.

Romania, too, proved an eye-opening experience. Our programme took us from the grim capital of Bucharest with its industrial pollution and child beggars underlining an endemic poverty to

Brasov, a central city in the Carpathian Mountains where the bullet holes from the unrest in 1987 were still visible in the walls of public buildings and on to Cluj-Napoca in north-west Transylvania.

Romania is a huge country and its agricultural potential is enormous. Yet it was a land of enormous contrasts. At that time Romania had more acres of glasshouses than Holland yet because of a marketing infrastructure that had remained unchanged for generations we learned that more than 80 per cent of all the food produced never travelled further than twenty miles from the point of production, being consumed in local markets. No doubt things will have changed dramatically by today. When we made our programme the driving ambition throughout the nation was to join the EU that everyone saw as a way out of grinding poverty. Economists and farming leaders we spoke to reckoned it would take up to twenty years before the dream would be realised. They were wrong. Romania became a member in 2007 bringing total EU membership to 27 nations embracing half a billion people from the Irish Sea to the Black Sea.

I have two abiding memories of our brief time in Romania. The first was finding, in a poor suburb of Bucharest, the grave of Nicolae Ceausescu, the former Secretary General of the Romania Communist Party. Ceausescu ruled Romania with an iron grip from 1965 until he and his wife, Elena, were captured and shot by a hastily assembled military firing squad on Christmas Day 1989. They had been fleeing the mass protests that marked the fall of communism in the country. When his body was first interred, the grave carried no name and was marked with a rudimentary cross crudely fashioned from a piece of water pipe. Now Romanian communists have added a memorial to a man that some hardliners still regard as a national hero.

My second constant reminder of the country is a painting of a Romanian Orthodox Church in a rural setting. In the foreground of the small white church is a flower meadow and in the background a hint of wooded hills. Overall it conveys an image of rural solitude and peace.

It was one of a group of paintings by a local artist called Chiselita on display on the wall of a small restaurant where the

Landward team had a meal on our last night in Cluj-Napoca. We spoke no Romanian and the waiter in the restaurant had only a rudimentary grasp of English. Somehow, Eric Robson and I conveyed to him our wish to purchase two of the paintings on display. Somehow, too, we managed to persuade the waiter to telephone the painter to discuss a price.

In the end, we left the restaurant with two of the paintings. The price? Let's just say that, on my return to Scotland, having the painting framed cost more than the original purchase price.

Looking back over those years it's interesting to note how the volume of BBC Scotland's programmes on rural matters has altered. I make no observations on quality or expectations on the BBC's production staff but during the years I had Eric Robson as part of the team – and Colin Cameron as an enthusiastic and supportive head of department - the *Landward* department, with a production team never more than three, produced no fewer than seventeen documentaries in addition to the normal yearly 26-part series. To the best of my knowledge that volume of output has never been repeated.

If Eric Robson proved to be the consummate television professional - Jan Ostrowski reckons Eric was able to talk to a camera within hours of his birth - from time to time television production also throws up amateurs whose passion and enthusiasm for their subject makes them compelling viewing. Bob Orskov was such a man.

I had known Dr Bob Orskov slightly for a number of years but well enough to know he was a remarkable man. Then based at the Rowett Research Institute in Aberdeen, Bob had been one of a family of twelve born and brought up on a small dairy farm in Jutland on the west coast of Denmark. Working as a miner to raise funds for his education he had put himself through university. When I met him he was head of the Feed Resources Unit at the Rowett but his work took him all over the world – usually working on contracts for bodies like the Food and Agricultural Organisation of the United Nations.

On one occasion we met by chance and he told me he was going to China within a few months and why didn't I come with him and make a film. He explained that what he was about to start was an ambitious project to try and help five million Chinese farmers build a better future by treating straw with urea to provide nutritional animal feed. As a bonus, food previously fed to animals would thus be diverted into the human food chain. I thought about it and it looked as if the budget might stand it. And so it was that in the summer of 1996 Ken Gow, Colin Maclure and I found ourselves in China.

It was to prove a remarkable experience. Because of Bob's contacts at the highest level we were able to film in many places where it would have been impossible had we been trying to gain access without him. On our last night in Beijing, Ken Gow and I had dinner with Adam Brookes, then the resident BBC correspondent in China and later to become a BBC correspondent in Washington DC. I explained where we had been. He expressed surprise and told us that he doubted if he and the other main media correspondents would have been allowed to travel as freely as we had.

Our visit to China also threw up the occasional bizarre experience. I hadn't realised it but the Chinese, like the Japanese, love karaoke. One evening Ken, Colin, Bob and I were guests of Chinese agricultural officials. We were in a small anteroom beside a large busy restaurant. When our meal was over, our hosts said: *And now we sing.* We looked at each other in puzzlement. The doors opened and two waiters wheeled in a karaoke machine. We were invited to perform. I pleaded temporary insanity and refused but the Chinese grabbed the opportunity eagerly and gave us renditions of a variety of western pop songs – all sung appallingly. At least I knew when not to open my mouth.

The earlier meal had been memorable. Course after course came through the swing doors and placed in front of us. I enjoyed it all – even though the origin of some of the items was perhaps better left undisclosed. There was one dish I questioned – deep-fried scorpions. They sat there in front of us, still perfectly formed with little twin pincers held erect. *Ah*, said our hosts, *you will enjoy them – and it is good for your hair. Please eat two or three.*

I can't remember Bob's reaction but Ken and Colin declined. With rapidly approaching baldness now a fact of my life I felt I had nothing to lose. I ate eight. The following day Ken and Colin said my hair had never looked lovelier.

As we left him at Beijing Airport – Ken, Colin and I on our way home via a little rest and recuperation in Hong Kong, Bob was on his way to Africa on yet another project to help the people of the developing world. He had great plans for future filming for us – in Cuba, Africa and Outer Mongolia. It all sounded very compelling but there are only so many hours in a day.

In the event, our brief visit to Hong Kong on our way home was also to prove a memorable experience. Today visitors to Hong Kong can expect to arrive in comfort at Chek Lap Kok, one of the world's most modern airports. But it was still under construction when the *Landward* team flew in from Beijing. During its lifetime of service between 1925 and 1998, Kai Tak was internationally notorious for being one of the most difficult airports to land at as all flights had to negotiate mountains and city skyscrapers in the north before landing on the only runway that jutted out into Victoria Harbour. All this was meat and drink to Ken Gow who over the years had tried to imbue his colleagues with his passion for all aviation matters. During recording breaks all over the world when the sound recordist would stop proceedings while an aircraft would pass overhead, Ken would inform anyone who cared to listen what kind of aircraft it was, who made it, how many passengers it could carry and how far it could fly on full fuel tanks.

Not surprisingly then, Ken was particularly delighted to find he was flying to Hong Kong on a Dragonair Lockheed Tristar L-1011 with three Rolls-Royce RB211 engines and with a three man South African crew. Some way into the flight I had a quiet word with one of the flight attendants about Ken's passion for flying – especially on this particular aircraft, a wide-bodied jet first made in 1968. She said she would see what she could do. Shortly afterwards Ken, to his obvious delight, was invited onto the flight deck flourishing only his Guild of Television Cameramen membership card as proof of identity - this was long before security became as strict as it is today - and invited to sit in the jump seat for the rest of the flight as we approached Kai Tak through the Hong Kong skyscrapers, seemingly just clearing the washing lines below our wings, and the landing beside Victoria Harbour. When Ken emerged from the cockpit he looked like the cat that had not only got the cream but everyone else's share as well.

As he later explained to me in detail, the landing at Kai Tak might be exciting enough from the passenger seats but it was out of this world from the flight deck. The procedure was for the aircraft to descend with the Instrument Landing System (ILS) heading for a chequerboard painted on a hillside. At 300 feet, a tight visual right hand 50-degree turn was made onto the runway seconds before touchdown.

I suggested gently that was more information than I needed to know but I promised to buy him a beer to celebrate. He agreed that that seemed a reasonable gesture. At a personal level, I was delighted that Ken had found his time in the jump seat of the Tristar so memorable. Over the years he had proved a staunch and skilled colleague always prepared to go the extra mile in the interests of the programmes he was involved with. His time in the cockpit seemed little enough reward for what he always gave in return.

Never one to miss an opportunity, our visit to Hong Kong en route back to Scotland had a greater purpose than just rest and recuperation. We were there to meet James Smith, the son of a Fife miner who over the years had risen to the top of the international hotel industry and was now general manager of a string of luxury hotels in the Far East. As a committed Scot he was also a great supporter of quality Scottish produce and when possible had tried to offer Scottish beef and lamb in his hotels.

By coincidence, Scottish marketing agencies were trying to expand sales into that part of the world and so we took the time to look at the story from the standpoint of a potential buyer of Scottish meat. Not only did James turn out to be a helpful and articulate interviewee but he was the most generous of hosts during our short time in Hong Kong.

The night before we left Kong Kong, James together with his wife Julia and daughter Debbie took Ken Gow and me to dinner in a restaurant favoured by locals rather than tourists. It was one of those restaurants where tanks of live fish compete for space at the entrance and it is expected that diners choose their fish in advance of being seated. We tried not to look the fish in the eye as we pinpointed our chosen delicacies. It was a memorable evening in good company but the highlight was yet to come.

After dinner, James Smith suggested Ken and I join the family for a nightcap in his luxury flat in hills high above the city. It seemed too fine an offer to refuse. And it was there he introduced us to the art and practice of Champagne Sabrage.

Sabrage is the ceremonial opening of a champagne bottle with a sabre. A Champagne bottle holds a considerable amount of pressure. Apparently, early bottle designs used to explode and the makers kept making the bottles thicker until they could contain the pressure that is caused by the release of carbon dioxide during the fermentation process.

With sabrage, the sabre is slid along the body of the bottle toward the neck. The trick is to hit the bottle with a clean and confident stroke. The bottle is held at about 45-60 degrees to the horizontal. Using the blunt edge of the sabre, the force of the sabre hitting the lip separates the collar from the neck of the bottle and the cork and collar remain together after separating from the neck.

The technique became popular in France during the time of Napoleon when the sabre was the weapon of choice for Napoleon's cavalry – the hussars. At that time Napoleon's victories gave ample opportunities to celebrate. He is reported to have stated: *Champagne! In victory one deserves it; in defeat one needs it.*

Beside the hearth in James Smith's Hong Kong apartment was a coal scuttle full to the brim of cork and collars from previous nightcaps over the years. Watching him execute perfectly the act of sabrage was so impressive that Ken and I found it necessary to ask him to repeat the performance after the first bottle had been consumed.

Sabrage proved an impressive nightcap indeed when performed by a master. But as they say in all the politically correct programmes – don't try it at home.

Champagne nightcaps apart, our visit to China had been a success – a strong story that we were able to turn into a 30-minute film at a modest price. Part of the reason for its success, of course, was the infectious enthusiasm for his work of our subject, Bob Orskov. He was so good, I believed, that if ever we got another chance to film with him overseas we would grab it with both hands – but next time we would do it differently. Next time Bob Orskov would be the presenter.

Two years later, in 1998, we got our chance. Bob Orskov was going to Vietnam and he could fix things to ensure we could gain access to all the work he was doing there. The theme was sustainability of farming systems and once again I was able to balance the books to make our filming possible. Bob Orskov proved a natural.

Once again I had Ken Gow and Colin Maclure in the team as we began our film in Hanoi before moving to Hue in central Vietnam and ending in Ho Chi Minh City in the south.

For anyone involved in the green movement in the western world, Vietnam could offer a template for the future. We filmed large duck ponds where the excrement from thousands of birds fed thousands of fish. And we filmed on small farms where the gas from human effluent was used to fertiliser fruit trees. It was not a savoury subject – but it was an important one and it made a strong programme. Bob Orskov was a star with a commitment and energy that would set an example to those half his age. Now well into his 70s he has spent a working lifetime travelling the world trying to build better lives for the subsistence farmers of the developing world. I used to describe Bob as Danish by birth, Scottish by adoption but a citizen of the world by inclination.

For all the food production and farming priorities that underpinned all our filming work, there were often insights into history and human triumph against all the odds. During our filming in Vietnam we met a senior agricultural expert who had been a member of the Vietcong during the war when North Vietnam was fighting South Vietnam and the USA between 1959-1975.

After one fierce engagement this member of the Vietcong had been seriously injured and had lost a lot of blood. In the absence of plasma, his fellow soldiers had saved his life by injecting coconut milk into his vein. Coconut milk is sterile and using it created a vital lifeline until he received better medical attention in a field hospital in the jungle.

Despite our territorial ambitions, *Landward* was by BBC standards a small programme and a cheap one in cash terms. I reckon that the programme continued its unbroken run for more than quarter of a century for a variety of reasons. First, it didn't cost a lot; second, it fitted neatly into the public service ethos that the BBC espoused; and third, we didn't rock any broadcasting boats. The programme was a known product at a known price and we could be relied on to deliver the goods 26 times a year – every year, year after year. And if there was any enthusiasm left over – and there always was – we would produce a few extra programmes as well.

I took a quiet satisfaction in that. Also, I had satisfaction in knowing that the success of the programme and the enjoyment and information it brought to its loyal audience wasn't only due to me as producer. It was due to a whole team of people who had given so much to public service broadcasting over so many years. I have mentioned many of them in the preceding pages of this book but it would be remiss not to make special mention and underline the enormous commitment to the programme of Rob Shortland for 20 years the video editor who, in technical terms, put it all together in polished form ready for broadcast. Over the years he proved a master of his craft, always up to and often ahead of the latest technology in a rapidly changing business. I owe much to all the presenters, cameramen and sound recordists on location but Rob Shortland's editing abilities ensured that his colleagues' skills reached the nation's living rooms in a final streamlined and accurate form.

I have paid tribute to the professional skills and commitment of the BBC staff cameramen like Ken Gow, Jim Patchett and Colin Maclure, who proved stalwart colleagues over so many years and to whom the BBC owes much. Due thanks must also be given to the small army of freelances I worked with over the years, chiefly Jan Ostrowski and Terry Black who came to be part of the *Landward* family during my time with the BBC – and later in many commercial video productions since I retired. I jokingly referred to Jan and Terry as the North of England branch – Jan lives near Newcastle and Terry near Carlisle in Cumbria. Whether at home or abroad, Jan and Terry were splendid colleagues and friends who always went the extra mile to do a good professional job, often in difficult circumstances.

Looking back over the years, one stalwart young assistant producer-director to join my team, albeit only for a brief spell, was David Kerr. From the start his star shone brightly and his early talent was confirmed when he, together with Eric Robson, produced a two-part series called Lights in the Glen on the renewed vigour within the crofting communities of Scotland. David was soon to leave my team to seek fresh challenges in London where he cut his teeth directing television commercials and comedy programmes. At the time of writing he has just directed his first major movie with Johnny English Strikes Again, a comedy spy spoof starring Rowan Atkinson. I have no doubt that David's talent will ensure he remains a sought-after director for many years to come.

I have much to be thankful for, too, to the many Productions Assistants who worked on *Landward* over the years. Some, like Jeni Warburton and Janie Innes departed with their respective husbands for new lives in Australia (was it something I said?); Irene Gibbons who went on to find a new role in religious affairs television; Sarah Johnson became an award-winning producer before taking up medicine; Alison Bruce found a new career in BBC sports broadcasting; Jenny Seymour became a producer herself in BBC Radio Scotland; Jenni Collie enjoyed success as part of the BBC Natural History team in Bristol and for several years was an important member of the production team on the highly successful *Big Cat Diary* programmes from Africa; and Maggie Mutch, having thankfully chosen not to get lost after all in Volgograd, became a successful freelance Production Manager in the independent sector working with high-profile figures in the entertainment industry like Sir Bruce Forsyth and Piers Morgan.

The last of my PAs was Noreen Harding, a friendly and hard-working girl who, like me, had cut her broadcasting teeth in local radio in the north of England. She was my PA at a time of great change and challenge in the BBC at a time when the BBC kept not only reinventing the wheel but tried to impose new multi-skilling wheels as well. Noreen was ready for it all and threw her shoulder to any new task or challenge asked of her. She had all the skills and more required of a traditional PA and, for a brief period, she also proved herself an able and committed picture editor.

My assistant producers/directors also proved to be stalwart colleagues. I have mentioned most of them with the exception of Jane Fletcher, an able and engaging girl who went on to enjoy a career as a BBC television producer in the south including responsi-bility for the long-running *The Sky at Night*, and Susy Dale, des-tined to be the last of the long *Landward* line. A fine journalist with a strong personality Susy made a memorable member of the team before moving on to pursue a future in newspaper journalism. She was to be the last Assistant Producer in my team. Thereafter, the role was changed when Ken Rundle joined me as a full-time staff reporter and correspondent. Ken was to prove a tower of strength over the next few years – he was a man with a deep knowl-edge of food and farming and a wealth of contacts at all levels in the industry. The *Landward* programme became immeasurably stronger editorially as a result of Ken Rundle joining the team and it was a shame that such a strong journalistic talent should have left the BBC earlier than he needed to. Thankfully, Ken landed on his feet after leaving the BBC when he became Communications Director with Scotland's Rural College. The BBC's loss was another organisation's gain.

The strengths and talents of all my colleagues eventually created opportunities for me outside the normal run of making pro-grammes. In 1997, for example, I was privileged to be Chairman of the Guild of Agricultural Journalists of Gt. Britain, a year that coincided with Britain's turn to host the annual Congress of the

International Federation of Agricultural Journalists at Macclesfield in Cheshire.

Our patron and main speaker at the conference on the future of world food production was the Princess Royal. As Chairman I was delegated to spend the morning with her and was suitably nervous. I needn't have worried. She was charm itself and I found talking to her both easy and natural.

I had less time to converse with her brother, Prince Charles, when the following year I was fortunate enough to be invested with the MBE for services to agricultural broadcasting. With Andrea and our two daughters Anna and Ailsa in attendance at Holyrood Palace, I took my turn in the queue and in due course was granted twenty seconds and a handshake. As I was shuffling along in the queue I recognised one of the men involved in the recording of the investiture. It was Cameron Crosbie, a former freelance sound recordist with whom I had worked many years before and who now was contracted to record these formal events at Holyrood. It was good to meet him again after all those years. As they say, it's a small world.

My last overseas programme was in 2000 – Ken Gow and I went to Australia with presenter Fergus Wood, a farmer and businessman. Fergus, like Bob Orskov, was not a broadcaster by profession but by dint of his natural enthusiasm for all things rural – and the all-important ability to talk articulately in front of camera under pressure - there was no doubt that he could have made a living out of broadcasting had he chosen that particular path. Fergus is a farmer near Aberfoyle in Stirlingshire and an acknowledged expert on wool production and was one of the pioneers who tried to get cashmere production off the ground in Scotland. We had filmed together before in Scotland and in France and he had proved a natural on television. I decided he was the man to present a history of the Australian wool industry. And that's precisely what he did – and superbly well.

Once we had finished filming with Fergus he flew back to Scotland to pick up his normal farming activities and his burgeoning political involvements which included becoming Provost of Stirling.

Ken and I stayed in Australia to wait for the arrival of another star *Landward* presenter Lindsay Cannon, the Galloway farmer's daughter and freelance presenter who had contributed so much to the success of the programme over the previous ten years. Lindsay's remit was beef production and we found that despite all the brouhaha back in the UK in the wake of the BSE crisis, Australia had much to teach us especially in the area of traceability and provenance of meat supplies. Ken and Lindsay did a superb job and I was satisfied that we had another good programme in the can.

Ken, Lindsay and I ended our filming by staying on a large houseboat on the Murray River and thanks to some help from a local farming agency it was arranged that we end our film by recording in a hot air balloon early one morning over the river. To be more accurate, two hot air balloons. The idea was that Lindsay and I would be in one hot air balloon so that Lindsay, wearing a radio mic, could introduce the programme with Ken recording her from the second balloon.

What I knew then but Ken and Lindsay did not was that, a few months earlier, I had decided to retire from the BBC. After much thought weighing up the pros and cons I had made my decision but had told nobody apart from my wife Andrea. Driving from the houseboat to the launch site for the balloons I was consumed by anxiety. This was to be my last overseas shoot for the programme. We were about to do something potentially dangerous. What if it all went wrong. Ken conversationally asked me if I had checked this and checked that. Because my fevered imagination assumed things might not go well, I was unusually terse with one of the most conscientious and hard-working cameraman in the television business. I immediately felt guilty but if Ken noticed my irritation, he was too much of a gentleman to mention it. We proceeded to the launch site.

In the event my natural instinct to worry was unfounded. The shoot went perfectly. The balloons rose in the still early morning air. Below us was the broad stretch of the Murray River with the vineyards stretching for miles around. Lindsay's radio microphone was switched on and from his balloon Ken filmed Lindsay's pieces to camera as I crouched down in the basket so as not to be seen. After all, I'd had the walk-on part on the Russian train and you can only have so much of a good thing.

The balloons landed beside a vineyard and Lindsay, Ken and I celebrated our safe landing with an early morning glass of champagne. What else could we have done? Sadly it was also to be one of Lindsay's last overseas filming assignments for *Landward*. She continued presenting but was eased out of the *Landward* team a few years after I retired – new management making their mark I suppose, however unwise that mark might have been because Lindsay was held in high regard and affection by the programme's core audience of Scotland's farming and rural population. However, I'm delighted that Lindsay – a keen climber and hill walker - went on to run her own business as a qualified French mountain guide near Chamonix.

As Lindsay and Ken left for Scotland with the recorded tapes safely under their wings, I had one more visit to make. Andrea had flown out to Australia to join me when my work was over and together we flew on to New Zealand to visit our friends Colin and Doreen Follas.

It was to prove a memorable and happy visit and it was good to see Colin's commercial video production business thriving. Andrea and I stayed in their home near Auckland and were delighted to wander through their beautiful seven-acre acre garden accompanied by Brie, their affectionate Golden Retriever. Perhaps the highlight of our visit was when Colin called in a favour from a friend of his who happened to own a helicopter and we were flown to a restaurant on an island off the coast. Happy days.

It was to be the last time I saw Colin. Shortly afterwards he developed cancer and underwent chemotherapy treatment from which he later appeared to be making a recovery. Andrea and I invited Colin and Doreen to our daughter Anna's wedding in Scotland on May 24th, 2003. They planned to come but shortly before the event Colin took ill again and was unable to travel. He rang our home in Auchenblae on the morning of the wedding and wished us well for our big occasion and said how much he and Doreen would have liked to share the happy event with us. It was a sentiment that Andrea and I echoed.

We never spoke again. He died shortly afterwards. Wherever he is, I hope he's in the midst of laughter and one-legged ducks.

All Work and No Play?
– No Fear!

Despite the pressure of work and never ending deadlines over many years, it would be wrong for me to convey an impression of a life of unceasing toil. All work and no play makes Jack a dull boy is a proverb that has been handed down over the generations. I took it to heart as often as I could. I always found time to play.

In my 30s and early 40s I enjoyed revisiting the game of squash that I had first been introduced to as a schoolboy. In the early 1980s two farming cousins John Milne and John Forbes bought the County Hotel in Stonehaven and developed a squash club. I was hooked from day one and began to play three or four times a week – invariably with a lot more enthusiasm than natural talent.

Occasionally in life, one development leads to another. As far as squash was concerned, my problem was that I wasn't fit enough. So I began running to build up stamina in the forlorn hope of trying to keep up with some of the talented youngsters. Within six months I was as fit as a flea and running marathons – over three years I completed six. Sad to relate, however, whatever improvements running may have made to my fitness it did nothing for my abilities on the squash court other than to ensure that my new-found stamina meant my frantic hurtling around the court tended to last longer.

A second offshoot sprang from my squash playing activities. The editor of *The Mearns Leader,* the local weekly newspaper, asked if I would consider offering regular reports of the squash club's activities in the Grampian Leagues. Thus began a ten-year stint as the local squash correspondent writing under the pen name of Yellow Spot. Sad to relate, this departure from my normal journalism went unremunerated. Equally sadly, a twisted knee during a game eventually brought an end to my ten-year love affair with chasing a little ball around a court like a demented and uncoordinated chimpanzee.

So what next for a thwarted sporting hero? By this time I was deeply involved with a charity called the Royal Scottish Agricultural Benevolent Institution. This was Scotland's only charity specifically concerned with helping those who had depended on the land and who had found themselves in dire straits because of accident, illness or redundancy. As the charity was approaching its centenary year we looked for a project that would raise both money and awareness of the charity's work throughout Scotland's farming and rural communities.

I floated the idea of a charity walk across Scotland – a 13-day sponsored trek along the 212 miles of the Southern Upland Way from Portpatrick in Wigtownshire to journey's end at Cockburnspath in Berwickshire. The idea was accepted and so began for me a major logistical exercise in gathering support from throughout rural Scotland and planning the detailed daily walks. In the event it was a great success. More than 100 hardy souls joined me for the walk – some joining for only a day, others for perhaps three days or more. One stalwart was Hugh Mann who farmed near Edinburgh. He was 70 years old but his advancing years only spurred him to greater efforts and Hugh walked with me every step of the 212 miles. He was a real hero. By the time all the money had been collected the RSABI charity gained more than £20,000. Somehow, we felt all the sweat and sore feet had been worth it.

A pleasant spin-off from this marathon walk was that my old friend Fordyce Maxwell, Agricultural Editor of *The Scotsman*, asked me to keep a daily diary of the walk that he would publish once we had completed the task in hand. And so it was that each evening in whatever small hotel or bed and breakfast I happened to be staying in, Andrea – who drove ahead to each day's destination to make ready whatever blister medication might be necessary - produced my laptop from the boot of the car and I would chronicle my impressions of our day's exertions. Accordingly, on Monday, July 21st, 1997, the following diary appeared in the paper:

Friday, 4 July:

Arrive May Farm, Portwilliam. Beware all imitations, this is the farm, a hallowed patch of The Machars of Wigtownshire – so long since it was home, still sharp in the memory. The Ayrshire cows and Beef Shorthorn bull are long gone, my mother and father gone too, but their legacy is a third generation putting down roots at the May. Out towards Wigtown Bay and Cairnsmore lies the bleak expanse of the moor – memories of heather burning in spring, childish panic as a circle of fire closes round, reassurance as my father appears through the smoke and a child's hand slips into what seems a giant's fist. It's not only the whaups of the Machars that endure as I think about tomorrow.

Saturday, 5 July: Portpatrick Harbour

Two bacon rolls down, 212 miles to go. The first 16 volunteers arriving including Ian Purves-Hume, the RSABI's energetic director, and Hugh Mann of Carrington Barns, Gorebridge, who plans to walk all 13 stages. At 70 he looks – and is – fitter than the organiser. The wheeling gulls on the cliffs towards Killantringan lighthouse mock us and the skeleton of the ill-fated Craigantlet sticks gloomily above the water line as we take our first steps. Six miles out, a bonus – a horsebox on Mulloch Hill above Stranraer with beer, beefburgers and Galloway cheese generously provided by local farmers John and Jean Ross.

Sunday, 6 July: Castle Kennedy

A grand start to Sunday's nine-mile stage with a formal approach to the White Loch. A family affair with sister Monica, brother-in-law John McTurk plus the enthusiasm of nieces Katie and Hilary calculated to dispel any weakening resolve. We are also joined by the journalist Bob Ross and his wife, Jeanette. Through the tree-lined coolness of Glenwhan Moor. Sad to see the old stone dykes, the lunkie holes where Blackfaces once passed. Where now the shepherds who walked those hills before the trees came.

Monday, 7 July: New Luce

A new batch of walkers, but the indomitable Hugh Mann goes on as the initial euphoria turns to the pragmatism necessary for the 17 miles ahead. Farmers' wives outnumber farmers but another batch of enthusiastic walkers from the Scottish Office's agricultural section, led by Willie McGregor, balances the sexes. Ian Salmon of Montrose meets his first Blackie ewe. Not hard to persuade him that it's easier to make a living from beef, barley and daffodils than from one of nature's more suicidally-inclined species. Hugh Mann and I agree that John Buchan and Rider Haggard will make a comeback but he also quite likes Jeffrey Archer. Suspect heatstroke. Seven hours later, beer, bath and bed imminent.

Tuesday, 8 July: Bargrennan

Hugh mercifully of sound mind after a night of enforced isolation. He had a parrot for company in his B&B and life in the hills above Bargrennan can't get much more exotic than that. This is a big day – 22 miles. At 0815, more volunteers, this time from the Howe of the Mearns – John and Mary Forbes and John Milne. Disaster strikes early – no clear waymarker for the crucial first left turn and I lead the party astray. Blood pressure rises – 10,000 employees in the Scottish forestry industry but never one when you want one. Eventually find the trail and begin the long trek to Dalry. Splendid scenery above Loch Trool, good weather and fine company but it's a hard, hard walk. Mary Forbes calls a halt for lunch overlooking Loch Dee – beautiful but now virtually lifeless because of acid rain. From the recesses of his small rucksack, John Milne - ever resourceful and generous - produces a bottle of claret. After seven hours slog, someone says with feeling that he'd rather face a batch of government forms to fill in than another walk. Journey's end in sight we think – but we find there's still another mountain to climb.

Wednesday, 9 July: St John's Town of Dalry

This is the longest section – 25 miles to Sanquhar, although a second opinion suggests it could be closer to 27 miles. Only four of us today – me, Hugh, Andrew Dewar from Penicuik and Angus Jacobsen whose farming interests include herding cashmere goats on the cliffs at Inverbervie. It's a long hard trek today. Muscles scream at the imposition of one more hill but it's grand open country seen to best effect in glorious sunshine. Angus fills his water bottle from a hill burn and swears that a caddis fly and a water boatman will maintain his protein requirements. Are we the Four Just Men or the Four Horsemen of the Apocalypse? A horse, a horse, my kingdom for a.........clearly hysteria is setting in.

Thursday, 10 July: Sanquhar

The shortest day, eight miles, but a tough slog up from the town to the hills beyond or, as one experienced walker claims, "a good grunt." How right he is – but worth it to see the forestry blocks round Clenries farm, a tribute to farmer Billy Elliot's pioneering work linking land and trees. Another fine turnout of volunteers, including Allan Leiper, a Wigtownshire pig farmer who establishes common ground with Hugh Mann – their fathers were both former presidents of the Scottish NFU. Other new faces are Simon and Kate Duffin, trout farmers. Allan advises Simon on the wisdom of keeping a pig or two to get rid of trout waste. Wanlockhead below and we're there by 2pm. I don't care what anyone thinks – I'm going to bed. Almost 100 miles covered but the stamina reservoir is lowering rapidly in the intense heat.

Friday, 11 July: Wanlockhead

Muscles screaming again on the long haul to the top of the Lowther Hills. Then a drop – and up again. Low cloud base means that this is the first day without baking heat. Another batch of walkers from The Department. Tremendous support so far from the Scottish Office's agricultural section from offices in Ayr, Hamilton and Dumfries. Farmer support reinforced by an old friend, John Harle of Aberdeenshire, with more than 200 Munros behind him. But he's not the only fit man today because

Adrian Hamilton is here – trout farmer, former international skier and Gulf War veteran. Hugh Mann outlines his plans for the definitive study of south of Scotland landladies, a potential best-seller. I begin to weary and feel more than my 52 summers but failure is not an option. Look on the bright side – only another six hours to go.

Saturday, 12 July: Beattock

Last night's steak in Moffat has fortified the inner man and we set out on the 21 miles to Tibbie Shiels at St Mary's Loch with new spirit. Fresh faces today include Johanna McLeod from Scottish NFU headquarfters and Alasdair Hutton, former MEP and former Territorial Army major. Another fit man, he's beginning to match John Harle stride for stride. Walking down Ettrick Water is pure pleasure, diluted only slightly when I throw away the walker's stick and try to be a farmer's boy again by helping move a reluctant suckler cow and calf from field to steading. More exhausting than walking and doesn't leave much in reserve for the long haul up to the ridge of the Loch of the Lowes and from there down to Tibbie Shiels. But we make it. Bliss – and two bonuses ahead – only 12 miles tomorrow and a 10am start. Bring on the unguents Andrea.

Sunday, 13 July: St Mary's Loch

Splendid Tibbie Shiels breakfast but outside it's pouring. Just a little dew from the hills, says Hugh. Stoic to a fault, that man. Turnout of 27 walkers today including my good pal Fordyce Maxwell and fellow journalists Andrew Arbuckle and Liz Snaith plus Landward's right hand lady Noreen Harding. NFU stalwart Mike Scott arrives with several Border farmers including Robin and Jen Forrest and family members. But the hero of the day is undoubtedly the Scottish Agricultural College chairman Sandy Inverarity, not one of nature's natural walkers and braving the elements despite a painful hip. He makes it though. Nine days down, four to go. We might make it too.

Monday, 14 July: Traquair

Boots barely dry from yesterday's deluge but we're assured that trench foot is only a remote possibility. Another great turnout including BBC Scotland's Colin Cameron and son Neil both fighting fit after a cycling holiday in Italy. Also with us today is Deirdre Hutton, chair of the Scottish Consumer Council. All Scottish scenery is good but the uphill slog from Traquair is rewarded by a view of what must be some of the best – a breathtaking landscape with the Tweed way below and the Eildons in the distance. Then on past the Cheese Well and another splendid vista over a brief lunch at the Three Brethren. A carpet of wild flowers accompanies our slow downhill descent into Galashiels. They must have known we were coming.

Tuesday, 15 July: Galashiels

More great support from old friends with George Blakebell here to introduce his Edinburgh walking pals. Nigel Miller keeps up the farming strength. What a revelation this trek is proving – all those years racing up and down and across the country chasing schedules at high speed and I think I know Scotland. Yet how little I've really seen. How little, too, we know people until we walk in their shadow. Allan Leiper has marched across Scotland with the best of them and has been raising money from the RSABI for more than 40 years. Andrew Dewar, a joiner who joined us by chance at Portpatrick and stayed, is raising money for his daughter, a volunteer worker in India.

Wednesday, 16 July: Lauder

More farming support from Carrick McLelland and Tom and Mary MacFarlane. They have a proprietorial interest as part of today's route takes us through their land at Flass in the Lammermuirs. A pleasant surprise as that North-East farming stalwart Eddie Gillanders joins us, breaking off a holiday. Again, it's the ladies who lead the way – the commitment of Jen Forrest, Trish Mobbs, Anne Russell, Marion Cunningham, Eileen Dykes,

Janet Dunn and Adelaide Borthwick has been splendid. Not forgetting Jerry Mobbs who has led consistently from the front in recent days despite a tightly bandaged ankle. Allan Leiper and Hugh Mann are already talking about walking the West Highland Way.

Thursday, 17 July

The final day – almost 18 miles from Longformacus to Cockburnspath. Robin Forrest, Fordyce Maxwell and Ian Purves Hume are back with us today while an old journalist friend Ian Morrison and his daughter Lesley also join us. Farmer numbers bolstered by Doug Niven who sets a furious pace. I slow him only slightly by discussing a potential Landward film about his farming interests in the Czech Republic. Quiet euphoria. A piper and a reception is waiting at Cockburnspath. But the objective was simply to get here. It has been a memorable and wonderful two weeks. Hugh Mann has been the star – a man of humour, courtesy and determination. However tired, he has never grumbled. For the many walkers the trek has endorsed Lewis Grassic Gibbon's maxim that the best things in life are the warmth of toil, the kindness of friends and the peace of rest. It seems an age since we stood with John and Jean Ross looking at the wreck of the Craigantlet – 14 beds, 212 miles, 636,000 (give or take a few) footsteps, eight counties, 52 litres of water. Now – the North Sea and the other side of Scotland. For a few seconds it's hard to focus. Sea breezes catch you like that sometimes. We turn inland to Cockburnspath and a fine reception in the village hall. Journey's end.

Little did I know then that the Southern Upland Way walk was to be the forerunner of many more long distance walks to come. With the prompting and support of my friend John Forbes and other farming folk in the Mearns I began to organise a charity walk in June each year. Over the years a group of about 30 or so regulars known as the Kinneff Reelers (Scottish country dancing was the group's winter activity) covered hundreds of miles over hills and glens and thanks to the generosity of many, succeeded in raising tens of thousands of pounds for a variety of good causes.

If the rigours of 212 miles of the Southern Upland Way had proved a major physical challenge through the hills of southern Scotland I was to discover that I had yet another physical task to accomplish – this time in the south of England. By 2004 I was closely involved with the Guild of Agricultural Journalists Charitable Trust and we trustees were keen to raise money and profile for the charity. And so it was that I came up with another madcap idea – walking the 186 miles along the Thames Path from the Thames Barrier in central London to the source of the Thames in Gloucestershire.

Once again I was joined by journalistic colleagues for different days of the trek; once again my long-suffering medical and moral support team in the form of Andrea went on ahead of me to ensure a hot bath and a glass of wine were waiting at the end of each day's long walk; and once again I kept a daily diary for posterity. I share it with you now:

September 5: Thames Barrier to Whitehall

Only 1115am but the music of corks popping from bottles of the best English sparkling wine confirm that my bluff has been called at last. Three months after tentatively suggesting the idea, this is day one of a ten-day trek to raise cash for the Guild of Agricultural Journalists' Charitable Trust. Councillor Brian O'Sullivan, the Mayor of Greenwich, generously gives up part of his Sunday morning to officially start the walk as does David Croston, of the English Beef and Lamb Export agency, our main sponsor. Andrea is there to see me off and cousin Helen and husband Roland have generously come north from Brighton to wish me well. Once my long-time colleague Keith Huggett has photographed our small group from every conceivable angle, I set off for the 10-mile first leg into Whitehall joined by journalist friends Diane Montague, Peter Bullen and Don Gomery.

Despite the heat, we make good progress along the south bank of the river resisting the temptation to drop in for a refreshment at the Anchor & Hope. We stay with the river and walk past the Dome that we're told boasts the largest roof in the world. Cormorants skim the surface confirming the availability of fish in an ever-cleaner Thames. Across the river is Canary Wharf with its distinctive tower that irritatingly takes an age to recede into the background. Other minor irritations include frequent dog-legs around yet another multi-million pound development and the apparent absence of signs to keep our small group on the right road.

Past the Cutty Sark, through Deptford and Rotherhithe with the London Eye now in the far distance serving as a reminder of journey's end – at least for today. The sweeping transformation of derelict buildings into domestic housing over the last 10 years is increasingly obvious and the crowds enjoying a hot Sunday afternoon slow our progress as we approach central London. Even so, based on an average walking speed of 3mph the concensus of our small group is that today's walk with its frequent dog-legs has been more like 12 miles than 10 miles. I've arranged to have a quick shower in the Farmers Club in Whitehall and then join Andrea, Helen and Roland for tea and sandwiches in the Savoy Hotel. I feel I've earned it.

September 6: Whitehall to Putney

Today, I'm on my own – but at least it's the shortest leg of all. With an overall average of 18 miles a day to cover, today's 9 miles to Putney will help to build stamina. The first landmark today is Westminster Bridge that was the first between Putney and London when opened in 1750 despite attempted sabotage by ferrymen. Admiring the views of Westminster across the river, I start badly by missing a sign and find myself in the grounds of St Thomas' Hospital with the proper route running parallel above my head along the Albert Embankment. Press on and eventually I get back on track past Lambeth Palace only to find myself caught up in more dog-legs to circumvent prestige residential development work along the Nine Elms Reach. Around Battersea Power Station and the Dogs Home then back to the river via Battersea

Park and the huge Buddhist Peace Pagoda. Despite strong walking boots, the constant pounding on tarmac and pavement makes for aching feet. But an early bath today and the application of appropriate unguents and snake-oil to my feet by my wife, Andrea, who has generously agreed to drive ahead each day to the next hotel or B & B leaving me to carrying only the essentials for daily survival – water, apples and a mobile phone.

September 7: Putney to Shepperton

This will be the longest walk so far – 23 miles. I begin at Putney Bridge, famous as the starting point of the Oxford and Cambridge University Boat Race, and I'm pleased that within a few hundred yards I leave tarmac behind and for the first time I am on a towpath where the going is slightly less hard on my feet. Past Harrods Depository and on the left is the Wetland Centre run by The Wildfowl and Wetlands Trust to create a unique visitor attraction near the heart of London. There are thirty wild wetland habitats within this 1090-acre site that provide a refuge for over 140 species of wilds birds along with many butterflies and amphibians.

At Chiswick I cross to the north side of the river for the first time but in a little over a mile I return to the south bank via Kew Bridge and skirt Kew Gardens en route to Teddington Lock. Teddington has the longest weir and the largest locking system on the Thames and marks the transition between the freshwater Thames and the the tidal Thames. At this point the jurisdiction for the river passes from the Port of London Authority to the Environment Agency.

Teddington Lock is where I meet Phil Saunders, a key part of the sponsoring agency. Phil's a narrowboat enthusiast and, with his friend Peter, plans to follow my progress from here to Lechlade in Gloucestershire offering cups of tea or coffee and general support when required. We reckon that despite a cruising speed of around 6mph compared with my walking pace of half that, the time taken for the narrow boat to pass through locks should ensure that over any given day we will be more or less evenly matched. My rendezvous with Phil and Peter is captured for posterity on camera by retired colleague George Thomson and his wife Betty who have come to wish us well.

Wildlife abounds on the river now. The cormorants are still with us as are swans, coots, the occasional crested grebe and an abundance of ducks. But across the river there is no sign of the rich and famous that inhabit the £1 million plus homes straight out of the pages of glossy magazines.

Kingston Bridge sees the path take the north side of the river and on past Hampton Court Park with its wonderful palace but no time today to explore the famous maze. Back now to the south side via the Hampton Court Bridge and a long walk beside the Thames via Molesey Reservoirs and Sunbury Lock. Past the Swan at Walton where songwriter Jerome Kern met his wife. And back to the north side at Walton Bridge, reputedly the site of a ford crossed by Julius Caesar.

At Shepperton, a major hitch. This is the end of today's walk but it emerges that our hotel is more than a mile from the path. One extra weary mile before bath, supper and bed. Break out the unguents Andrea.

September 8: Shepperton to Maidenhead

A comparatively light day today – only 17 miles. Still reasonably fit and despite aching heels, no blisters are apparent – a tribute to strong woollen socks and run-in boots. Under the M3 then past Penton Hook Island, a burial ground during the Great Plague of 1665, under the M25 and its thundering traffic and then look across to Magna Carta Island, the site of the signing of England's earliest constitutional document. King John came to Runnymede to seal the Great Charter on June 15ᵗʰ, 1215. The right to navigation on the River Thames is recognised in Clause 23 of the charter as an extension of Edward the Confessor's Ancient Laws on navigation rights. Without that foresight I may not be enjoying the support of Captain Phil and my back-up narrow boat.

In sight of Windsor Castle the Albert Bridge takes the Thames path back to the north side only to see it swing back south via the

Victoria Bridge affording great views of the castle for a further mile before once again taking the north bank via the bridge between Windsor and Eton.

Two passings dogs take exception to my presence and make an assault on my ankles. I'm glad I have my "leveller" - a walking pole more suited to the Scottish hills than the Thames Path but invaluable for fending off unwelcome attention by man or beast. Seeing I mean business, they beat a reluctant retreat.

I continue along the north bank and under the M4 and then under the Maidenhead Railway Bridge, built by Brunel in 1839 to carry the Great Western Railway. The bridge is noted for its broad, flat arches which, with a width of 128 feet, are the widest brick-built spans in the world. Clapping your hands under the bridge produces a remarkable echo.

Day four ends at Boulter's Lock, one of the busiest locks on the river, which became popular in the late Victorian and Edwardian eras as a mecca for punting.

September 9: Maidenhead to Reading

At 24 miles, this will be the longest day's walk of all – but there's a bonus. I lighten my load by putting my rucksack in the narrow boat that will be within sight all day and there are plenty of locks where I can catch up with Captain Phil and my water bottles. Today is hot – and tiring - and I'm relieved to see the elegant sweep of Marlow's white suspension bridge come into view. I need my hat but I can't remember picking it up from my room at Boulter's Lock. A quick detour into Marlow and a replacement is speedily purchased for £14. Within 10 minutes I catch up with the narrow boat where Phil and Peter pass me water – and my lost hat that I'd placed safely in the rucksack. Possibly heat exhaustion or natural stupidity.

Keep walking. Don't give in. Past Hambleden Mill, dating from the 16th Century, then Henley Reach, the site of the Royal Regatta Course. There's more than a mile of a long straight stretch of the river here – an obvious attraction to oarsmen – and in 1829, the first of ten boat races between Oxford and Cambridge took place between Hambleden Lock and Henley Bridge.

More than eight hours after setting out from Boulter's Lock, I reach Caversham on the opposite bank from Reading. How quickly can I bath and eat? In bed by 9pm. Bliss – and still no blisters.

September 10: Reading to Wallingford

Today's stretch is 18 miles. The first point of historical interest is Mapledurham Mill, the only working flour watermill left on the Thames. After lying unused for thirty years, this 15th Century mill was restored in 1977. It has a wooden shaft made of oak and a waterwheel of elm. The mill can grind a tonne of flour in six hours – about the same time as I will take for today's trek. On the far bank of the river, the Mapledurham Lock was the first lock on the river to be mechanised in 1956.

Yet another detour takes me through Purley – street after street of identical houses and neat gardens but no people. It's like a ghost town. Surely everyone can't catch the 0715 into the City?

I cross to the north side of the river via the Whitchurch Bridge, one of only two surviving toll bridges across the river. Vehicles pay a small charge but I'm pleased that pedestrians cross for free.

This is the point that I leave the river for a couple of miles and face the only real uphill part of the route so far, eventually climbing a few hundred feet above the river before once more descending towards the Goring Gap with the Chilterns on the north side of the valley and the Berkshire Downs on the south side.

Now back to the south side of the Thames for the seven-mile walk into Wallingford, once again being re-routed away from the river for a couple of miles to bypass a conservation area. Was it today's hills that made me go slower or is the distance inaccurate. By the time I reach Wallingford I've been walking for more than seven hours which would indicate I have covered more than 20 miles rather than the official distance of 18 miles.

September 11: Wallingford to Oxford

Today's 23 miles promises to be another long tiring slog. Apparently William the Conqueror crossed a ford at Wallingford in 1066 on his journey from Hastings to London. The river still bustles with pleasure craft and wildlife but the going now is increasingly rural and beautiful – Paul Nash painted here with some of his locally inspired work now in the Royal collection. Between Abingdon and Oxford there's almost 10 miles of lonely walking, the country stillness broken only by the occasional rowing coach shouting advice through a megaphone at Oxford University oarsmen.

Around Oxford the Thames is known as the Isis. Why? Nobody can tell me. No matter, that refreshing pint in the Head of the River pub has never tasted so good. But more refreshment still to come – my EBLEX sponsors have organised a small barbecue in a riverside pub and colleagues Peter and Wendy Ryder and David and Elaine Steers have kindly come to offer me their support. Their company is good but the atmosphere is slightly dampened by the cold wet conditions – almost like a summer night in Scotland.

September 12: Oxford to Newbridge

Company again on this stretch as I'm joined for the 13-mile section to Newbridge by long-time John Deere PR man Steve Mitchell and his wife Adrienne. At Pinkhill Lock we strike out into the country on another detour to avoid a conservation area and lose sight of Captain Phil and his back-up narrow boat for an hour or so. After the long trek of the day before, the company of Steve and his wife sees this section soon completed.

September 13: Newbridge to Lechlade

Two more days to go and 17 miles to cover today. I'm joined by Guild of Agricultural Journalists' stalwart Mary Cherry and her niece Anna. It's a red letter day for Anna – not because she's walking with me but because today marks the launch of a pop single by her two youngest children. Already her eldest daughter based in New York is a successful songwriter whose work has been performed by Madonna. I am suitably impressed but quietly wonder if I can retain enough of this new musical knowledge to impress my own children when I return to Scotland.

Mary and Anna have to turn back after a while but I have been grateful for their company and support. Now I'm on my own again – apart from Captain Phil and his ever-present offer of a freshly-brewed cup of tea. I don't resist.

September 14: Lechlade to Thames Source

Time to set out on the final 22-miles to the source of the Thames. But first a farewell to Captain Phil and Peter. From this point on, the river ceases to become navigable for narrow boats and Phil and Peter have to turn and head back down river. I will miss them, not least because I will once more have to carry my own rucksack.

So I set out from Lechlade's Ha'penny Bridge named after the toll pedestrians were once charged. For this last leg I have the company of freelance journalist David Jones, another canal enthusiast who regales me with stories of his own narrow boat which is presently being fitted out to his own specification – including the installation of a diesel engine which has spent the last 50 years working one mile underground in a South African diamond mine.

This is truly the loneliest part of the entire Thames Path – no people but three herds of cattle in quick succession to pass around with a weather eye cocked for a recalcitrant bull.

Soon after Lechlade, the river turns into a stream and before long little more than a weed-filled ditch. I forgo my normal sustaining apple or banana in favour of handfuls of juicy ripe blackberries which have been a feature of the more rural parts of the walk. There have been tons for the picking – but no pickers. Despite the concerns of conservationists about urban sprawl, this is still a green and pleasant land.

Close to journey's end now but I'm lost. David is still en route but his feet hurt and he has urged me to press on. Desperately anxious to pick up the proper path again I spot a pleasant blonde striding towards me. She turns out to be a Daily Telegraph journalist on a day off and she soon has me back on the right road.

At last, a distant wave. Andrea, cousin Helen, her husband Roland and the Guild's Nick Bond are waiting at Thames Head with an appropriate bottle to celebrate the end of another marathon walk. Within ten minutes, David too has completed the final leg. We've left a glass for him. After 34 crossings of the Thames past 41 splendidly maintained locks, I've finally reached the end of the road. Most importantly of all, when the final cheques reached the charity our efforts had secured almost £4500 to boost our funds.

Re-reading this diary some years later I am saddened to record that four of my colleagues who supported me on the walk – Peter Bullen, Don Gomery, Phil Saunders and Keith Huggett – have all since died. They are much missed.

And Finally...

The late Aubrey Singer, a former Deputy Director General, famously offered a piece of advice about surviving life in the BBC - *don't aim too high, don't take it too seriously, don't stay too long.*

There used to be a rule that a planned BBC career was in five-year phases. Not for me. I stayed ploughing the same furrow as *Landward* producer for almost 25 years. Presumably by some standards I couldn't be accused of aiming too high. Taking it too seriously? Maybe I could justifiably be accused of that. Having the complete freedom to make a film about a subject and then offering my idea in the shape of a completed television programme to tens of thousands of Scottish families on a Sunday afternoon was clearly a privilege and was one that I did take seriously.

Staying too long? Some of my colleagues may have felt that I might have overstayed my welcome. If they did they were too diplomatic to drop any hints. Certainly, I never felt the years drag by. I was lucky. I loved what I was doing and, latterly, had the great good fortune to be decently rewarded for what I was enjoying. I also had wonderful supportive colleagues and looking back I just wonder where all the years went.

In a changing world, today's BBC is a different organisation. Certainly, some of the anecdotes of the BBC of years past would not fit easily in the politically correct world of today.

I also suspect that there's less of a sense of innocent mischief abroad in the BBC today. I can't imagine a repeat of the occasion when, on the morning of a visit to one of the network centres by the Chairman of BBC Governors, some cynic had posted a notice:

The signs "push" and "pull" will be removed from the swing doors when the chairman visits. He will choose which way the doors open.

And the broom of political correctness that sweeps every nook and cranny of the BBC today would no longer allow some of the perceived double entendres that from time to time would drop unbidden into reports and raise an eyebrow or two across the nation.

One tale concerned the radio reporter sent to interview an old crofter who had just celebrated her 100th birthday. In addition to a long life, another of her proud boasts was that during her marriage she had given birth to three sets of twins.

Goodness, said the reporter, *twins every time?*

Heavens no laddie, came the reply on tape, *hundreds of times there was nothing at all!*

And interpretation is all. Many years ago the late TV chef Fanny Craddock was creating on camera a simple creation for the nation's men-folk who might on occasion have to fend for themselves in the kitchen. Her creation was doughnuts.

It was the last item on the programme and as Fanny Craddock showed the final mouth-watering product to the camera with a flourish, there was just time for the presenter to step in front of the studio camera and close the programme thus:

And for all you men out there, may your doughnuts look like Fanny's!

Even we supposed professionals in the communications industry slip up when we think we are in command of the situation only to be firmly put in our place. On one occasion the *Landward* team was filming in Finland. On our first night in Helsinki I had gone to dinner with an official of the Finnish Ministry of Agriculture to confirm one or two matters about the filming schedule over the next three or four days. The two of us had a memorable meal in a fish restaurant beside the harbour and my enjoyment of the dinner was enhanced by the fact that my host paid the bill. Every little bit of budget saving helps.

As I left I noticed the sign above the restaurant read Ravintola. I scribbled a reminder and resolved to return to the Ravintola at the end our week's shoot, this time in the company of our presenter Ross Muir.

Filming on farms in central Finland went well and our last night found us back in Helsinki. I looked forward to a repeat of the wonderful meal I had enjoyed several days earlier and Ross and I eagerly jumped into a waiting taxi outside our hotel.

Our driver looked round enquiringly. Unusually for a Helsinki taxi driver he didn't speak English. I made a stab in the dark:

The Ravintola Restaurant please.

He responded in Finnish. Clearly he had no idea what I'd said. In the manner of the British abroad I repeated my destination – this time slowly and loudly:

The Rav-in-tola Restaurant please.

He looked baffled and shook his head and beckoned the hotel concierge who had been standing watching this frustrated exchange of dialogue between taxi driver and hotel guest.

The concierge, who spoke perfect English, opened the door of the taxi:

Is there a problem Mr Anderson?

Yes, I said with a rising note of exasperation. *I'm asking him to take us to the Ravintola Restaurant but he doesn't seem to understand.*

There was a hurried exchange between the two Finns before the concierge sought further clarification.

Mr Anderson, the taxi driver wants to know which restaurant you want to go to.

I've told him twice – the Ravintola Restaurant!

Yes, Mr Anderson, he knows that. But which one? You see, Ravintola is the Finnish word for restaurant!

Ah well, you can't win them all.

Mind you, sometimes you can't win at all. On an earlier filming project in Sweden, Ross Muir and I were being driven north by an official with the local Ministry of Agriculture. Our journey took us through mile after unvarying mile of pine trees with just the occasional glimpse of a small lake to break the monotony.

From time to time we passed a warning sign indicating that elk were a likely road hazard.

Conversationally, our driver informed us that he was a member of an elk-shooting syndicate and that every year for the previous ten years he had taken a week's holiday and gone camping with some pals deep into the Swedish forests to hunt elk.

And how many elk have you shot? Ross politely enquired of our driver.

Mr Muir, he replied, *I have never even seen an elk!*

The BBC motto proudly emblazoned on the corporation's coat of arms is *Nation Shall Speak Peace Unto Nation.* Over the years filming in almost thirty countries I came to believe that filming in foreign parts can build bridges of friendship and understanding between people. A smile and a friendly handshake work wonders around the world and I always maintained that filming issues relating to food and farming production helped create a greater knowledge of and empathy with other nations than any package holiday on a foreign beach ever could.

Of course, some preconceived notions about a nation's characteristics are either confirmed or overturned by personal experience. I filmed in Germany several times and was always impressed by the precise organisation and discipline of our hosts even though a sense of humour was occasionally lacking.

Sometimes the German sense of humour disappears entirely when they travel. I had been filming the Royal Smithfield Show in London when Ross Muir and I returned to our hotel late one evening after a long and indulgent supper in a nearby restaurant. For reasons lost in the mists of time, I was wearing my kilt.

Despite the lateness of the hour, the hotel foyer was full of German visitors checking in and waiting for the lifts. No doubt they'd had a long journey and disliked the late check-in as anyone would. The foyer was silent. Hardly anyone spoke to anyone else despite an adventurous *Gute Nacht* from we two BBC men as we picked up our keys from reception.

We took the lift to the sixth floor. The lift was full of Germans - all silent. When we reached our floor the doors opened and the lift disgorged Ross and me plus yet more glum-looking Germans and their suitcases into the corridor and around the lift doors.

You'd think something might make them smile, whispered Ross.

Who knows, I replied. *See you at breakfast. Goodnight.*

With that I headed one way down the long corridor and Ross the other, leaving the still silent pack of Germans hovering in the corridor.

A few seconds later I halted in my tracks:

Hoi! You! called a distant but familiar voice.

I froze and turned.

There, some thirty feet away were the Germans and thirty feet beyond them was Ross hobbling towards me as fast as he could with his trousers at his ankles and shaking his fist in my direction.

Come back Scotchman, he cried in a second-rate Anglo-German accent with an added touch of Hollywood overkill. *I vant my money back! I vant my money back!*

No doubt he thought it might bring a rare smile to the faces of the German visitors. Or maybe they watched the unfolding incident with horror. I didn't stop to look as I high-tailed it to the safety of my room.

I was never in any doubt that I could outrun my stumbling pursuer. After all, a Scotsman with kilt up can always run faster than a man with trousers down. In any event, I wasn't worried – on the basis of having known him for the better part of forty years I reckoned Ross was the archetypal alpha male.

Next morning the Germans were at breakfast. If they recognised the kilted Scot from the night before being pursued for financial reimbursement for heavens knows what kind of service they didn't convey it. In any event the kilt was nowhere in sight - it was in my bedroom at the bottom of my suitcase.

Whether in jest or in serious mode, the matter of money is never far from the surface in the broadcasting business. Every producer claims to be short-changed by the management mandarins and is forever pleading poverty.

There is an anecdote told after one General Election when the producer of a breakfast programme invited a newly-elected MP onto the programme to discuss his policies and the future of mankind in general as seen by the fledgling Parliamentarian. The general thrust of the next morning's interview and the time of arrival at the studio were discussed and agreed.

Just one thing more, said the producer, *about money – we're a bit tight on budget at the moment. Would £30 be all right?*

Absolutely, said the new MP, *I'll bring it with me.*

So there we are – more than half a century down life's working road and increasingly conscious that in all certainty I'm a lot closer to the end of things than the beginning.

Where did all the years go? Maybe I should ask the twenty-three presenters, forty-nine cameramen, fifty-seven sound recordists, twenty-four picture editors, twelve production assistants and twenty-two directors who shared my working life in television.

Wherever life takes you it's important to try to hang onto the friendships built over the years. A group of former BBC colleagues endorse that principle enthusiastically when we meet around Christmas every year for a long and liquid lunch involving a heady mix of nostalgia, character assassination, innuendo and slander – a fine preparation for the season of goodwill.

And so I grow older and can look back over the years with pleasure. Not everyone is so lucky. At my boyhood home of the May Farm a cruel twist of fate intervened to ensure my sister Monica and her husband John were destined not to grow old together. After years of hard work as a successful Belted Galloway breeder – in 2013 John picked up eight different championships with the same heifer, a feat never before achieved – John and Monica were looking forward to new horizons: John, having voluntarily relinquished the tenancy, was now farm manager for Mochrum estate owner David Bertie who had taken over the estate following the death of his cousin Miss Flora Stuart; while Monica, having retired from her senior speech therapist role with the National Health Service, was catering organiser for seasonal shooting parties on the estate.

However, on Saturday morning, October 25th, 2014, John had fed his beloved Belted Galloways as usual and was changing to head north with Monica for a weekend in Edinburgh to see their daughters Katie and Hilary when he collapsed and died following a major heart attack. He was only 60.

He was cremated at a private family service at Roucan Loch Crematorium in Dumfries on Tuesday Nov 4th and a few hours later hundreds came to Penninghame St John's Church at Newton Stewart to pay tribute to his life as a farmer, stockman, rugby player and coach, husband, father, uncle and friend. For his family and all who loved him, a bright light had been extinguished far too early

That picture of our four youngsters playing in the snow still has pride of place on my bedside table. More than thirty years on, Anna, Angus, Andrew and Ailsa have all grown to adulthood. Anna and Keith have children of their own – our beautiful granddaughters Lucy and Holly. Ailsa, too, is married - to Darren - and they are the proud parents of Alana, Ellie, Harris and Daisy.

Andrew and Laura married in the summer of 2014 followed by Angus and Kelly in the spring of the following year. The strange peripatetic lifestyle of their father over many years did not stop all our youngsters turning out to be fine human beings of whom Andrea and I are immensely proud.

Like all parents, Andrea and I worry about what the future holds for the next generation. In many respects, possibly our generation has been the luckiest of all. I never had to bear arms, was never unemployed and enjoy a comfortable retirement. Would that I could wish the same for my children and their children. Yet we live in testing times and selfishly, I often echo Maurice Chevalier's song all those years ago in the musical Gigi: *I'm glad I'm not young any more.*

Farming in all its aspects has dominated my life. From my boyhood days growing up on the May Farm in Galloway to my first twelve years in newspaper and magazine journalism followed by almost thirty years working in radio and television with the BBC then almost ten years running my own video production company, farming has run through my life like a sustaining artery.

Biased in favour of farming as I am, I get concerned when food production and rural affairs very often appear to take a back seat when the priorities of society are being assessed and legislated for.

Three vital elements are necessary to sustain life on this fragile planet – fresh air, clean water and a few inches of topsoil scattered, often unequally, round the face of the earth. Crops grown on that topsoil, linked to the husbandry skills of our farmers, fill the bellies – or not in too many tragic cases - of countless millions. For that reason I endorse the sentiments of a car sticker I saw years ago on a station wagon in South Dakota that proclaimed simply: *Never criticise a farmer with your mouth full.* Food production is of strategic importance to everyone on this planet – after all, as one geopolitical economist has calculated, mankind is only four meals away from anarchy.

And so we have one lucky man's life story recounted in a few thousand words. A hectic and fun-filled journey and occasionally there's a celebration for reflection – like the 50th anniversary of BBC television broadcasting in Aberdeen of which I have been proud to have played a small part for half that time and, in November 2013, the 40th anniversary of the launch of BBC Radio Carlisle (now Radio Cumbria) where my BBC career began.

I will end this account where my working life began. A few years ago I was in Edinburgh and walked alone from Princes Street across North Bridge and into the original *Scotsman* building, now a five-star hotel. I walked down a flight of stairs and into the old sub-editors' room that had been transformed into a glitzy cocktail bar with bottles of expensive malt whisky arranged round the walls. I ordered a drink and sat and let the memories wash over me. I looked down and there was the same parquet floor that I saw on Remembrance Sunday 1961, my first day as a copy boy. All these years later even the cigarette burns were still clearly visible. If I half closed my eyes I could see the subs' faces as they worked, wreathed in cigarette smoke, brows furrowed in deep concentration against the approaching deadline for the first edition. And what was that noise away below my feet – a low rumble that seemed to come from deep within the very earth itself. Was that the thunder of the mighty printing presses that used to daily punctuate my young life more than half a century ago? Maybe it was, maybe it was...

Lightning Source UK Ltd.
Milton Keynes UK
UKHW020234031220
374510UK00008B/376